public communication

public communication

RODERICK P. HART
GUSTAV W. FRIEDRICH
WILLIAM D. BROOKS
purdue university

harper & row, publishers
new york, evanston, san francisco, london

to our parents

Sponsoring Editor: Walter H. Lippincott, Jr.
Project Editor: H. Detgen
Designer: Jared Pratt
Production Supervisor: Will C. Jomarrón

public communication

Library of Congress Cataloging in Publication Data
Hart, Roderick P
    Public communication.
    Bibliography: p.
    1. Public speaking. I. Friedrich, Gustav W., joint author. II. Brooks, William Dean, 1929– joint author. III. Title.
PN4121.H264   1975   808.5'1   74–8292
ISBN 0–06–042685–3

contents

unit III. problems of communication in public settings 169

epilogue: the systems of public communication 263

preface

It takes a certain amount of arrogance to write a book of this sort. Arrogance because we have presumed to write for college students— a most demanding public audience; because of the onerous task we have taken upon ourselves—that of explaining some of the complexities of public communication; but, primarily, because we are, in this book, trying to teach *a way of thinking* about communication. After all, it does not take much audacity to write a textbook where the facts carry the primary pedagogical burden. It takes not a little humility to write a cautious book, in which careful inferences and hypotheses (as opposed to passionate preachments) abound. Ah, but to talk about *thinking*—that's arrogance.

What would you do if you were asked to say something intelligent about communication in public settings? Would you simply detail the findings that have emerged from speculative and behavioral research? Or would you scotch all of that and instead list the many brands of communicative elixir? Alternatively, would you assume, as we have, that a textbook is a very limited vehicle for communicating information and that it has done its job if it presents a tolerably efficient way of thinking for approaching communicative acts? Would you assume that lists, principles, studies, theories, and so on, are quickly forgotten, but that the *style of thinking* that a college course encourages lives on after the facts are interred with the student's intellectual tastes? We have assumed these things, and others.

We feel that a textbook on public communication *cannot do* certain things, that classroom teachers are uniquely equipped to deal with some aspects of public communication because their relationship with the student is always immediate and in-context. Furthermore, a teacher, not a textbook writer, can adjust his or her teaching to the individual needs of students and to the specific contexts within which the student does his communicating.

Thus, we do not intend to preempt the job of the classroom teacher who can best treat such situational matters as delivery and articulation and such specialized issues as style and outlining. We have written this text with an eye to the roles that the *classroom instructor and the student* play in the process of teaching public communication. It expresses our belief that teacher, text, and student should investigate public communication *in concert*, each doing the job for which he is uniquely suited.

Matters that relate specifically to dyadic, small group, and mass communication are not discussed in *Public Communication*. Although we believe that the general principles of spoken interaction espoused in this book are applicable to all communicative contexts, we have singled out public communication for special scrutiny. Thus, this book is especially well suited to the needs of students in public speaking or persuasion courses and, when appropriately supplemented, to the requirements of any broad-based introductory course in speech communication.

In suggesting that *the way we think about communication determines our success with spoken interaction*, we have included three general "think-probes." Unit I asserts that to understand what makes public speaking "public," to appreciate the essential nature of human speech, and to be aware of the vagaries of communication is, in a very lifelike sense, to take hold of certain attitudes toward what makes public communication *effective*.

Unit II argues more pragmatically. We treat the resources most available to the public communicator, resources that, if effectively exploited, can make talking something more than a monumental chore. By viewing the "potentials" residing within public audiences, within listeners' perceptions of the speaker, and within the remarks actually made by the speaker, we suggest that *it is the manner in which these resources are approached intellectually* that makes or breaks public communication.

Finally, Unit III discusses three of the most common "problems" faced by the public speaker. We treat the communicative approaches available to those who seek to reduce the complexity of information, to sustain the motivations of others, or to overcome resistance to persuasion. In so doing, we present what we think are practical and theoretically defensible techniques for dealing with such communicative problems.

Deciding what is essential to say in a book is, of course, taxing. We omit discussions that present theory for the sake of theory. Also, we consider the unit discussions to be central to our endeavor because they present self-contained materials in addition to previewing what is to come. A list of books and other references are given in end-of-text Bibliography. We have carefully cited materials that the beginning or intermediate student of public communication could profit from directly and immediately. Because many textbooks often fail to tie it all together, we have included an Epilogue in order to leave the reader with a general, workable perspective from which to approach public communicative acts.

Although we do not offer "tips," we do stress *practical modes of thinking about communication*. We have tried to avoid abstruse material that has little obvious relevance to the situations into which everyday communicators get themselves. In addition, we have tried to effect a blending of traditional rhetorical concepts and those arising out of behavioral science approaches to public communication. In general, we have attempted to stick rather closely to extant findings and theories which focus on public communication, yet hope that we have avoided being pedantic in so doing.

In this book, we have departed from the traditional method of including discussion questions and exercises at the ends of each chapter. Because we feel that the *instructor* of a course should make decisions relative to questions, exercises, and assignments, we asked Professor Robert Doolittle of the University of Wisconsin-Milwaukee to assist us in bridging the gap between theory and practice. He has produced what we feel is an excellent instructional guide entitled *Public Communication in the Classroom*.

In this rather extensive volume (which accompanies *Public Communication*), the classroom instructor will find that each chapter is summarized propositionally. In addition, for each chapter, prologue, and epilogue, Professor Doolittle has constructed "think" questions, application questions, and recall questions. Furthermore, for each chapter in the book, the Guide contains research probes, numerous activities in speaking and criticism, as well as a number of stimulating exercises the instructor may find useful in making the theoretical material in the book clear, concrete, and meaningful to his or her students. We feel that the Guide will become an indispensable asset to those teachers and students who choose to read *Public Communication*.

When writing this book, the authors profited from the wisdom of many. Some years ago, Carroll C. Arnold, Donald K. Smith, and Paul

Brandes piqued the authors' curiosity about public communication in ways that few others in the field could. More recently, J. Jeffery Auer, Gerard Hauser, and Donald Ecroyd made insightful comments on earlier versions of the manuscript. Also, the love and cooperation of wives and children helped to make the writing possible, as well as pleasurable.

R.P.H.
G.W.F.
W.D.B.

UNIT I

fundamentals of communication in public settings

UNIT I

There was a man with nothing to say
    And no way of keeping still.
"I like to listen to my own voice,"
    Said he, "And so I will."

"If I had to wait for something to say,"
    Said he, "I would be so old
Before I got to make a speech
    That everything would have been told

A thousand times. Then who would come
    To listen, and rejoice
At the nothing at all I have to say
    In my rather remarkable voice?

I can sound it high. I can sound it low.
    I can say 'harrumph!' so loud
It booms like a ton of TNT
    Set off in a thundercloud.

I can whisper and hiss as soft as sleet
    When it falls in the silent sea.
I can wink and imply on the sneak and
    The sly—
    So slyly and sneakily

That the people I bribe to listen and cheer
   Are so thoroughly overawed
By my artistry that they look at me
   And no man dares applaud.

—For fear, of course, they might break
   The spell
Of the truly remarkable way
I fill the room with the boom-boom-boom
   Of my nothing-whatever-to-say.

With the whisper and hiss and the sneak
   And sly
And the ever rising swell
Of my boom-boom-boom as I fill the room
   With the nothing I tell so well."*

I f the poet is correct, why would "a man with nothing to say" presume to stand in front of people with his non-message? If he is misguided in his criticism, why was the poet so blind as to miss the obvious quality of Agnew's speeches? Whether or not the poet is correct, there are other puzzling questions. For example, why do people come at all to an occasion whose focal point is public communication? How is it possible that an audience can be so spellbound by a public speaker that they dare not applaud for fear of breaking the spell? Finally, why would a poet of some repute and a magazine of the stature of *Saturday Review* publish a poem focusing on public communication? Is it really that important? Apparently so.

*John Ciardi, "About Making Speeches: For Little Spiro," Copyright 1971 by Saturday Review Co. First appeared in *Saturday Review* February 6, 1971. Used with permission.

basic elements of public communication

As we will see in Chapter 1, public communication has become one of the most popular forums for entertainment, elucidation, and escalation of ideas, theories, political philosophies, religious beliefs, fashions and fads, and so on. We use public communication to warn and cajole, to admonish and inspire, to herald and condemn.

But more than that, we use speech as a tool for getting our public work done. For some complex reason, we literally surround ourselves with talk. This talk is capable of creating and breaking spells and is powerful enough to start wars, end wars, and then commence them again. It is capable of inciting and quelling riots, able to launch or retard mass mobilization, such as the Jesus movement, neonazism, feminism, civil rights, and racism. Talk is seemingly capable of making and breaking a person's career overnight. Talk can also rend asunder the dreams, hopes, and aspirations of millions—and then rebuild them slowly. The reasons talk is used to accomplish this myriad of goals, why it is talk, more than any other human modality, that can bring so much delight and scorn to interested publics, will be discussed in Chapter 2.

In most cases it is not talk alone that produces such bountiful crops of public concern. Rather, it is the variety of effects that talk has upon people that keeps a complex and diverse society in touch with its own elements. It is communication—that endless process of talking, listening, and retalking—that determines the extent to which mutual understanding and concerted effort will win the day over those who preach divisiveness and ignorance. Thus, in Chapter 3 we discuss the much-discussed, but little understood, process of communication.

the implicit meanings of public communication

The concern of Unit I is threefold. We wish to discuss how (1) human speech is used (2) to engender and sustain human relationships in (3) public situations. But before we do so, let's consider what a public communication situation "means" in a very general sense. That is, what fundamental and generalizable explanations can we make of any situation in which a person talks to a group of listeners? More precisely, what *implicit meanings* are imbedded in an act of public communication? While the following list of implicit meanings of public communication is surely not exhaustive, it may be instructive.* In an

*The senior author is indebted to Professor C. C. Arnold for originally stimulating some of the thoughts presented here.

elementary sense, most instances of public communication mean that:

1. *the speaker perceives that some problem exists.* Here, "problem" means any set of conditions that the speaker feels requires change. We talk because we need to alter some portion of the environment in which we function. The "problem" can be as commonplace as the annual need to "rededicate ourselves to the principles of Americanism" on the Fourth of July, or as rebellious as a plea to take our Americanism out of Southeast Asia.

2. *the speaker perceives that some problem exists which can be overcome by talk.* Not all problematic situations can be resolved through communication. We cannot, in a single speech, change the ecological habits of 200 million Americans. Still, when most sensible persons face a body of listeners, they must have some feeling that their message could at least begin to change a situation that they, the speakers, see as undesirable.

3. *the speaker perceives that some problem exists which he cannot overcome by himself.* Public communication is a pronounced social experience. It implies that *collective* effort is needed if the speaker is to reorder his environment in the way he desires. Although she could regale herself with laughter by "just thinking," comedienne Joan Rivers must realize that her need for self-fulfillment or her need to entertain others (or whatever else motivates a stand-up comic) can only be achieved by engaging some particular *others* in discourse.

4. *the speaker perceives that some problem exists which he cannot overcome with just a few other people.* This book focuses on *public* communication—situations in which a speaker addresses a sizable audience. By deciding to do so, a speaker apparently has reasoned ahead of time that simply talking to Uncle Jeb and Cousin Sue is not sufficient for getting his job done. Such a speaker apparently seeks to influence some *sizable* portion of his social existence.

5. *the speaker perceives that the topic is important enough for him to risk public exposure.* There are surely better ways of making a living than by standing in front of 60 pairs of eyes, 43 of which close two minutes after the speaker has opened his mouth. When a person ventures to address a sizable public, he must somehow feel that the rewards to be garnered by the effective presentation of his message outweigh the possible "costs" of having himself and his ideas scrutinized in public.

6. *the speaker perceives that the topic is important to a number of other people.* Many of the things that we feel or know need not (perhaps should not!) be visited upon unsuspecting others, but this does not seem to be part of the ground rules for public communica-

tion. A person who presumes to address a body of auditors must have some feeling that a significant number of people can find potential import in what he has to say.

7. *the speaker is willing to open himself up to the possibilities of change.* As W. C. Fields should have said (but did not), public communication is not a one-way street. When addressing an audience, a speaker implicitly realizes that he too can be affected by the communicative surroundings. He may be shouted down. He may be elected president of the fraternity. He may be encouraged to believe even more strongly in his message. Because communication outcomes are not predictable in any significant sense, change is always the name of the game for the enterprising speaker.

8. *the audience is willing to open itself up to the possibility of change.* This proposition is perhaps so implicit that it frequently is overlooked. We seem to forget (as auditors or as observers of communication) that when a group of persons gathers together for the purpose of hearing public discourse, they are making an "implicit bargain" with the speaker that goes something like this: "I'm here, and you can try to change me—but you'd better make it good!" Furthermore, speaker and audience "agree" (except in especially turbulent times) beforehand that only *symbolic* influence will act as an agent of change in public communication surroundings.

We could probably continue the list of the "implicit" messages of an instance of public communication. However, this list should suffice to give you some idea of the manifold and complicated dimensions cutting across communicative acts. For the wary observer of human behavior, there is more than first meets the eye in public communication. By being aware of these inexplicit meanings of public discourse, you will, hopefully, be able to keep your own experiences as communicator in perspective.

communicating in public

CHAPTER 1

What has won the millions of workers for Marxism is less the literary style of the Marxist church fathers than the indefatigable and truly enormous propaganda work of tens of thousands of untiring agitators, from the great agitator down to the small trade-union official and the shop steward and discussion speaker; this work consisted of the hundreds of thousands of meetings at which, standing on the table in smoky taverns, these people's orators hammered at the masses and thus were able to acquire a marvelous knowledge of this human material which really put them in a position to choose the best weapons for attacking the fortress of public opinion. And it consisted, furthermore, in the gigantic mass demonstrations, these parades of hundreds of thousands of men, which burned into the small, wretched individual the proud conviction that, paltry worm as he was, he was nevertheless a part of a great dragon, beneath whose burning breath the hated bourgeois world would some day go up in fire and flame and

the proletarian dictatorship would celebrate its
ultimate final victory.[1] . . .

And he went about all Galilee, teaching in their
synagogues and preaching the gospel of the kingdom,
and healing every disease and infirmity among the
people. So his fame spread throughout all Syria, and
they brought him all the sick, those afflicted with
various diseases and pains, demoniacs, epileptics, and
paralytics, and he healed them. And great crowds
followed him from Galilee and the Decapolis and
Jerusalem and Judea and from beyond the Jordan.

Seeing the crowds, he went up on the mountain,
and when he sat down his disciples came to him. And
he opened his mouth and taught them. . . .[2]

There is not much that Hitler and Jesus could agree on, yet apparently both shared an appreciation for the power of public
communication. Separated by ideology and century, both seemingly
knew that they could unleash incredibly potent social forces by talking to their contemporaries in public settings. Their remarks call attention to at least two important assumptions underlying this introductory chapter. First, *an essential and powerful element in changing
a society and in informing the masses is face-to-face public communication; and second, this communication occurs at various levels and
in various settings*—ranging from the formal lecture audience, through
the informal tavern gathering, to the mass demonstration. In reading
this chapter, we hope that you will acquire an understanding of and
appreciation for the significance of public talk, the types, strengths,
and limitations of the various communication settings, and the important, distinctive features of *public communication*—the unique
concern of this book.

the practical significance of public communication

There has not been a time in recorded history that public communication has *not* been an important vehicle for our progress, education,

[1]Adolph Hitler, *Mein Kampf*. R. Manheim, tr. (Boston: Houghton Mifflin,
1943), pp. 472–473.
[2]Matthew 4:23–5:1.

and in many senses, our enjoyment. Inventions such as the printing press, radio, television, and the like, have mediated public communication and thereby extended its coverage. Furthermore, man's increasing understanding of himself has made public communication more sophisticated than it was in the days of beer hall gatherings or mountain-top sermons.

PUBLIC COMMUNICATION BACK THEN

On the surface then, some may be tempted to believe that the importance of nonmediated (i.e., face-to-face) public communication is waning since television has become so widespread and accessible to almost every American (and to a large portion of the people of the world for that matter). When reading of the great speakers and the dramatic speaking events of the 1800s and early 1900s (Scope's trial, the Chautauquas, etc.), we might be led to believe that few comparable forms of public communication exist today. Indeed, public speaking did enjoy a position of high prestige and wide acceptance before the arrival of radio, television, and movies. Prior to the advent of these technological innovations, most of our public communication, whether for information or entertainment, was home-grown and live. It was in-person, face-to-face communication. Readings, recitations, orations, political speeches, and debates were popular forms of education and amusement and were as much in demand as were piano players, magicians, dancers, and banjo pickers.

In the beginning of this century, nonmediated public communication was "in vogue" and people traveled great distances by horses or train to hear such public exhibitions of talk. From the mid-1800s through the early 1900s, extravagantly ornate opera houses, theaters, and town halls were built in cities across the land to accommodate these flashing, dashing communicative impresarios and their appreciative audiences. There were the famous—the "stars"—and there were landmark, sometimes carnival-like public communication events in this era. Indiana's James Whitcomb Riley, for example, first appeared to read his poems in the Dickson Opera House in Indianapolis in 1880, but was later booked into theaters and town halls in almost every state in the nation. There were hundreds of others like Riley across the land.

Other popular stages for public communication in the late 1800s and early 1900s were the Chautauqua and Lyceum movements, which were sort of public speech circuits, traveled by both the famous and the infamous. Nebraska's silver-tongued orator, William Jennings Bryan, gave his famous "Cross of Gold" speech scores of times in Chautauquas across America.

PUBLIC COMMUNICATION TODAY

Today, communication is not limited to face-to-face situations—we have worldwide electronic communication, television saturation, and packaged entertainment. And it is understandable why some have said that live, in-person public speaking is as extinct as the dodo bird. Nothing could be further from the truth! Not only is public speaking alive and well, but it is thriving as it never has before despite—and perhaps because of—the coming of the mass media. *Per person*, public speech consumption is higher today than ever before, including the era of the late 1800s. Even platform lecturing, one small aspect of nonmediated public communication, is a booming, million-dollar industry today. Political figures, journalists, authors, entertainers, business leaders, and proponents of all sorts of "isms" have found the lecture circuit of the 1970s to be a virtual gold mine. More than one presidential loser has paid the campaign bills by going on the lecture circuit. We, as a people, have *not* lost our enthusiasm for in-person public speaking as a significant social institution. Teddy Roosevelt once called the public speaking platform America's fourth great institution, surpassed only by the home, school, and church. This statement remains true today, no matter what has happened, or may be happening, to the other three institutions.

No one knows exactly how many speeches are given each year in the United States, but conservative estimates made for one group, The International Platform Association, run as high as 500,000. Speeches are given by persons representing literally thousands of organizations, groups that are large and small, governmental and private, commercial and philanthropic. For example, Senator William Fulbright (1970) states in his book, *The Pentagon Propaganda Machine*:

Besides using all of the modern tools for opinion molding, the military makes use also of the oldest—public speaking . . . [using more than] 1000 speakers a month within one Army command alone . . . in an almost steady stream, they have been speaking to Rotary Clubs, Reserve Officers Meetings, at ship launchings, and almost anywhere a responsive audience might be expected to gather. . . . The Navy's Office of Information every two years publishes a booklet titled "Outstanding Navy Speeches." In the preface of one of the most recent, the Navy Chief of Information [says that] "navy men and women are delivering more and better public speeches than ever before." (pp. 128–129, 133)

Indeed, according to the CBS special, "The Selling of the Pentagon," the war in Vietnam might have lasted as long as it did because of the "traveling colonels"—military personnel who toured the chicken-and-peas circuit thumping for continuance of the war.

If ever there was a fear that mass media extravaganzas would run public speaking out of town, that fear has now been buried. Indeed, public speakers are seemingly created and nurtured by the television screen. Instead of killing off the public platform as was at first predicted, TV has actually stimulated the demand for "live" speakers. In 1972 alone, there were upwards of 25,000 professional speaking opportunities in the business and convention fields alone—ranging from closed seminars for a handful of top-echelon executives to the annual open meetings of the National Education Association, which brings out a whopping 10,000 registrants.

The second largest sponsor of paid lecturers is education—from kindergarten assemblies to graduate school forums. About one in five of all elementary and secondary schools have at least one public program annually. The average number of speaking programs is running as high as five per institution. This totals up to 130,000 programs each year. Add to that another 200,000 programs on the junior college, college, and graduate levels, and it seems that the machinery of education is being well lubricated by the juices of eloquence![3]

Such public speaking statistics are staggering. In one week, for example, there were 40,000 paid speaking engagements in New York and 30,000 in Chicago. In addition, some U.S. senators make as much as $35,000 per year on the lecture circuit.

the social significance of public communication

All this talk—this public talk—with which we are being inundated is not talk for the sake of talk. There is a reason for it—man has no other means as efficient as public communication for solving his problems, for creating and maintaining organizations, or for collectively making and implementing decisions. On the other hand, public talk is used to start wars, to fester public wounds, and to visit all sorts of social and political plagues on suspecting and unsuspecting publics. Through public communication man deals with his environment-at-large. Thus, whether we like it or not, there are few tools other than public talk with which to maintain the delicate balance between community and jungle.

PUBLIC COMMUNICATION AS PROBLEM-SOLVER

Sociopolitical experts tell us that in the near future a means must be found for bringing newly emerging countries into the contemporary framework, that of a highly developed, technological, and automated

---

[3]Allan M. Widen, "TV Ups Lecture Industry," Gannett News Service release, *Journal and Courier*, Lafayette, Ind., July 21, 1972, p. 4.

world. Methods by which these peoples and states may be integrated smoothly into a world society must be worked out and, most importantly, *articulated*.

For example, anthropologist Margaret Mead is among those who have pointed out, that great numbers of people are being moved, in the short span of 20 to 30 years, from something akin to the Stone Age into an unabashedly technological era. Soon, young people in such societies may be able to say, "My father was a stone carver, but I'm going into internal medicine!" Satellites, supersonic planes, and telecommunications do not merely make such rapidly changing situations probable, they make them inevitable. These changes can occur smoothly and efficiently *only* if public communication is able to give voice to these unique challenges that are placed on contemporary humankind.

Another challenge encroaching upon us is that of creating governmental systems which permit diversity and dissent within a semblance of uniformity and majority rule. We are being called upon to build a society for all—not just for the rich and well-educated, but also for the educationally and economically unfortunate. With the rapid change that now characterizes our day-to-day lives, and with the rate of technological innovation being what it is, we must develop a *public* atmosphere conducive to allowing patterns of human behavior to change in pace with the material changes that affect society. Speakers by the hundreds have called attention to the fact that man has inadvertently let the rate of technological change out-pace our more distinctively *human* progress.

Moreover, these technological changes have made the world one. Many of our time-honored boundaries, borders, and rules belong, for the most part, to *pretechnology*. Technology has made many such delimiting artifacts obsolete. The paradox we now seem to be facing is that on the one hand we accept and encourage technological revolutions that inevitably make the world a "global village"; yet on the other hand we are being blinded to the human needs about us created by technological escalations.

It takes no great insight to see that substantial technological changes require prodigious human accommodations, and we, in *public* ways—in our organizations, institutions, and governmental systems— are being called upon to provide for such human changes. The vehicle which is increasingly bearing the brunt of such burdens is public communication.

Public communication does not exist in a vacuum but rather is part of the social and political mosaic. It is an essential part of every organization and every society in the world. For that reason, it is essential that we come to understand and to use effectively and constructively communicative ways of making human contact. This is the major sociological premise upon which this book rests.

Communication at some level and in some form is a process common to all living things. It is found in its most complex and sophisticated form in man. Communication is man's key instrumentality—his primary means—for forming relationships, for understanding his world, and for creating his institutions and organizations. At the risk of sounding philosophical, let us state that our societal evolution and perhaps our collective survival rest on the ever-burdened shoulders of public dialogue.

the range of communicative settings

Let's look at public communication from another vantage point, by considering its relationships to the other types of speech settings which impose upon us daily. What do we mean by communicative setting? What possible communicative settings can we get ourselves involved in? How do such settings differ from one another? What are the strengths and weaknesses of each?

A communicative setting is all too often confused with the media comprising communicative acts. *A communicative medium is a channel or vehicle by means of which ideas reach receivers.* Radio signals, letters, motion pictures, printed pages, the flag—these are media. Advertisers use such media as newspapers, magazines, direct mailings, television, radio, and billboards. All these are communication media. *"Communicative setting" refers to the environment within which a communication act takes place.* It can be defined by considering the physical and psychological surroundings of the receiver.

The five most common communicative settings are: (1) person-to-person, (2) small group communication, (3) speaker-to-audience, (4) group-to-group communication, and (5) mass communication.

PERSON-TO-PERSON COMMUNICATION

In person-to-person communication, it is the individual who constitutes the basic unit of interaction; the interaction is characterized by the participants' mutual (oftentimes rapid) gaining and relinquishing of sending and receiving roles. Such communication settings often operate at the dialogical, as opposed to monological, end of the continuum. One-to-one communicative settings often involve persons who know each other, like each other, and who share mutual interest or concern via their interpersonal communication. They may be lawyer and client, psychiatrist and patient, teacher and student, mother and daughter, sister and brother, or Batman and Robin.

SMALL GROUP COMMUNICATION

A second common communicative setting is small group interaction. As in one-to-one communication, the small group setting is characterized by its participants' tendencies to alternate the sending and receiving of overt messages. Again, communication in small groups is often not monological, or one-way, but is instead two- or multi-way. Any meeting of three people to a dozen or so, in which all can talk freely face-to-face about some common objective, constitutes the archetype *small group setting*. Business and industry use small groups in much of their decision-making procedures. Seminars, committee meetings, task forces, group therapy sessions, and discussion or study groups are familiar small group settings.

SPEAKER–AUDIENCE COMMUNICATION

A third communication setting, the one of which you will get a heavy dose in this book, is the speaker-to-audience (or, as we call it, public) setting. This setting is often characterized by its monological and institutional constraints. It is monological (one-way) in that the audience expects to listen (hence, they are named *aud*ience) and the speaker expects to and is often granted the privilege of monopolizing the talk. Such sending and receiving "rules" are not, of course, the only distinctive feature of public communication, but they are the most readily noticed. Later in this chapter, we will examine in greater detail the nature and unique characteristics of the public speech setting.

GROUP-TO-GROUP COMMUNICATION

A fourth communicative setting, group-to-group communication, appears to be a direct outgrowth of the global interconnectedness mentioned earlier. Such communication is discussed popularly today under the names cultural or intercultural communication depending on whether it takes place between cultures or between subgroups within a culture. As labor negotiations, student-administration confrontations, and United Nations dialogues continually demonstrate, such communicative settings often stretch the fragile thread of communication to its breaking point.

MEDIATED COMMUNICATION

One further distinction between communicative settings should be made at this time—the distinction between mediated and nonmediated communication. *Nonmediated communication refers to face-to-face communication with no physical intermediary separating the communicators. Mediated communication is that sort of communication engaged in by persons who are not in the presence of each other, but who are, in fact, separated by time, place, and electronic technology.* The mediators of their communication, the go-betweens, are, most commonly, the various devices of the mass media. Any one of the four communication settings we have identified above could be "superimposed" on television, radio, newspapers, magazines, books, or shown via films (e.g., the late night talk show). Such mediating forces, we are told by telecommunications proponent Marshal Mc-Luhan, are doing much to change the way we regard and participate in the events of the world around us.

distinguishing among communicative settings

Are these four or five levels of communication totally different from one another? Does courting Sweet Sue alone in the moonlight *differ fundamentally* from the president's wooing of the Rhode Island electorate come voting time? Most communication teachers and scholars answer in the negative. It is held in the field that: *The behaviors engaged in in "private" communication are different in degree, not kind, from those engaged in in public communication.* This is our thesis, as well. Public communication simply escalates from our "less crowded" communication contacts.

PUBLIC AND PRIVATE COMMUNICATION

We accept such premises and we believe that it is important that you as a student of communication appreciate their two important implications. First, public speaking, group discussion, as well as more intimate conversations, utilize skills that are common to and transportable from setting to setting. Second, there are differences—sometimes of degree only—between such settings that are critical and that necessitate the adapting and adjusting of acquired communicative skills. The practical point we are trying to make is simple: the zillions of conversational experiences you have had in the past will stand you in good stead as you grapple with the problems associated with public speech experiences.

Because the differences among these communication settings are differences of degree only, it is sometimes difficult to see where the characteristics of one setting end and those of another begin. If you are having such trouble, good! To focus on "settings" rather than on *communicative problems*, is the surest way to confuse your speaking priorities. The late James Winans, one of America's pioneers in speech communication, illustrated this point well when he said back in 1938:

Let us imagine all speeches and all memory of speech-making to be blotted
out, so that there is no person in the world who remembers that he has
ever made a speech, or heard one, or read one; and there is left no clue
to this art. Is this the end of speech-making? Here comes a man who
has seen a great race, or has been in a battle, or perhaps is excited about
his new invention, or on fire with enthusiasm for a cause. He begins
to talk with a friend on the street. Others join them, five, ten, twenty, a
hundred. Interest grows. He lifts his voice that all may hear; but the crowd
wish to hear and see the speaker better. "Get up on this truck!" they
cry; and he mounts the truck and goes on with his story or his plea.

When does the converser become a speechmaker? When ten persons
gather? Fifty? Or is it when he gets on the truck? There is, of course, no
point at which we can say the change has taken place. There is no change
in the nature or the spirit of the act; it is essentially the same throughout, a
conversation adapted, as the speaker proceeds, to the growing number
of his hearers. There may be a change, to be sure, if he becomes self-
conscious; but assuming that interest in story or argument remains the
dominant emotion, there is no essential change in his speaking. It is
probable that with the increasing importance of his position and the
increasing tension of feeling that comes with numbers, he gradually
modifies his tone and his diction, and permits himself to launch into a bolder
strain and a wider range of ideas and feelings than in ordinary conversation; but the change is in degree and not in kind. He is conversing with
an audience. (pp. 11–12)

Obviously there are some critical differences between our two-way
conversations and our communicating to a public; but as Winans implies, the way we *think* about communication and our attitude toward
the talking experience are the primary determinants of our enjoyment
of communication in *any* setting. A closer look at some of those differences would be in order now.

VARIABLES DISTINGUISHING COMMUNICATIVE SETTINGS

The rationale for this section is simple: By identifying *important*
variables which help us distinguish among communicative settings,
we can take advantage of the special strengths of each setting and
make insightful adaptations to them. Following are six important
variables that help distinguish among communication settings and
which may assist you in seizing upon the unique communicative demands of public communication.

opportunity for interaction between the speaker and the receiver
This is the first important factor that varies among communication
settings. In the dyadic, person-to-person encounter, one has significant opportunities for mutual give-and-take, for mutual message-

sending; but in mediated, mass communication settings, one has virtually no opportunities for immediate verbal *inter*action. In mass communication, the speaker can make guesses about his receiver *before* the message is constructed and sent. In two-person (dyadic) communication, both sender and receiver are able to monitor one another's reactions so as to tell (sometimes) whether the other is interested, understanding, accepting, or agreeing. Immediate feedback, both verbal and nonverbal, provides *immediate* reward or punishment to the talking partners in such settings. In dyadic situations, both communicators have maximum opportunity for interaction and maximum opportunity to understand or become frustrated by the other. This possibility for immediate monitoring of reactions probably helps to explain why employers prefer face-to-face settings for selecting employees, solving problems, and for giving instructions relative to accomplishing some task. Memos, reports, typed credentials, and routine written notes are too easily misunderstood and even ignored, since *interaction* possibilities are minimal.

Not only is dyadic communication efficient in that understandings can be monitored by personal and contextual cues and by various other "checking out" procedures, but the greater *amount* of verbal interaction in the person-to-person setting can *sometimes* help to create an intimate communication climate. Some researchers have suggested that there is a direct connection between amount of interaction and the resulting amount of liking or interpersonal attraction between people. Perhaps it is for this reason that salesmen prefer the dyadic setting, ostensibly hoping that a "liking relationship" may develop because of the opportunity such settings present for pronounced verbal interchange.

In the small group setting, interaction potential remains fairly high, but obviously not as high as in dyadic situations. After all, there are more fingers in the communicative pie. As we move to the public speaking setting, the opportunity for *verbal interaction* between speaker and audience decreases even more. In public communication, the listener expects to remain quiet and listen and the speaker expects to retain his role as speaker. Such "institutionalized roles" are, to some extent, breaking down in our age of dissent, but generally public speakers *do not expect* listeners to interrupt them, return dialogue, or in other ways usurp the speakers' roles as primary message senders.

Such built-in interactive features have their limitations. In public situations, speakers have less of an opportunity to know their listeners, and hence in many cases make imprecise adaptations to *groups* of individuals. Such handicaps are, however, offset by still other distinctive features of the public communication setting. Through the stability of his role as primary message sender, the speaker controls to a great extent the information listeners receive about him and his topic. Also, the speaker knows that he has a carefully allotted amount of "interaction time" and can, therefore, *plan how he will lead or direct the thoughts of his listeners* so that they will come to understand and accept his point of view.

Political speakers, for example, often prefer the public communication setting because it *usually* guarantees them noninterruption and enough time to present the totality of their arguments. It is said that perennial presidential candidate Norman Thomas favored the public speech setting to any other because he felt that, without interruption and with enough time, he could convince the most resistant audiences of the value of his Socialist position, or, at least, cause them to stop wincing at the very thought of socialism. Apparently, he never had the time to do so.

Thus, when the *amount of reciprocal interaction* is judged to be critical to the desired outcome of the communication encounter, judiciously choosing among speech settings becomes a highly relevant task.

the role and influence of the speaker

This second factor also varies from setting to setting. We have known since the early writings of the Greeks that the speaker's own influence (*ethos* or credibility) has much to do with the effectiveness of communication. As with opportunity for interaction, most public communication settings have special liabilities. Touch, direct eye contact, and subtle vocal and physical behaviors are more accessible to receivers in dyadic communication settings than they are in the public speaking situation (and to some extent) in the mass communication setting. Intimate knowledge of a speaker, then, is not likely to occur when one must address a large number of persons simultaneously.

Although the public speaker risks losing intimacy, he can *alone* do much to control his projected image through the use of specific, carefully chosen cues. Listeners always determine for themselves the speaker's projected image, but in public settings they are often limited to the cues the speaker himself is willing to provide voluntarily.

opportunity for the speaker to gain information about the receiver and to adjust to the receiver

Obviously, the speaker's chance of successfully communicating is improved as he gains information about his receiver and adjusts his communication to the receiver. And it is also obvious that a speaker can get to know a receiver best in the face-to-face, dyadic setting. As one moves from two-person, to group, to small audience, to large audience, to mass audience, specific knowledge about the receivers usually decreases, and in addition, one's ability to know exactly *how* to adjust to receivers often diminishes.

In the public speaking situation, the speaker attempts to get information about his receiver's attitudes, values, and positions *before* he prepares his speech. Thus, prespeech audience analysis becomes important as a means of compensating for the decreased opportunity of the speaker to gain information about his receivers *during* the interaction. Since the *public* speaker's knowledge of his receivers often is limited, the probability of his making uncorrectable mistakes increases.

Even if the speaker is able to obtain information from the audience via their nonverbal feedback during the speech, it may be difficult to understand the real meaning of such a flurry of signals. Also, adjusting easily to such a bevy of new information during a speech is difficult. Furthermore, when a group is large, the speaker receives much information from the audience that is either contradictory or difficult to generalize because of the sheer *number* of cues generated by a collection of individuals. Thus, the speaker's opportunity to know and to adjust to the receiver is increasingly limited as one moves up through the "numerical" levels of communication settings.

the effect of group membership on the receiver
This fourth variable is another that changes from one communication setting to another. Sometimes, a person's orientation to a message or a speaker, or to that speaker's position on an issue is determined by one or several of the groups with which he or she identifies rather than merely by their own experiences and insights. It is much more difficult for us to change those attitudes that we *share* with a group than those attitudes we hold "alone." Being the social animals we are, we tend to conform to those groups which are of immediate importance to us. This seems to be especially true when members of that group are seated about us—as they are in public speech situations. (Does it bother you to ask a question in a large lecture hall?)

Probably, the small group and the small audience settings offer the greatest opportunity for the group members to affect the receiver in obvious ways. On the other hand, "private" speech settings permit or require (whichever is the case in a given situation) the person to be isolated from the physical presence of fellow group members, thus cutting down on the "interference" a speaker must deal with communicatively.

Not only can the speaker in the two-person setting capitalize on his receiver's isolation, but he can remind the receiver of *their* shared groups' opinions and of *their likenesses and common grounds.* The practice of isolating the receiver from the pressures of groups to which he belongs is a common practice for psychotherapists, police interrogators, salesmen, and numerous others—a kind of "stand on your own and be influenced only by me" approach.

There are situations in which a speaker might choose to make the pressure of the group work *for him rather than against him.* In such a case, a speaker might choose the small group or public situation. After all, one is not able to control for the presence of group members in the mass communication setting, and they are not physically present in dyadic situations.

An example of the utilization of this "groupthink" phenomenon is often seen in the typical religious revival meetings. One of your authors has attended Billy Graham crusade meetings in Seattle and Kansas City and in both meetings was impressed with the creation of group influence. The audience became unified by appeals made to common *group* values; *group* expectancies were created or emphasized so as to become prominent in the awareness of members of the audience; singing, reading, and praying together became a *group* mandate. This technique is not unique to Billy Graham's crusades, but is also used more subtly by political "preachers" in their electioneering rallies. ("Vote for me for the good of the community.") Group membership appeals have been used effectively by Stokeley Carmichael to solidify collective opinion in the youthful audiences he addresses, as well as by countless other speakers. So, as with the other variables we've discussed, this variable of *group* identification and influence may be a factor of overriding importance in *public* speech settings.

opportunity for the speaker to control the
receiver's exposure to the message

In some speaking situations, for example, the mediated, mass communication setting, the receiver himself entirely controls his exposure to the message. He can turn off the television or radio, he can decide to ignore the commercial on his way to the refrigerator to get a snack, or he can decide to finish reading the paper while the Man from Glad regales us with his success story.

While exposure is quite selective for the listener in the mass communication setting, this is not true in the public speaking situation. There are significant social constraints placed upon members of a public gathering. For example, listeners in such circumstances are "expected" to be reasonably attentive and acquiescent, and are not encouraged to drag out the latest *Playboy* to prevent themselves from slumbering through the Reverend's sermon. Also, such listeners normally have only one *public* set of verbalizations visited upon them— that of the speaker. Of course, all receivers can tune-out and think about tomorrow's movie at any time, or in some other acceptable way manage to diminish their exposure to the public message. To a great extent, however, listeners in public settings open themselves up to being "captivated" by the *speaker's* message.

In the small group and dyadic communication settings, the receiver has even less chance to flee from messages sent his way. A listener can and will be dealt with *directly* if the speaker perceives disinterest or rejection on his part.

the number of persons reached via communication

This "numbers game," the final variable related to setting, is perhaps the most obvious factor pertaining to communication setting. The ability to reach a large number of people is obviously a major advantage of public and mass communication. As increasingly large numbers of persons share in the decision-making and governing processes, and as businesses, industries, and services are designed for large numbers of people, it becomes necessary to communicate more messages to more people in shorter periods of time. Only public and mass communication can accomplish such a task on a large scale.

Let's recap our discussion by considering the apparent distinctives of each setting:

In summary, we have seen that the private, **two-person setting:** (1) permits a good deal of verbal interaction, (2) is oftentimes a good vehicle for establishing intimacy, (3) allows for instantaneous and specific adaptations to the receiver involved, and (4) can isolate the receiver from the presence and subsequent effect of group members.

The **small group setting** offers opportunity for high verbal interaction, and can provide for its participants group approval and a sense of participation. Group standards, influences, and pressures may be present, however, as persons come together in small groups. Also, it is difficult for one to curtail his exposure to the messages in the small group setting.

In the **mass communication setting**, there is no immediate human interaction (at least none except delayed and indirect), little or no opportunity for the speaker and receiver to know each other; thus, on-the-spot communicative adjustments are impossible to make; only a modest opportunity to control the salience of group memberships is available to the mass communicator and he can exert no control over the receiver's exposure to his message. A general image of manipulation seems to characterize many mass media attempts to communicate, and the message can reach large numbers of people.

Since this book deals with *public* communication, let us now take a more detailed look at the unique characteristics of speaker-audience situations.

the distinctive features of public speech settings

All salesmanship, all oratory, whether it be a parson in his bloody pulpit boring his audience to bloody death, and making them want to get away from his misery; or whether it's a heckler screeching with all the crowd giggling in front of him, this is hypnosis. And I'm always conscious ... of deliberately utilizing an audience in this way. For example, I'll pick out one person. He will act as a scapegoat for the whole of the crowd, because then it will relieve the crowd to know that their own anxieties are taken away, piled on him, and they can all insult him through me. And if this is done with sense of humour in order to keep a balance in the crowd, it's pleasing to the crowd, and quite often it's pleasing to the person I pick out because quite often they are masochists. . . .[4]

These remarks were made by one of the dozens of itinerant, ragamuffin speakers who regularly engage in soap-box oratory in London's Hyde Park. While we can learn many lessons from such colorful ramblings, one message seems to stand out—*there is a rather unique geography and sociology to public speech settings*. As our Hyde Park speaker indicates, there is a unique *gestalt* surrounding public communication. For example, even though individuals make up a group, a group is more than the sum of its individual members. Groups take on their own characteristics, their own standards of behavior, and adopt their own roles and patterns of communication. How else could we explain the differences we all see between the S.D.S. rally and the conclave hosted by the Housewives Against Obscenity?

In public communication, where the concern is with an individual attempting to influence the attitude or knowledge of a public, many principles associated with informal, private, and dyadic settings are relevant; but upon closer inspection we can see that public settings are also unique in some ways. In this section we will examine these distinctive aspects of public communication on the assumption that we can increase our chances of using public discourse effectively if we are intimately acquainted with its special characteristics.

GENERAL CHARACTERISTICS OF PUBLIC COMMUNICATION

Public communication occurs, generally, in "public," not in "private" places. This is not as much double-talk as it may first appear. Sociologists such as Erving Goffman (1963) have defined "public places" as any region in a community that is fully accessible to members of that community. Private places, on the other hand, are places where only members or invitees gather. Examples of public places might be

[4]Heathcote Williams, *The Speakers* (New York: Grove, 1964), pp. 142–143. Copyright © 1964 by Heathcote Williams.

streets, parks, restaurants, theaters, shops, meeting halls, and dance floors. Private gathering places include, for example, offices, factory floors, kitchens, and living rooms. Thus, one of the unique characteristics of public speech is that it normally occurs in public places, with all that this implies in an institutionalized, organized society.

Another distinction of public communication is that *the event, the communication encounter, is a pronounced "social" occasion.* This is not true, necessarily, in the small group and dyadic settings. The sociologist distinguishes between the more private meeting of two persons or of a small group and the meeting of several persons in a public place. The latter is called a "social occasion" by students of human behavior. Such meetings are bounded in regard to place and time and typically are facilitated by fixed equipment. Examples of social occasions are picnics, a night at the opera, a lecture in an assembly hall, and theater performances. Each such type of social occasion normally possesses its own distinctive *ethos*, spirit, and emotional structure which are carefully created and sustained. Such occasions (1) are usually planned in advance, (2) are guided by an agenda of activity, (3) have an allocation of management functions (some person or persons perform standard roles and do certain things), (4) have clear-cut and agreed-on specifications of what constitutes proper and improper conduct, and (5) conform to a preestablished unfolding of phases—certain things are done at certain times. Clearly, there are accepted roles, ways of behaving, and other constraints unique to public speech settings, many of which have already been discussed. As we have seen, public speaking occurs in a public place and thus is affected by constraints and expectancies different from those found in the dyadic and small group setting. Thus, when we see the apparent "choreography" of a well-planned political rally, we are seeing the stylized traits characteristic of public, *social* occasions. To test this out for yourself, just make a short list of the "do's and don't's" you adhere to in your lecture classes. In such a public speech setting, the order, rules, and communicative jobs are all well laid-out ahead of time, and woe to the student who dares violate them!

For another thing, *there are special norms that regulate behavior in the public speech setting.* That is, the public speech situation is part of an "institutionalized setting." It seems true that *social* occasions which must be held in *public* places must also subscribe to some kind of *public order.* Public order refers to the norms or rules that have been created to regulate interaction among those members of a community who may or may not be well acquainted. Public, face-to-face communicative encounters also fall victim to the establishment of norms, or rules of conduct. Goffman (1963) points out that "public communicative influences come under strict normative regulation which gives rise to a kind of communicative traffic order" (p. 24).

The norms of behavior for speaker and listeners may vary from group to group somewhat (e.g., you are "permitted" to ask questions in some lecture classes), but many norms are basic enough so that they are shared across all types of groups in a given society or nation. The "funny thing" that has happened to so many speakers "on the way to the speech" may, then, be a function of certain conventionalized rules for speech introductions. Unfortunately, all too often such values are adhered to *ad nauseam*.

In addition to these three traits which grow out of the "publicness" of public communication, there are many other defining characteristics of such a communication setting. Rather than go into them at this time, let us consider a list of "distinctive features of public communication" that may serve as a practical summary of what we have said so far. As we move on in this book, we will be stopping back, from time to time, to consider each of the following traits more extensively. Contrasted with dyadic and small group encounters, in *public communication we find that:*

1. The message must be relevant to the group as a whole—not merely to one or a few individuals in that group. In public communication, the "common denominator" must be constantly searched for by the speaker.
2. *"Public" language is more restricted,* that is, it is less flexible, uses a more familiar code, is less personal in phrasing, and is filled with fewer connotations than is "private" talk.
3. *Feedback is more restricted* since it is limited to subtle nonverbal responses in many instances.
4. *There is greater audience diversity* to deal with. In public communication we face the difficulty of entering *many* "perceptual worlds" simultaneously. (This will be discussed in Chapter 3.)
5. As the size of the audience increases, there is a greater chance of *misinterpreting feedback,* since there's so much to look for.
6. The speaker must do a more *complete job of speech preparation* since there is so little direct moment-to-moment feedback by which he can guide his remarks.
7. The *problem of adaptation* becomes paramount since one message must suffice for many different people.
8. *Audience analysis is more difficult* and necessarily more inaccurate when many people are interacted with simultaneously.
9. It is sometimes *difficult to focus attention* on the message because of the great number of distractions a public situation can entail.
10. A *greater amount of change* is possible in public communicative settings since the message reaches more people in a given unit of time.

intra-audience effects in public communication

No disussion of public communication would be complete without some mention of one of the most distinctive features of public speech settings. Intra-audience effects, *a network of messages sent and received by audience members themselves*, constitute one of the most interesting facets of public communicative acts. As an example, picture yourself in front of the television set ready to watch the "Tonight" show. Johnny Carson makes his appearance and amidst the polite applause, we clearly hear the refrains of Loud Clapper and Shrill Whistler. Quite simply, these characters serve to induce their fellow auditors in the studio to respond favorably and to join in the fun. But that's not all. The laughter and clapping of the studio audience serves, *in turn*, to encourage all the folks out there in TV Land to similarly enjoy the proceedings—a kind of rippling effect.

We saw another example of the intra-audience effect in *What Do You Say to a Naked Lady?* (the movie produced and directed by Allen Funt) when four "experimenters" and one "stooge" were brought into a room as five supposed participants in a job interview. On cue, the four experimenters wordlessly began to disrobe. In almost all instances shown, the naive subject also undressed even though he was given no verbal reason to do so.

Desmond Morris in *The Naked Ape* (1967) describes the same phenomenon more precisely when he discusses the responses of teenagers to their idols:

As an audience, they enjoy themselves, not by screaming with laughter, but screaming with screams. They not only scream, they also grip their own and each other's bodies, they writhe, they moan, they cover their faces and they pull at their hair. These are all the classic signs of intense pain or fear, but they have become deliberately stylized. Their thresholds have been artificially lowered. They are no longer cries for help, but signals to one another in the audience that they are capable of feeling an emotional response to the sexual idols which is so powerful that, like all stimuli of unbearably high intensity, they pass into the realm of pure pain.
If a teenage girl found herself suddenly alone in the presence of one of her idols, it would never occur to her to scream at him. The screams were not meant for him, they were meant for the other girls in the audience.
(p. 98; italics added)

A MODEL OF INTRA-AUDIENCE EFFECTS

As can be seen from these examples, the effects of auditors on one another can be powerful forces in public speech settings. Naturally, such listener–listener interaction does not always operate in a direction favorable to the speaker. The ways in which these intra-audience responses can complicate the speaker's job are represented in Figure 1. A politician, candidate King, is giving a campaign speech to an audience of seven people. The following model indicates some of the communicative reactions *and interactions* which may result from his speaking.

Although in reality intra-audience effects are much more complicated, our model depicts some of the *adaptive demands* forced upon our plucky politician by his very "busy" audience. The following short-hand comments are made available by our diagram:

1. From the speaker's point of view, Maryann is a "good listener." She is totally enthralled with the candidate's speech, hanging onto every word he says and is oblivious to her fellow auditors.
2. John and Carol, on the other hand, are "perfect listeners." Like Maryann, they are really "into" the speech but *in addition* are reinforcing the speaker's remarks (for one another and for Bob) by their approving chatter and applause.
3. From the candidate's viewpoint, Bob is inscrutable. Bob is quite interested in overhearing Carol's positive reactions to the speech and the negative reactions of Barbara, and hence he may not be paying much attention to the political oratory itself.
4. Barbara's reactions are also difficult to assess. She is being greatly affected by Grace, who appears to be really turned off by the speech. Because she needs immediate social support (she and Grace being members of the same sorority), Barbara is probably tending in Grace's direction. Because her feedback to the speaker is minimal, it's difficult to tell how Barbara will eventually react.
5. Grace is obviously a lost cause, what with her scowls, sarcastic laughs, etc.

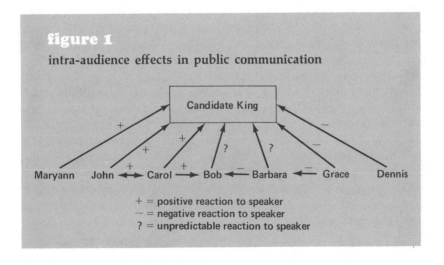

figure 1

intra-audience effects in public communication

6. Dennis is equally disturbed by the speech but is just grimacing, not overtly expressing his displeasure.

How should our speaker adapt to such a set of conditions? He can probably afford to direct his attention away from Carol, John, and Maryann for a while (since they are "with him" for the moment) and concentrate instead on Bob, Barbara, and Dennis. By soliciting their opinions for example, King might draw them into the conversation and hence discover and adapt to the sources of their disagreement (a technique that grade-school teachers often wisely use with unruly children). The remaining problem is, what is he to do with Grace?

Not all members of an audience have the same social power. There are, for instance, *opinion leaders* who have a great deal of influence on an audience. Thus, if Grace is a person of considerable clout, King might ask for her comments on an issue, hoping that this amount of personal attention will reduce her hostility. If Grace is *not* an opinion leader, the speaker is probably best advised to ignore her and to concentrate instead on more viable possibilities, hoping that the *group* of auditors he has "hooked" will then sway the one he has not yet been able to reach. The tireless, but tiresome, adage "ya' can't win 'em all" seems to be especially true of public communication, a situation in which the *complex, dynamic, social geometry of an audience* can do much to advance and retard the efforts of even the canniest of speakers. The issue of intra-audience effects, although interesting in and of itself, serves better to point up the complex *adaptations* forced upon a speaker by the "publicness" of public communication.

conclusion

In this introductory chapter we have attempted to describe the importance, depth, and scope of public communicative acts. Hopefully, we have shown how public communication affects us at just about every turn. We have tried to explain some of the ways in which public communication issues from our more private forms of spoken commerce and at the same time moves in its own unique directions. Above all, we hope that you appreciate the necessity of understanding the essential nature of public communication, for we feel that only with such an understanding, will you be able to explain to yourself your experiences when speaking in public. At the risk of sounding prosaic, to understand the nature of such speech-making is to ready yourself to consume and to conceive public discourse intelligently. In the pages that follow, we will attempt to assist you in fulfilling that mandate.

on human speech

CHAPTER 2

Peg: Hi.
Carolyn: Hi. Has the teacher gotten here yet?
Peg: No, and I wish he would. I'm nervous as
          a cat.
Carolyn: Me too. I've put off this speech course for
          five semesters. Finally had to take it.
Peg: Not me. I'm going to get it over with as
          quickly as possible. I *hate* to give speeches.
Carolyn: Yeah. People seem to look right through
          you when you're giving a speech.
Peg: Yes, and classroom speeches are so darn
          artificial. I mean who cares about another
          speech on drug addiction?
Carolyn: Yeah, I know what you mean. Although, I
          did give a speech in high school about the
          welfare system. It went over pretty good.
Peg: Yeah, but why a whole course in it? I've
          been talking all my life! Gee, I wish that
          teacher would get here and get things
          started.
Carolyn: Well, at least the kids in here look O.K.

	My roommate said that she really got to know the kids in her speech class.
Peg:	Maybe it won't be that bad. I wonder if they'll let us use note cards.
Carolyn:	I hope so. I always get so jumbled up when I try to explain something.
Peg:	That's what I mean. It's so artificial. I mean, when am I ever going to have to give a speech again for the rest of my life?
Carolyn:	Right. Although I guess I'll have to meet the public when I go out and do social work. But that's not the same as giving speeches. . . . Wow, that guy's five minutes late already.
Peg:	Hey, maybe he got scared too!
Carolyn:	Why should he? Teachers don't have to give speeches!
Peg:	Well, maybe this course will be good for me. Everybody says I'm too shy.
Carolyn:	That's funny, you haven't been shy with me.
Peg:	That's because you seem nice. I get up-tight when talking to strangers. Are you in a sorority?
Carolyn:	Yeah, how did you know?
Peg:	Oh, just some of the things you said made me think so.
Carolyn:	That's amazing. I didn't know it showed!
Peg:	Hey, maybe this course won't be so bad. At least we've got each other!
Carolyn:	Oh, by the way, I'm Carolyn Cross.
Peg:	I'm Peggy Franklin.
Carolyn:	Oops, here he comes. He doesn't look too bad. Maybe. . . .

Any of it hit home? Well, at least for Peg and Carolyn, the speech course promises to be quite a chore. Or does it? Beneath the veneer of this rather ordinary social conversation, what can we tell about Peg and Carolyn and, more importantly, what can we say about the problems and pleasures associated with the making and utilizing of human speech?

Let us begin by looking at a few of the somewhat questionable assertions they made from time to time. Peg claims that she hates to give speeches. Yet in the space of five minutes she has given more than a dozen "speeches." You say, however, that these were not "real" speeches—no standing up, no podium, no note cards, no sleepy audience, no speech teacher writing furiously, and so on. Yet Peg was "poised" for conversation, she was processing information intellectually (admittedly without note cards), she very obviously was trying to adapt to her audience, and, as we see later on, her audience was evaluating her utterances. So then, when is a speech a speech? Are the standing up, and the group of auditors, and the mass of feedback necessary to have a "speech setting," or are there common threads running throughout all of our spoken verbalizations?

We will be asserting in the pages that follow that the *behaviors* that Peg and Carolyn will engage in in their classroom speaking exercises are not different *in kind* from their sometimes mundane, sometimes exciting social conversations. We will be arguing that no spoken interaction can be "artificial," as Peg calls it, *unless* a speaker fails to make a perceivable investment in his message or does not attempt to demonstrate a semblance of meaningful commitment to his audience. We will contend that all teachers "give speeches" even though they sit on their desk, speak often in an interrupted fashion, and furiously smoke their pipes when speaking excitedly. We will try to find out why "giving speeches" is what makes us human and how speaking makes contact with other humans manifestly possible.

Peg claims that she has been talking all of her life. Yet she does not tell us that many of her talking experiences have been futile, boring, and sometimes, even painful. Most students of communication see a difference between "just talking" and talking effectively. After all, we all have been breathing since birth, yet how many of us, except for the Indian fakir, can *control* our breathing for biological (and as the Swami would have it) for meditational satisfaction? Similarly, we can *learn* to control our spoken verbalizations so that they have social impact.

Yet there is much that we can learn from Peg's and Carolyn's casual insights into human speech. Peg pointedly shows us that a certain amount of risk usually attends our talk. In this chapter we will explore some of the reasons for this phenomenon and try to understand why speech courses initially seem more scary than other academic enterprises. We will also attempt to explain why Carolyn received such a "good feeling" when communicating successfully with her high school speech class, why people seem to "see through us" when we speak, and why students seem to know each other well after having survived a speech communication class together. We will try to see why getting "jumbled up" when talking is a very common, natural, and in some senses, a very desirable set of conditions. We will investigate why Peg concluded simultaneously from Carolyn's *speech* that she was "nice" and a sorority girl, and how Carolyn was able to judge that Peg didn't "seem shy."

Perhaps most important of all, we will try to understand together why, after only a few short moments of *speaking*, Peg and Carolyn gave birth to a friendship and why Peg was motivated to say, "At least we've got each other." More than any other statement, this latter one demonstrates how we humans use the pleasures associated with speech to ward off the liabilities that spoken interactions sometimes entail; it also serves to show us that without effective communication, the chances for initiating and maintaining profitable social contacts are, at best, chancey.

speaking as a manifestation of our humanity

You would think that after having been around for thousands of years, we humans would have discovered finally what makes us what we are, what our peculiarly human characteristics are, what distinguishes us from other forms of life. Yet this does not seem to be the case. Scientists are continually finding strange but distinct parallels between man and his fellow animals—dolphins exhibit rather high order intellectual capacities, bees "communicate" with each other by a myriad of nonverbal "dance steps," and primates, when properly trained, seem capable of humanlike bodily dexterity. To date, however, researchers have yet to find an animal that "talks" in a full-bodied sort of way, save one, man himself.

This is not to say that if man could not talk, he would not be man. There are other ways of establishing our humanity. We live in social groups. We make tools that make other tools. And we are "rational." Of this latter point, the distinguished student of man, Mortimer J. Adler (1967) argues that to call man rational is to call him a talker, because "philosophers who, on the basis of common experience alone regarded man as the only logical or rational animal were, in effect, saying no more than that man is the only talking, the only naming, declaring or questioning, affirming or denying, the only arguing, agreeing or disagreeing, the only discursive animal" (p. 112).

Thus, by some method of intellectual and physiological happenstance, man seems to be unique in his ability to produce meaningful speech. Not only can A produce verbal sounds, but B can comprehend the utterances and react to them. Although the system often breaks down, man is distinctive in that he can create language systems and utilize his creation in the presence of other men, for pleasure, for profit, and, of course, for pain. *Put simply, we talk because we are human and we are human because we talk.*

It seems that ever since man began making these distinctly human noises, he has become enthralled by them, and sometimes uses his gift of speech in amusing ways. We find ourselves talking to cats who cannot return the compliment, yelling our lungs out at basketball players who cannot hear a word we say, and strangest of all, we "talk" to thumb-mutilating hammers even though they can neither hear nor talk back to us. Yet we do this because, in some sense, talking is "our" way of soothing, encouraging, and berating ourselves and each other.

And we take our talking seriously. We institutionalize people who continually talk to lamp posts and incarcerate those who use their talking ability to incite riots or to make obscene phone calls. Yet before we send these latter unfortunates off to the brig, we ask them if they have anything to *say* before sentence is passed. Even if they have committed a more serious crime, we still respect their humanness by allowing them "a last few words" before the pellet is dropped into the acid.

Although most of our talking is done in less threatening circumstances, human speech is important. As we will see later in this chapter, we use speech to find out about ourselves and to investigate the strange world of our fellow humans. Even when alone, we talk in order to simulate social conversation. Who can doubt that Robinson Crusoe spent much of his solitude talking to himself? Or that, as he constructed one of his endless contraptions, he sang, that is, used rhythmic, melodious *speech*, to entertain himself? All of this he (perhaps unwittingly) did to assure himself of his continued humanness.

In our everyday lives we continue to document the importance of our speaking ability. Society promulgates a host of talking rules ("children should be seen and not heard"). We use talking criteria to judge each other (he's "full of hot air" but she's "quiet as a mouse"). People incur censure for the quality of their speech ("he's a double-talker") as well as for the quantity of their verbalizations ("she just talks too much"). Sometimes, we use the same statement to describe totally different talking experiences—"we got nothing done; all we did was talk" or "we had a great time—just sat around and did nothing but talk."

At times, it almost seems as if we define all of our social experiences by describing our speaking activities. We engage in "heart-to-heart talks," "small talk," "man talk," "woman talk," and when all else fails, we "talk ourselves into it." All of these anecdotes carry the same message. Our talking is an inescapable part of our humanity.

It is the tool we use to describe our worlds, to define our comrades, and to change both our worlds and our comrades. While we can function without speech and still remain human, all reports indicate that a talkless existence is far from pleasurable. An intriguing claim that remains to be substantiated is that the suicide rate among those who went deaf during World War II was higher than the rate among those who were blinded. Even if untrue, the fact that such a proposition seems plausible demonstrates how man's "most human" gift penetrates and shapes his existence.

speaking as social contact

As you already know, we do not usually talk in a social vacuum. We talk to, at, for, with, and about *other people*. This sociability of ours is another important factor that makes us human. Yet the talking and social natures of man are inextricably intertwined; we talk because we are human but we also talk because we share this planet with other humans.

Many of our utterances can be seen as an attempt to define ourselves for others, to say: "Hey, look at me. I'm unique." At the same time, however, our spoken statements invite sharing from others by implicitly saying: "OK, I've said something. Now talk to me and tell me what you're like."

Of course, we want to say "more" than this when we talk to other people; often we want to change them in some way. We talk because we are not content with our existences, our listener's behaviors, or our mutual environment. "Pass the salt," "vote for Beame," or "I love you" are all attempts by us to assert our individuality *and* to change the world we share with other people. But this book is dedicated to the proposition that not all of our social talk is created equally. Ill-conceived utterances can and do rend the social fabric that ties us together. More about this later.

TALK AS SOCIAL SHARING

Whether or not we speak effectively, it is usually a set of social conditions that precipitates our talking—our social sharing. It is not accidental that speaking is the stock-in-trade of psychiatrists, school counselors, politicians, preachers, and teachers. When in the psychiatrist's office relating all of our feelings, we are attempting to *share* our problems with him and, in a sense, to make our problem *his* problem too. Our speech is the force that mediates and sometimes *demands* this sharing.

Oftentimes, the need to share ourselves with others becomes extremely important. Imagine that you have just learned that you have gotten an A in a course which you were sure you would fail. You are uncontrollably excited. What do you do? The answer is obvious. You talk, of course, to your roommate, to your parents, and if they are not around, you corner the guy down the hall with whom you have not spoken all semester. He smiles, gamely, and volunteers "That's nice. I'm glad for you." However, you are not really interested in his *response*. The important thing was to get the feeling *out*, to share it with someone.

Sometimes the pressure to talk becomes uncomfortable. Who can ride a crowded elevator from the twentieth floor to the street level without feeling the tension generated by the 20 nontalkers as they stare mindlessly at the elevator door? But should some brave soul make a statement, no matter how foolish it is, there's an almost audible sigh of relief from the reticent multitude. People make us talk. Who can endure more than five minutes in a small room with a stranger without muttering some inane pleasantry? Just one statement, of course. That's enough to acknowledge his humanity and our *social* responsibility.

The fact that talking implies social sharing sometimes takes on important consequences. Newspaper headlines seemed to shout out the news when the U.S. and Russia had agreed to discuss nuclear disarmament. And mind you, the two great powers *had said nothing* to each other at that point. They simply had *agreed to talk*. The left-wing responded joyously, seemingly because they realized the great amount of potential *sharing* that such a talkfest could entail. The right-wing also seemed aware of this sharing aspect of the talking experience and warned that the U.S. delegates might share too much, like so many warmed-over Yaltas.

Perhaps the most vivid manifestation of the social import of speaking is the decision *not* to talk. The angry person gives his or her unfaithful spouse the "silent treatment," as if to deny social obligation toward the offending person. Thus, it is not surprising that the ultimate punishment in modern prisons is solitary confinement—a place where talking, where social sharing, is impossible.

speaking as a naked me

Can you find anything strange about the following dialogue?

Nancy: Hi, Jack, how are you?
Jack: Things are copasetic. Is the feeling reciprocal?
Nancy: Yeah, I'm fine. Are you going to the game with me?

Jack: Such forms of diversion appear trivial to one mainly concerned
         with intellectual pursuits.
Nancy: Ya, but are you going?
Jack: As mentioned previously, one cannot enjoy pastimes that con-
         tribute nothing to the intellectual life.
Nancy: Oh, I guess that means you're not going with me.
Jack: Correct, even though such invitations are pleasurable in a sense,
         one must guard against totally peripheral activities.
Nancy: Good-bye, Jack.

Several things are important here. The main item to note is that Jack
is obnoxious. Why? At least one reason for our receiving such an
impression is that he seems disembodied, as if he has stepped outside
of his skin, and has somehow detached himself from his feelings.
There is no "me" in his speech pattern—no "I" or "myself." This,
combined with his pseudointellectual vocabulary, makes his talking
seem pompous. Of greater importance for our discussion of human
speech is the fact that his words depict him as *depersonalized*. Studies
by Gibson et al (1966) show that on most occasions normal speech
is literally peppered with personal pronouns.

SPEECH AND PERSONALITY

Thus, one of the inescapable aspects of speaking is the inordinate
amount of me-ness that goes with my spoken words. When I talk,
I talk. There is not much way of escaping from spoken words, since
it is *our body* that produces them; it is *our eyes* that see some of the
results of our words on other people. Because there is an inescapable
element of the individual speaker in everything he says when talking,
speech behavior is an especially good mirror of personalities, attitudes, and feelings.

   You can easily document the interconnectedness of your speech
and your person by trying, like Jack, to carry on a conversation in
the third person for five minutes. It seems funny. It seems as though
someone else were speaking for you. As if your body were being
used to convey a message that someone else had created. You feel the
impulse to say: "Now, wait a minute, *I* want to say something."
Although con artists, espionage agents, and professional actors can,
with practice, "step away from their messages" and speak someone
else's part, they undoubtedly feel some tension, at least initially, when
choking off *their* feelings and *their* motivations.

   This is an aspect of speech-making that is so subtle that it often
goes unnoticed. Yet before anyone will believe us or be taught by us,
they want to know *how much of us* is going with the message we
utter. It is for this reason that Gerald M. Phillips of Pennsylvania
State University observes that, in a sense, speech improvement means

personality change. Not any radical change necessarily but, because I am so closely connected with the "speeches" I make, I cannot help but be different after I have spoken.

SPEECH AND PERSONAL INVESTMENT

Some researchers have looked at schizophrenia as an attempt by disturbed persons to deny the me-ness of their spoken verbalizations. R. E. Laing (1969), the noted psychiatrist, states that "A good deal of schizophrenia is simply nonsense, red-herring speech, prolonged filibustering to throw dangerous people off the scent, to create boredom and futility in others. The schizophrenic is often making a fool of himself and the doctor. He is playing at being made to avoid at all costs the possibility of being *held responsible* for a single coherent idea or intention" (p. 177). We have italicized the words "held responsible" because this is the point we are trying to make here—that we are inextricably connected to and *made to stand with* the words we speak.

When you think about it, you really cannot plagarize a speech. You can take your roommate's old outline into speech class and read it, but it is *you*, not your roommate, who will feel the exhilaration of having communicated successfully. It is *you* who will feel the increased social acceptance precipitated by the speech. On the other hand, if you have chosen poorly when picking roommates, it is *you* who will feel the boredom. It is *you* who must deal with the negative feedback from your audience. It is *you* who must stand and feel embarrassed when your listeners perceive your lack of personal involvement. All of this while your roommate, the creator of *another message*, is completely uninvolved in the way that *your* message is received.

An interesting way of looking at the blending of personality and speech behavior is to consider the similarities and differences between speaking and writing. In 1966, Carlsmith and his co-workers conducted an interesting research in which they asked one set of subjects to write a short essay advocating something with which they disagreed, while another group was asked to give counter-attitudinal speeches. The researchers were investigating cognitive dissonance which, in part, involves the tension we feel when we appear inconsistent to ourselves. The results indicated that those who spoke falsely began to favor the positions they advocated in their speeches. This shifting of attitude was not nearly as dramatic for those who were asked to write essays.

Our previous discussion should help you to interpret these findings. Whereas the writers could tell themselves, "Oh, what the heck, that *wasn't really me* writing the essay. The experimenter forced me to write it. *He*, in effect, was the one who wrote it," the *speakers* probably had more difficulty devising such justifications for their actions. After all, it was *their* minds that modified their speeches while speaking. It was *their* mouths that made the words and *their* eyes that watched for the feedback. And it was *their* hands that got sweaty and *their* legs that shook as they gave their orations. Because they were so intimately connected to their spoken messages, it is little wonder that the speakers were so tempted to accept the ideas they had spoken.

As Arnold (1970a) points out, a speech is an action, not a product. We do not "make" a speech as we do an essay. We *are* our speeches. Business executives will attest to the fact that the easiest way to dismiss a troublesome subordinate is to tell the employee: "Put it in writing and I'll send you a memo." This allows the executive, when responding, to castigate a disembodied product rather than engage in the *personal, human activity* which spoken confrontations necessarily entail. It is probably for this reason that the late psychologist Haim Ginott advised parents who have "had it" with their kids to write occasional "hate letters" *to themselves* rather than to display their resentments in *spoken* confrontation with their children. Because our talk is *us* in a very real sense, it is usually the warmest and most tender vehicle for saying "I love you," and often the most cutting and cruel way of saying "Get lost."

Perhaps the best summary to this section is provided by speech students themselves. One of your authors often asks his students to put themselves in the following situation: "Suppose that you had something difficult to tell your parents. Would you rather write them a letter or talk to them in person?" While most of the students choose to talk it out, all seem aware of the problems associated with speaking: speaking does not give you enough time to construct completely your message, nor does it allow you to "say it and forget it"; it gets you flustered more easily; it forces you to deal with your parents' negative reactions. In other words, *talking gets you personally involved.* The following statement, or some paraphrase of it, appears in almost every answer received: "If I didn't talk to them, my parents would think I was chicken—or that I didn't care about them." At the risk of sounding prosaic, it seems to us that these students have been trying to make but one point: *when I give you my talk, I necessarily give you a bit of me in the bargain.*

speaking as a risky business

Some people contend that the most natural thing about talking to others is that it is fun. If this is true, then the second most natural thing about speech is that it is sometimes a scary proposition. Some of our most common day-to-day experiences center around the mild (sometimes not-so-mild) fear associated with the speaking act:

"I'm scared to death to give this speech. I know I'll just fumble all over myself."

"But I've never had a job interview before, how will I know what to talk about?"

"I just know how they're going to react. I'm really afraid to tell them."

"But I've never been to a wake before. What should I say?"

All of these are common situations, and not very grueling when you think about them. Most of us grit our teeth, put our brains in gear, and get through the experience, somehow.

THE RETICENT INDIVIDUAL

For some people, however, speaking, and sometimes the very *thought* of speaking, can present seemingly insurmountable problems. At many institutions around the country, researchers are now beginning to study the maladies of the excessively reticent individual, a person who sees the gain to be derived from communicating far outweighed by the act of speaking itself. In other words, they feel that speech forces them to risk more than they want to risk. Gerald M. Phillips, whose notion of speech improvement as an agent to personality change was discussed earlier in this chapter, has for many years conducted special speech classes for students exhibiting an unusually high amount of fear about speaking. One comforting discovery he has made is that some degree of anxiety attends all communicative activity; this appears to be true for both normals and reticents (Phillips 1968). However, highly reticent individuals seem to exhibit certain characteristics more often than do those not so afflicted. Highly reticent people exhibit excessive shakiness, perspiring, and other physical symptoms of nervousness; an inability to talk to "important" people (professors, employers, etc.); self-perceptions of extreme shyness; a tendency to be overly apologetic; an inability to talk to parents; and (as you might expect from our previous discussion) a preference for writing exercises as opposed to speaking activities. If you see yourself here, do not be alarmed. We all have such feelings and engage in such behaviors from time to time. Highly reticent individuals, however, behave in these ways both *excessively and consistently*—it is not an on-or-off behavior for them as it is for most of us.

We bring up this issue of excessive reticence for one basic reason. Speaking problems as dramatic as these clearly point to the "little tensions" and risks that talking necessarily entails for "normals." Some readers may find our use of "necessarily" puzzling. After all, we all have had many enjoyable conversations where fear, tension, and risk were not present. Our rejoinder may sound like just another professorial equivocation. It does seem true that all of our oral communicative activities involve some sort of risk or tension but *it is our capability of dealing with the tension that varies greatly*, and in many cases, the pleasures of the communicative experience minimize our perceptions of the tensions. Knowing *why* such tensions exist in the first place, however, seems to be the first step in developing an ability to cope with these unpleasant, but necessary, portions of the speech experience.

FEAR AND THE SPOKEN WORD

Our first clue to why speaking sometimes is fearful comes from our previous discussions of the "social" and "personal" natures of the speaking experience. *Because speaking forces me to put myself on the line in front of others and because I value myself and others, speaking by its very nature involves risk.* If the risk is great, tension develops. If the tension mounts steadily, fear ensues.

Consider the proposal situation, a situation where risk, tension, and fear traditionally are present. He, by asking for Her hand, risks not only rejection, but also being thought foolish or presumptuous. She is his one true love, and hence tension is produced because a valued relationship hangs in the balance. And because all of this is so tenuous and uncertain, because he cannot predict her response, the fear of the unknown looms large.

This example gives rise to two subpropositions about the risks of talking. The first is that *the fear associated with talking will be high when we are acutely aware of being evaluated.* In other words, when we are placed in situations where it becomes *obvious* to us that others are judging our words, we tend to become unnerved. As sociologist Erving Goffman says in *Interaction Ritual* (1967):

> ... When a person volunteers a statement or message, however trivial or commonplace, he commits himself and those he addresses, and in a sense places everyone present in jeopardy. By saying something, the speaker opens himself up to the possibility that the intended recipients will affront him by not listening or will think him forward, foolish, or offensive in what he has said. (p. 37)

What Goffman is saying is that the risk of being judged adversely is always present when we speak. But as anyone who has ever attempted to explain away a speeding violation to a hard-nosed cop knows only too well, we are sometimes *especially* aware of the talk-and-judge procedure that humans engage in.

What increases our awareness of this evaluation procedure? There are several factors. Tension seems to increase when

1. *the person we are talking to is especially important to us.* This is one way of explaining the tension some students feel in a public speaking exercise. The teacher is grading, the peer group is sizing you up, and you yourself are especially conscious of your words. ("Boy, is this going over like a lead balloon.")
2. *the size of the audience is larger than normal.* The application to the classroom speaking situation is obvious. Here, a great *number* of evaluations of us are being made simultaneously and the complexity of monitoring such judgments becomes difficult. However another variable to be taken into account here is the composition, not only the size of the audience. After all, we would much rather speak to a roomful of friends than face one Dean of Students!
3. *there is an imbalance in the status of those engaged in conversation.* This probably explains why it takes us so long to "warm up" when talking to some of our teachers. Because they have a certain amount of "power" over us, we cannot help but feel that they are judging *everything* we say—even our hellos and goodbyes!

All these situations have one thing in common—a sudden consciousness of the judging of our verbalizations and, ultimately, of our very personalities. The "risk" involved is that the judgment will be negative. This is perhaps why lulls in conversations, those awful "dead" spots during an otherwise convivial evening, are especially painful. Suddenly, we are made to realize that people have been sitting back and judging us, and that these judgments were previously camouflaged by the very chatter we now so passionately desire to have resumed.

The second subproposition is that *the fear associated with talking will be high when we are not able to predict the outcomes of the interaction.* This springs from the very nature of fear itself. When in doubt, fear! This is reasonable, since for most of us maintaining the status quo will do very nicely, thank you, if our only other option involves embracing a hazy and possibly painful future. While the unknown could contain more good than bad, we rarely seem to make book on it.

The unknowns in the speaking situation are many. In addition to the sometimes tortuous search for things to say and ways to say them, we also have to decide what our feelings on the subject are and how the listener will react. Thus, total unpredictability seems to be the nature of communication. We can try to control for as many such factors as possible, but the tensions connected with speaking seem high when

1. *we do not know (or are unsure of) how we feel about ourselves.* This may seem like a strange proposition, but one of the most unnerving of human prospects is to find out something about ourselves that others have long since observed. It is probably for some such reason that many persons fear sensitivity training and psychiatric counseling sessions, even though such a revelation can, of course, be pleasurable. Both situations present two risks: (a) "I'll find out something about me that I'd rather not deal with" and (b) "You'll find out something about me that I'd rather we didn't discover simultaneously."

2. *we don't know or are unsure of how we feel about the audience.* The archetype situation involves conversing with strangers. Because each of us lives in a very unique world, we necessarily meet and engage an "unknown quantity" whenever we talk with another. Strangers simply add to the unpredictability of the situation. First meetings are often awkward for us, for we are never quite sure what we might be risking by talking to this new addition to our lives.

3. *we are unsure of the dynamics of the speaking situation.* Life is filled with examples of this type of talking tension. How does one behave when meeting "Her" parents for the *first* time? What do you say to a professor *outside* of the classroom? How do you manage yourself when speaking to your girlfriend and to your parents *simultaneously?* The many unknowns that an unfamiliar speech setting sometimes involves can wither the hardiest of us.

COPING WITH FEAR

At this point two questions should be puzzling most readers: (1) With all these risks and tensions present, why should I ever open my mouth? and (2) How do I cope with these risks and fears? The answer to the first question is obvious from our initial discussion in this chapter. As humans, we have no other choice but to speak. The second question is a bit more difficult to answer. We could of course, simply avoid talking to people who are important to us, whose status is higher than ours, whom we do not know. Obviously, such a solution is patently impractical.

Like all human problems, the antidote to fear seems to be knowledge and experience. By reducing the "unknowns" in the speaking situation, we will increase our chances of having a pleasurable interchange. Becoming aware of our own uncertainties and limitations will better enable us to deal with them. We will begin to get a feeling for the range and complexity of human behavior only by meeting different people. By thrusting ourselves into various types of interactions, we will be in a position to meet the challenges of new and strange speech settings. And last, by knowing as much as possible about the nature of human auditors, about both our self-image and our social image, and about the practical demands placed upon all speakers, *we will be able to put the tensions associated with talking in their proper perspective—as necessary, but not unconquerable, portions of the speaking experience.*

Thus, the psychology of the speech classroom is not very different from the psychology your mother used with you when, as a four-year-old, you felt sure that a gaggle of goblins laid in wait in your closet, ready to spring out when the shadows lengthened. If she was sensible, she invited you to come with her, hand in hand, and investigate the nature of dark closets. While the closets are just as dark in spoken interactions, experience (in the form of sensitive classroom speech activities) still seems to be the best hand-maiden.

speaking as a jack-of-all-trades

In a way, this sums up all we have said before. Speech *does things* for us. It tells us about our humanity, about ourselves, and about our fellow humans, but above all, speaking is our attempt to control our environments. We talk because we want to share our joy, our knowledge, our boredom, or our frustrations, and because we want to maintain or modify our social environments by such sharing.

In a delightful book entitled *Speech and Man* (1966), Charles Brown and Charles Van Riper retell the tale of the lad who, by the age of five, was yet to utter a single syllable. His parents were beside themselves with worry. Where had they gone wrong in producing a child who would not speak? One morning at the breakfast table, Silent Sam gave vent to his verbalization: "This oatmeal is damned lumpy." Uncontrollably excited, his parents posed the obvious question: "For five years you've said nothing. Not even baby talk. Why? Why? Why?" The answer came readily: "Until now, everything was alright!"

The implication of this story is not that kids have it too easy these days, but rather that we speak when we *have to.* We speak because it is one of the few nonviolent ways of changing the social world around us. And being the unsatisfied beasts we are, we do a lot of talking: "Hamburger again, Mom?" "May I see your license, Miss?" "But you do love me, don't you, Mary?"

Speech, then, has many functions, not all of which are mutually exclusive. In *Speech and Man* (1966), Brown and Van Riper have constructed a handy set of categories for looking at the functional aspects of human speech and it is to these that we will now turn our attention.

SPEECH AS EMOTIONAL EXPRESSION

In a very real sense, speech is an outlet for our emotions. Swearing at hammers which mutilate fingers helps in that it takes some of the anguish outside of our bodies. The husband rants and raves after a hard day at the salt mines while his wife sits demurely and lets him blow off steam. Her chance will come the next day at the coffee klatsch where the women gather to disparage their salt miners!

With the advent of Esalen, T-groups, encounters, sensitivity sessions, and the suburban bargain-basement therapy clinic, Americans have found a new and sometimes profitable way of expressing their emotions through speech. All such outlets are based on the fundamental assumption that speech is the healer and helpmate to the psyche, just as anxiety is the building block of neuroses. Good bartenders have long understood this therapeutic aspect of human speech and are, perhaps, the unsung heroes of the mental health community with their "Yes, Mr. Sullivan, I know exactly what you mean." If we are to believe contemporary psychotherapists, it is important that we continue to establish and maintain settings and institutions where expressive speech is not just tolerated, but encouraged, by sympathetic and known spoken responses.

SPEECH AS A SEARCH FOR IDENTITY

If asked, "Who are you?" how would you respond? Most likely you would reply by stating your name, occupation, dominant personality characteristic, political party affiliation, or some such objective description. This is not an idle question. As Brown and Van Riper contend, much of our oral communication is an attempt to find an answer to the query, "Who am I?" With the depersonalization of society, with the myriad of social roles each of us is asked to play daily, and with the growing complexities of rapidly changing ideas and mores, "Who am I?" becomes perhaps the *only* question worth asking.

And we "ask" this question over and over again, always veiling it in some sort of conversational guise ("Oh, those other people gave a much better speech than I did, don't you think?") or burying it beneath the cloak and dagger of courtship ("Well, now, you probably

think I'm just another one of the empty-headed sorority girls").
These are attempts to get data about ourselves from the speech behaviors of others—without getting burned.

The fact that we often say things that surprise us, probably indicates that we also learn about ourselves by "listening" to *our own*
words. If we were not so egocentric in our speech patterns and concerned with establishing our personal identities, why would 40–80
percent of all of our oral statements contain the pronoun "I"? As
Brown and Van Riper (1966) say: "Listen, if you will, to the staccato
of the perpendicular pronoun in the speech about you: 'And I said to
him, I said . . .' 'I'm the kind of person who . . .' 'I think that . . .'
The 'I's explode like popcorn in the conversational pan" (p. 36). And
what could be a more *natural* way for finding out about ourselves
than by listening to our very own speech or to the spoken remarks
made about us by others?

SPEECH FOR COMMUNICATION

In *The Naked Ape* (1967), Desmond Morris discusses why infants
cry. According to him they cry because they are in pain, because they
are hungry, because they are alone, because they are in unfamiliar
territory, because they want to change their physical surroundings,
and because they are frustrated. What better beginner's list is there
to explain why adults attempt to *communicate*. Common to all of the
infant's screams is some kind of built-in knowledge that *he needs
the assistance of others* to meet the demands that this world has
placed upon him.

The communicative aspects of orality probably override all speech
functions. After all, billions of us have been placed in a world that
can comfortably accommodate only half that many—and told to work
it out together. Together! Somehow, we have been charged by the
fates to take all of those magnificent thoughts stored within us and,
by using the fragile, halting tool of human speech, make those meanings someone else's. What could be more difficult or frustrating?
Perhaps, not making an attempt.

Quite obviously, this book will deal heavily with the communicative potentialities of human speech. Communication is an unwieldly
process, yet at times it is dramatically effective. Communication presumes an almost computerlike intellectual ability on our parts, yet we
take it in stride. Most of all, communication demands a tolerance for
individual differences before even elementary social sharing, not to
mention social cohesion or social change, can be accomplished. Because all of us are so enamored at times with the expressive and
egocentric aspects of human speech, speech for communication fights
a Herculean battle for its place in the sun.

SPEECH FOR CONTROL

Put simply, control speech takes our talk and puts it to work—preaching the Good News, constructing a Third Reich, cleaning up the local polluter, or putting pressure on congressmen, doctors, lawyers, Indian Chiefs, and other influential members of the community. Control speech is the speech of saviors and demagogues, of kings and paupers, of courters and courtees. It is a practical use of oral communication designed to make some sort of dent in the rigidity and lethargy of both the Establishment and the counter-culture. Control speech is an attempt to modify existing conditions, to right wrongs, or to create new ones in their stead.

It is not entirely accidental that speech is used as a vehicle for controlling our social environments. Again, we must consider the options. If we did not use speech, what would we use—bombs? torture? coercion? It is interesting that even in totalitarian societies, control speech is used in fantastic proportions. To document this, we need only look at the greatest "controller" of them all—Adolph Hitler. Hitler, more than most totalitarians, had a native understanding of the tremendous potential of control speech.

Fortunately, lovers of peace and charity have also latched on to the ways in which control speech can be harnessed, and have been engaging themselves in the market-place of spoken confrontation with the would-be murderers and dictators.

SPEECH FOR THOUGHT

Just as speech is the outgrowth of mental operations, so is it the informer and sustainer of thought. Circular, you say? Precisely. When we talk, we are at once drawing upon what we "know" and at the same time adding to that store of knowledge.

There are those who argue that we never really "know" something until it can be *said*, clearly, lucidly, and articulately. There is much to be said for such a position. After having traversed the campus hundreds of times, can you give a stranger precise, well-phrased directions to the Student Union? Or how many times have you found yourself attempting to explain a math formula to a friend, only to discover that in the middle of the explanation, you did not know it as well as you had originally presumed. And who can forget the tremendous satisfaction we derive when we are finally able to "put it into words"?

Speech-for-thought also has more serious consequences. For many years, Russian psychologists have been investigating the interrelationships between thinking and speech. Roughly stated, their conclusions are twofold: (1) speech patterns seem to be good indicators of mental development, and (2) the ability to verbalize can assist the individual in growing intellectually. They have found, for example, that patients, whose mental disorders have impaired their motor ability, can significantly increase their mobility by *saying out loud* what they are trying to get their bodies to do. The same principle of transference operates in the psychiatrist's office. Sometimes by simply *putting it into words* (which is often a painful procedure in itself), patients are better able to understand the causes and dimensions of their disturbances. Anyone who has ever read aloud the essay he had composed to see if "it seems as though I know what I'm talking about," has some feeling for the speech-for-thought phenomenon.

SPEECH FOR PLEASURE

Aside from the psychiatrist's couch and Hitler's rallies, we humans talk because talking is fun. We engage in bull sessions, in talk dates, and in gossip parties simply because it is enjoyable to exercise our speaking capabilities. In *Games People Play*, Eric Berne (1964) argues that the ultimate function of human speech is simply to structure time, to have something to do. Certain people, among whom are preachers, teachers, and politicians, seem to do nothing but talk. Judging by the popularity of such professions, it is apparent that people derive much satisfaction by structuring their time in such a talking fashion.

Here we seem to come full circle to our initial discussion in this chapter. We talk because we are human animals and at the same time social animals. We make small talk because it is rather enjoyable to while away the time "just talking." Desmond Morris sees this small talk phenomenon simply as an elaboration of our animalistic need to groom each other. What else could explain the all-too-human piece of dialogue Brown and Van Riper (1966) cite as an example of the very ordinary pleasures associated with human speech?

"Whatcha going to do now?"
"Oh, I dunno. Just take it easy."
"Take it easy, eh? Won't make any nickels that way."
"Who wants nickels? I'm a dollar man, myself."
"Yeah?"
"Yeah." (p. 121)

THE MULTIFUNCTIONS OF SPEECH

We should not view these six functions of speech as being mutually exclusive since most of our spoken acts are motivated and guided by more than just one such function. For example, besides providing diversion, our small talk often gives us insight into ourselves and may help us understand something we have never really grasped before. Or, we may sit down for a pleasant evening of chatter and wind up exhorting our guests to join the Peace Corps. There are times when we misperceive the speech function most appropriate to a particular setting and that sometimes makes for problems. The businessman who cannot suppress the impulse to "talk shop" over the dinner table is apparently unaware that dinnertime conversations are usually set up for "pleasure speech." And many a popular mobilizer has been accused of primarily seeking ego-gratification with his public exhortations, rather than adhering to his task of changing public policy. In short, the complexities and interrelationships of man's speech functions are simply outgrowths of the complexity of social man himself.

conclusion

In the public speech situation, the situation about which Peg and Carolyn have such ambivalent feelings, the nature and functions of human speech become dramatically apparent. The public speaker is made aware (sometimes painfully) of the amount of personal investment effective speaking demands. The size of his audience vivifies the amount of social sharing that speech entails. The knee-knocking and occasional stammering of the student speaker dramatizes the risks we run when confronting one another in a talking situation. But our sense of controlling our environment that public speaking offers, and the emotional and intellectual rewards brought about by such communication experiences, can make the whole exercise seem worth it, even if sometimes we feel that our spoken products are only so much oral graffiti. *In short, public communication exercises make the pains and pleasures associated with all of our oral communication easier to see, to understand, and to deal with, than do our more frequent but more casual conversations.*

To understand human speech is to be in a position to control it intelligently. As Brown and Van Riper say, speech is a miracle. It makes us unique. It makes us happy. It comforts us. And it gives us social power. It both *says* things and *does* things. ("I do" is a good attestation to the utilitarian power of speech.) Thus, before anyone *uses* this miracle tool, it would behoove him to know something about it. After all, what self-respecting Saturday handyman begins to build his dream house before looking at the instructions for his electric saw?

Perhaps the most fitting way to end this chapter is to again quote from Brown and Van Riper who, more than most of us, truly understand the powerful impact of human speech:

Because speaking is so commonplace, only those who have been deprived of normal utterance seem to appreciate its magical powers. The stutterer, struggling desperately to answer a casual question, knows. The cancer patient whose larynx has been removed finds suddenly that all existence has changed because the air pressure that once permitted speech to emerge from his mouth now merely swishes silently out through a hole in his neck; he knows how much he has lost. The speechless person with aphasia resulting from a stroke or automobile accident knows but he cannot tell us. In certain ancient cultures the tearing out of a victim's tongue was the ultimate punishment, worse than death itself. It is through the use of speech and language that we live together, work, earn our livings, win our mates, and find our meanings in the pinpoint of time and space that we inhabit. Yet few of us ever give our speech more than casual attention; few of us ever view it as the most important instrument we will ever learn to manipulate.[1]

[1]C. Brown and C. Van Riper, *Speech and Man* (Englewood Cliffs, N.J.: Prentice-Hall, 1966), pp. 1–2.

communication: the world mediator

CHAPTER 3

Dad: Well, now you've done it! A high school student caught smoking marijuana! Why, you've ruined your family's good name in the community, made a laughing stock out of me at work, destroyed your mother's social life ...

Mom: Now, David, don't get so upset, remember that Bobby is our little boy.

Dad: Little boy? He's turned into a pot-smoker!

Bob: Oh, and I suppose that drinking is OK, huh?

Dad: Don't you sass me. Why, when I was your age I had respect for my father. You're just like all the rest of these kids—don't care about your family or our standing in the community, or ...

Mom: Now, David, this isn't getting us anywhere. We've got to come up with a solution.

Bob: Well, I've got a solution. I'm going to get out of this house.

Dad: That's a silly solution. What we've got to do is impose a curfew on you. Watch your friends. Get you a job so that you're too tired to smoke that stuff.

Mom: Now, David, we've got to remember the psychological implications of our decisions on Bobby's adjustment to his peer group. Freud says that . . .

Dad: Listen, Margaret, now don't you start with all that fancy stuff. That adjustment junk is a bunch of nonsense. I should have disciplined this kid until he knew what respect was.

Bob: I'm getting out of here. All you do is pick on me. You never understand my side of things. You're always persecuting me and . . .

Dad: Persecuted you, huh? Why I've given you everything money can buy.

Bob: That's it, Dad. Tell me how it is with you Establishment-types. You don't even care why I smoked.

Mom: Now stop it, you two. We're not getting any-where. Would anyone like coffee? I made some sweet rolls this morning. You know, the kind with raisins that Bobby likes so much.

Bob: Mother, don't think that you're going to change the subject. And stop calling me "Bobby."

Mom: Oh, dear, now you're against your mother. The woman who cared for you when you were sick with the measles. Oh, what is this world coming to?

What we've apparently got here (in our admittedly contrived dialogue) is a failure to communicate. But is this really a *communication* problem? From the looks of things, we might just as easily call this a noncommunication problem. Perhaps because frequent and intimate dialogues did not "grease the communication machinery," Mom, Dad, and Bob now find that they can only make words at one another, not share experiences, expand horizons, or, for that matter, even get through three minutes of conversation.

Or could we more accurately term this a "talking" problem, in the sense that some of the functions of talk are being used at the expense of others? This is certainly an example of talking for expressing emotions, and obviously, not a case of speech for pleasure—and can anyone doubt that speech for control is being used? Even Mom, through her weakness and inability to face the problem, does a fine job of making her presence felt. In a sense, we can see our little dialogue as an instance of speech for thought—by hearing himself assert his uncompromising position, for example, Dad perhaps achieved great insights into the righteousness of his stand.

More crucially, is this verbal montage a case of speech for *communication*? To our way of thinking it is, in the sense that meanings were generated in human minds through the use of words, and interpersonal relationships were affected by symbol-using humans. In short, Mom, Dad, and Bob had an inkling of where each "stood" at the conclusion of the interaction. Unfortunately, this kind of "bare boned" communication did not tell each of them where they *could* stand relative to one another or how their person-to-person relationships could be made more productive through talk.

Thus, even by the crudest criteria defining *effective* communication, the interactants fail miserably. Meanings were not shared. No sense of commonality was established—the "community" part of *communi*cation was nowhere to be heard. It is unlikely that the three participants received any rewards from their encounter. Even Dad, who apparently "won," achieved a decidedly Pyrrhic victory—it is doubtful that future attempts at communication between him and Bob would be enhanced by the interaction in which they have just engaged. Who can doubt that further and even more bitter verbal escalation would result from their forthcoming meetings? Perhaps the most devastating aspect of this interaction is not the lack of mutual acceptance, which is rare enough anyway, but the total lack of concern by all parties involved as to *why* the others feel as they do. Any chance for a fuller understanding of reasons, motivations, or "hidden" feelings was destroyed entirely through this instance of collective irrelevance.

It is not the purpose of this text to study the causes of this ruptured communication experience. In this chapter, we would like to look at perhaps the most basic factor which precipitated this three-way verbal assault—*the inability to perceive and the refusal to accept individual uniqueness and human similarities.* We feel that if Mom, Dad, and Bob were able and willing *to see* each other as the very distinct creatures they are and *to search* for common areas of concern and motivation, they would have been able to approach at least a rough-hewn type of understanding and perhaps, accommodation. After discussing the complexities of the worlds in which we live, we will turn to those aspects of the communication process which make talking a handicapper's delight.

communication and the worlds in which we live

For the past five years, one of your authors has been asking his students to name the three heroes in their lives. The responses to such a question are fascinating. Out of the 200 or so written responses to this query, many were predictable. Relatives were chosen 17 percent of the time, close friends 22 percent, actors 10 percent, and political figures 7 percent. Interestingly enough, more "traditional" hero-types such as literary, religious, athletic, and entertainment personages were seldom chosen. One of the most intriguing statistics emanating from this very informal study pertained to the category chosen most frequently: over 20 percent of the respondents indicated that they had no heroes whatsoever. When coupled with the miscellaneous choices (which, among others, include Mick Jagger, Henry VIII, Superman, Charley Brown, Abigail Adams, Earl Scruggs, and, of course, Bilbo and Frodo), it is evident that a great number of the students surveyed were quite resistant to identifying with the types of "super-beings" that so frequently were held in regard in times past.

The relevance of this to our recent discussion of the plights of Dad, Mom, and Bob may escape you at this point, but it is simple. Assuming that Bob is a worthy product of his culture—the era that has produced the antihero—it is not difficult to begin to see why Dad has such trouble conversing with his son. Dad, who probably identifies strongly with John Wayne, General MacArthur, Babe Ruth, and more recently, Archie Bunker, probably could not have (1) *predicted* his son's responses to our little questionnaire, (2) *understood* his son's reactions, and (3) certainly could not have *accepted* the values and attitudes underlying Bob's outlook on life. As we will be asserting throughout this book, *a speaker's ability to predict the behaviors of his listeners as well as his fortitude in understanding and at least partially accepting the values of those with whom he converses, is fundamental to any sort of effective interaction.*

ACCEPTING OUR DIFFERENCES

Some day, someone might become rich and famous by authoring a book entitled *The Games Students Play.* The book will deal with such topics as Excuses Students Use, Courtship in the Classroom, and How to Cheat Creatively. But Chapter 1 will have to be devoted to the Ostrich Game which takes place when the professor is looking for a response to his very convoluted and long-winded question. He looks around the room, searching for a student to call upon, but nobody will establish eye contact with him. The students are sanctimoniously scanning their notebooks, looking out the window, searching, gazing, staring everywhere and anywhere *except* at the professor. Should our pedagogue be offended by this mini-form of social isolation? Not at all. He should just be reminded that his students are playing the Ostrich Game, that well-entrenched, head-in-the-sand, classroom reaction that asserts: "If I can't see you, you can't see me, and hence you can't call on me since I'm not really here."

Absurd as this statement is, you know from your classroom experience that this type of behavior does, indeed, take place. Students, like everyone else, are in a very real sense imprisoned in a world of their own creation. They can engage in such ostrichlike delusions because they know, or think they know, that "others" can never really enter their world entirely because it is *their* world—they created it, they sustain it, and *they* will determine who or what is admitted through its portals. Their worlds, or more accurately their *perceptual worlds*, are perfectly capable of keeping out intruding professors.

We are taking the position here that each and every human being is "locked into" his own unique and sometimes very private perceptual world, that this makes him fundamentally different from all others, and that human interactions can hardly be profitable until such understandings are uppermost in the minds of persons involved in communication. Obviously, there is nothing new about this statement, except that, as with truisms, we tend to forget or overlook such wisdom at the time we should bear it most in mind—when we are *talking* to one another. Thus, we suggest that the most basic and most fundamental barrier to effective communication is the very human tendency to talk to others *as if they were ourselves*, as if they "lived" in *our* perceptual worlds.

THE COMPONENTS OF OUR PERCEPTUAL WORLDS

We can define a perceptual world as that *complex of forces that allows us to see what we see.* The components of our perceptual worlds are the "slices" of our beings that make us what we are. Some of these "slices" are depicted in Figure 2. Many of the terms used in the figure may be familiar to you, so a few brief, informal definitions might suffice:

past experiences: the real-life personal and social situations we have been part of

status: our social, economic, intellectual, and so on "standing" in the hierarchy of society *values:* those tangible and intangible "goods" that we esteem and seek

roles: the sometimes apparent, sometimes subtle social obligations we must meet; these include ordinary "tasks" (e.g., student) as well as "psychological duties" that we or others place upon us (e.g., subservient student)

reference groups: any collection of persons with which we strongly identify; includes both formal social ties (e.g., fraternities) as well as informal or imagined ones (e.g., a secret desire to be part of a subculture)

norms: often unspoken, but tacitly understood, "rules" that we follow in our day-to-day interactions with others

self-image: our total picture of our strengths, weaknesses, idiosyncracies, ambitions, etc.

social image: our conception of what *others* think of us

This is neither the time nor the place to study all the complexities and nuances of these and other features of our perceptual worlds. However, it probably goes without saying that all such forces are quite complex and are very important in making us what we are to

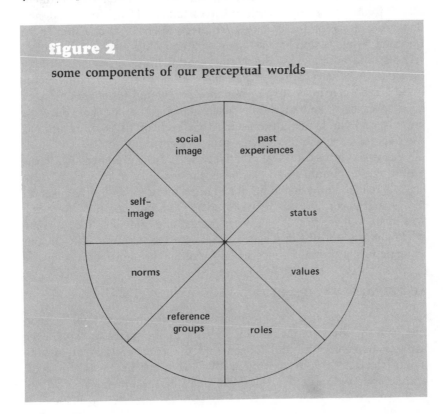

figure 2

some components of our perceptual worlds

ourselves, what we are to others, and what we *can* be both to ourselves and to others.

With just these few tools in mind we can begin to see why Mom, Dad, and rebellious Bob had such a difficult time when trying to converse with one another. We can see Dad drawing on his own past experiences ("When I was your age . . .") to little avail as Bob compares such remarks to his own values ("What's happening today is really all that's important"). We observe both Dad and Bob attack each other's reference groups ("Establishment-types" vs. "high school kids") with tragic results. Without much in-depth analysis, we can see Dad's self-imposed role of authority figure clash sharply with Bob's self-image of a rugged individualist. Perhaps saddest of all is Mom's struggle with the negative feedback her social-image receives. But all of this Monday-morning quarterbacking we are doing is somewhat peripheral, since it is most difficult to recognize possible areas of perceptual conflict when we are *engaged in the act* of communication. Being the very rapid, oftentimes confusing process that it is, communication very rarely affords those tranquil moments to which the poet Wordsworth addresses himself.

It should not be very difficult to imagine a completely different set of circumstances for our little trio of talkers. Had Mom, Dad, and Bob been aware of the countless studies that have shown that even fraternal twins, reared by the "same" parents, educated in the "same" schools, and adopted by the "same" social groups, *must inevitably turn out to be very different persons*, perhaps sensitive adjustments could have been made to the remarks our would-be communicators have so casually and carelessly hurled at one another. For, once we initially and fundamentally assume that each of us is quite unique, we *must adapt* to the unknown worlds we encounter daily.

But if the refusal to deal creatively with our differences is a basic problem in communication, so too is the inability to make our similarities really count in communication. Despite the baffling set of forces that encourages us to stand apart from one another, there is a wealth of values, past experiences, roles, and the like, that we can or do share with others. These features can become our allies in our struggle to try to make sense to one another through talk.

ACCEPTING OUR SIMILARITIES

Perhaps you have had the experience of seeing an exceptionally good film, one that literally makes you bursting at the seams to explain the show to someone else and to generate the same excitement in him. You rush back to your apartment, "tie" your roommate to the chair, and explode with every memorable detail of the movie. You do no' worry about orienting him at the beginning of your "speech," or placing the details in an understandable sequence, or even monitoring his responses to your talk; you simply tell it the way you feel it, remembering it as you do. When you have "wound down" finally, you slump to your chair with all of the satisfaction that speech for pleasure can give a person. Now, if your roommate is kind, one who is able to appreciate the richness and uniqueness of your experience, he will not throw a book at you for wasting his time while you "thought out loud." If he is especially kind, he will not even let on that he had not understood a thing you have said; instead, he will ask for a few more details, desperately hoping that after your moment of passion has passed, you will be reminded of interpersonal differences and talk *to him*, not *to yourself in his presence*.

Except for an excessive amount of human kindness, what, do you suppose, would account for your roommate's extraordinary restraint? Friendship? Compassion? Duplicity? All of these are possibilities. But an equally likely explanation of his forebearance might be that he can see a bit of himself in you—he can see some of his past experiences in yours. Although he has never seen "your" movie, he has had other experiences that have pushed him beyond the usual limits of human excitement. Your experiences and those of your roommate have been different, yet similar enough for him to make accommodations for you. Different but alike. Perhaps after all, such rugged approximations of experience are our only real basis for making safe bets in communication.

USING OUR SIMILARITIES

But similarities, even rough ones, do not simply "exist" between people trying to communicate effectively. Unlike kindly roommates, most listeners are not so willing to "extend" themselves in communication —*speakers* must demonstrate where their's and their listeners' views converge. *Speakers*, in all but the friendliest of circumstances, must build the communicative bridges and invite listeners to meet them half way.

Again, turning to the dialogue that opened this chapter, it is remarkable how little capitalizing on similarities occurred in this all-too-common verbal skirmish. Solutions could not be found; furthermore, Dad and Bob were unable to establish common methods of looking for them. Mom and Bob could not even agree on sweet rolls!

Yet the similarities were potentially "there," even though untapped. Locked deep inside of the three perceptual worlds, we can assume, were a host of commonalities, many of which could have been loosed in an effort to communicate effectively. For instance, although it is not apparent on the surface of the conversation, there was probably some amount of affection binding the three, although nothing *communicative* was made of such a fact. Bob and Dad both probably place value on just solutions, but justice never became a topic of conversation. All three members of the group were obviously trying to protect their social images but not one of them seemed willing to admit this, even tacitly, and hence the battle was waged. It is because these important areas of similarity were *not discussed* that explains some of the reasons for the ensuing turmoil.

MANIFESTING OUR SIMILARITIES: AN EXAMPLE

Communication contacts need not, however, resemble the opening dialogue. We are different from one another, but we need not crusade about it. Let us consider an instance of apparently successful communication to see how the *utilization of human similarities in communication can have a profound impact on our interpersonal relationships.*

Being of the Cowboy Bob, Captain Kangaroo era, most of you are probably unfamiliar with "Mister Rogers' Neighborhood," a delightful, contemporary show aimed at three- to eight-year-olds and appearing on 237 channels of the Public Broadcasting Service. This daily excursion into the mysterious world of little people has a number of important lessons to teach any serious student of communication.

Consider the premise. Fred Rogers, a forty-five-year-old ordained minister and professional musician, attempts for 30 minutes a day to communicate with children whom he can neither see nor hear. An even greater task is his attempt to convey some extremely sophisticated concepts to his audience and do so without boring them. Any of you who has ever tried to crack into the world of the four-year-old, probably has some idea of the communicative challenge that Rogers continually sets for himself.

What is perhaps most interesting about Fred Rogers' approach is that *he does not assume irreconcilable differences between himself and his audience.* Instead, he concentrates on similarities. Admittedly, as an adult he shaves, pays taxes, drives too fast on occasion, and engages in the numerous other daily routines that are part of the adult world. All such considerations, it is probably safe to say, lie well outside of the perceptual world of the tot, but Rogers remembers the child within us all. Different though he and his audience are (and Rogers is careful to acknowledge this on occasion), his intellectual propositions, his analogies and examples, and even his bodily movements and tone of voice are startlingly attractive to the child. Consider the lyrics from one of his songs and see if you could improve on his ability to stress similarities and hence reach some measure of communicative accord with his audience:

It's great for me to remember
As I put away my toys,
That Mothers were all little girls one time
And Fathers were all little boys.

My Daddy seems so big right now
He must have grown a lot.
Imagine how he felt one day
When he was just a tot.

My Mother's not so big as Dad,
But bigger than my sister.
I wonder if she ever had
A little fever blister? . . .

My Daddy didn't even have
A real electric fan.
He had to wait a long time too
'till he became a man.

My Mother used an ironing board
And play irons that were colder.
She often wished for big folks' things
But she waited, and got older.

So knives and plugs and hot things
Are OK for Mom and Dad,
'cause when they were a girl and boy
They played with what they had.

And I think I can wait now
And grow the way they do,
And I will use the grown-up things
When I'm a grown-up too. . . .[1]

Even if the poem does not bring a tear to your eye, it surely re-
veals a rare *communicative* mind at work, a man who is able to get a
reading on the past experiences, norms, values, and especially the
self-images of his listeners and, most remarkable, work within these
parameters in getting a message across to a somewhat alien audience.

We have been arguing in this section of the chapter that two very
human demons continually bedevil communication contacts. Oblivious Olga, that charming but inept wench who continually assumes
that others' worlds are but machine duplicated copies of her own, is
one of our problem communicators. Not to be outdone, however, is
Haughty Hal, who speaks his piece and literally dares his listeners
to find a semblance of common ground in his message. While such
quaint characters have a certain amount of charm about them, they
appear to do little to facilitate effective communication.

---

[1]Fred Rogers, *Let's Be Together Today.* Album produced by Small World Enterprises, Inc. Reprinted by permission of Family Communications Inc.

aspects of the communication process

Our previous discussion may appear to be more suited to a philosophy book than to one which purportedly deals with communication. We feel, however, that a very solid *communicative* reason has motivated our discussion of perceptual worlds. Unless a speaker assumes, initially and fundamentally, that he and his listeners live in very different worlds, he will have no need to adapt, no need to monitor feedback, no need to structure his messages with other human beings in mind—indeed, he would have no need to study the communicative techniques suggested in this book. In fact, if individual differences did not produce so many uncertainties for a speaker, he could just "think his thought," attach it to any language that seemed handy, and "place" his meanings directly into the crania of his listeners.

COMMUNICATION AS A BETTING PROPOSITION

Unfortunately, the world of human talk does not operate this way. We do not send or transmit meanings. Rather, we use a very fragile system of verbal and nonverbal symbols and thereby *induce* listeners to react to us. In reacting to us, listeners may or may not reconstruct the meanings that *our* worlds have captured. If we think about communication as a process of inducing, not sending, we are then forced to view talking as a choice-making proposition; for, in *induction*, the crucial question becomes: given what I know about myself, about my audience, about my topic, about my native language, and so forth, what options do I have when constructing a message for a person living in a world unknown to me? If we could *transmit* meanings—say, via ESP—certainty and "message fidelity" would abound. However, regular, everyday practical communication will have none of this feigned surety. There is a constant warning implied in communication: "If you stop considering alternative ways of saying things, if you cease to look over your options carefully, watch out. I'll be there to get you when you least expect it. I'll put you into contact with a sweet old lady in tennis shoes who, unknown to you, wrestles alligators on the side. And then you try to talk to her about garden parties!"

In connection with these remarks about uncertainty, let us consider a childhood experience you might have had: It's a hot summer's eve and you cannot sleep. You steal out of the house, being careful not to trip over the cat, and head for your favorite "thinking spot." You sit on that very special stump at Old Listening Lake and, being the twelve-year-old you are, quite naturally proceed to throw a stone into the quiet water.

Since it is the blackest of nights, you cannot see exactly where the stone hit, nor can you see the number of ripples it produced. You cannot see how high the water splashed nor can you gauge how quickly your unseen missile dropped to the bottom of the lake. All that your efforts have evoked—that is, induced—is a splash. The only "information" or "feedback" you've received from the water is a "ker-plunk." But you like the sound of the "kerplunk" and attempt to see if, by controlling as many of the "variables" as possible, you can, with another stone, reproduce this fascinating sound. So you try again. You look for a stone whose dimensions approximate those of your first weapon. You wait for the wind to die down and as you hurl your next projectile, you are careful to match the velocity of the throw and the amount of wrist-snap to that of your first effort. And what do you get for your trouble? You guessed it, a "kerploosh"!

A "kerploosh" and not a "kerplunk"? What's wrong with that lake? Doesn't it have the good sense to *interact* intelligently with the very best rock thrower in these parts? It is after all, the same lake on both occasions. Or is it? Was Old Listening Lake in the same "mood" in both instances, what with the wind, the floating logs, and the trout to bestir it? And how about your stone-encrusted *messages*? Were they the same in both cases? Since you could not "see" these little wavelets—the perceptual worlds of dark lakes being just as mysteri-ous as are those of people—you really could not assess the *covert feedback* the lake was providing. Meanwhile, what has happened to your stone? Is the water "digesting" your message even as you stand there? Is it *reconstructing* your beautiful stones into some sort of moss-and-sand-covered underwater creature? It is all too frustrating to contemplate, so you trudge on home and, this time, kick the cat!

COMMUNICATION AS COMPLEXITY

There is not much difference between the frustration our twelve-year-old feels and the anguish many of us experience in our day-to-day attempts to mediate our and others' lives through communication. Communication, as we have said, is a fragile instrument, not very precise, not very predictable, sometimes even not much fun. But com-munication *is* extraordinarily complex, and just when you think you have got the process "knocked," it throws you a curve ball.

We define **efficient** communication as *the process by which a speaker manipulates symbols within his perceptual world and, through a complex process of message exchange with a listener, alters the listener's perceptual world in ways the speaker desires.* Let us discuss the constituent elements of this definition one by one:

"efficient communication is the process by which a speaker . . ."
As we have said previously, communication is at best an *attempt*. It is
never a completed "product" as far as the speaker is concerned.
Like our twelve-year-old with the stones, it is a guess-throw-and-
guess-again proposition in which the speaker simply makes bets,
some intelligent and some not, as to what effect he will produce
in an auditor.

"manipulates symbols within his perceptual world . . ." It should go
without saying that we do not send "thoughts" to one another.
We can't do so because thoughts are locked within our perceptual
worlds and cannot "escape" on their own. They need "vehicles" and
the only such vehicle humans have been able to produce to date is
a very delicate and most imperfect system of symbols. Symbols—
those verbal and nonverbal "things" that stand for our thoughts
—are really all we have to go on in communication. Fortunately, we
get pretty adept at manipulating these symbols. Much as it does for
our stone-thrower, the process of learning and acculturation teaches
us, in approximate fashion at least, the "size, heft, and probable
impact" of the language systems available to us in communication.

**"and through a complex process of message exchange with a
listener . . ."** A stone is thrown, a "kerplunk" returns. As our twelve
year-old soon discovers, communicating with lakes is not simple.
Speakers (and stone-throwers) are only a part of the process, because
they must *interact* with other persons (or objects). The trouble is,
nobody ever really is sure what symbols (and stones) "do" to
their recipients or what the returning symbols (or ripples) "mean"
in any absolute sense. All that is known is that a stimulus produces a
response and, for humans at least, life becomes a process of ferreting
out what these returning symbols—this feedback—"mean" for our
perceptual worlds.

"alters the listener's perceptual world in ways the speaker desires."
Attempting to manipulate symbols and exchange messages is only
part of the story. Communication scholars often argue that we cannot
not communicate. Even a person sitting rigidly mute in a chair "says"
something about himself to others. While all of this is true, we *can*
fail to communicate *effectively*. From a speaker's standpoint, effective
communication occurs when the listener's perceptual world "absorbs"
a bit of the speaker's and is changed in ways deemed adequate by
the speaker. The hows and whys of accomplishing this seemingly
Herculean task are not known entirely, but succeeding chapters in
this book may give you some basis for laying your communicative
bets.

One of the feelings we hope you have garnered from reading these very sketchy descriptions of the components of communicative acts is one of *movement*. In communication, the mutual alteration of perceptual worlds in which speakers and listeners engage are done so *simultaneously*. When we attempt to elicit meanings in others through our talk, we *use, receive, create, and expend* symbols both as creators of messages and as receivers of communication. We *fire* symbols at one another and, while doing so, are ourselves bombarded by still other symbol systems. Others' remarks to us *trigger off associations* within us and these associations set off more associations. And all of this goes on so quickly that to say that "communication is where the *action* is" is an understatement indeed.

THE PROCESS DEPICTED

For many years, speech and communication scholars have been trying to capture these multiple interactions on paper by drawing pictures, or models, of the process of communication. If you have some spare time, you might look at a few. The drawings are elaborate, some even artistic, but somehow they just "sit there" on the pages of the book. The life, movement, passion, and frustration of *people interacting* does not come through. A visual model of communication is not so different from taking a stop-action picture of a quarterback and, with this picture, trying to illuminate the eventual outcome of the play.

Still, pictures have their value, and so we are going to try to put our definition of effective communication "to work" by "watching it operate" diagrammatically. But *you* will have to add the dynamism, the speed, and the humanity to our picture. Most importantly, *you* will have to add the complexity since we, as mere mortals, could never hope to depict all of the variables that interact when people converse. But adding the complexity should not be difficult—you have had experience with it. Each time you have said, "I can't talk to my parents about this. They'd never understand," you have acknowledged the complexity of the communicative act, and resigned yourself to not talking because you felt totally incapable of *managing or controlling* the multitude of feelings, attitudes, and experiences that successful communication demands of us.

With all these cautions firmly in mind, consider the phases of the communicative act as illustrated in Figure 3.

Two things about our model should strike you immediately. The speaker's "world" is elliptical and the listener's is rectangular. This is a clear, but inartistic, attempt to demonstrate the human uniqueness we have discussed previously. The second point to note is that the "insides" of the speaker's and listener's worlds are quite similar—

figure 3

the phases of the process of communication

speaker's perceptual world

listener's perceptual world

| exigence |
| interpretation |
| idea generation |
| message creation |
| symbolic manipulation |

context and message signals

| exigence |
| interpretation |
| idea reconstruction |
| message creation |
| symbolic manipulation |

they have the same basic intellectual apparatus although this equipment is "used" differently. Let us now consider each of the phases of the communicative act, realizing all the while that the *process interrelatedness* of the phases of communication necessarily make our picture a very modest and incomplete one.

the exigence phase

Quite simply, this stage of the process gets things started. A communicative exigence, according to Lloyd Bitzer (1968) is *any social problem that can be alleviated by human discourse.* The undeserved, failing grade on your exam constitutes the exigence that "calls forth" your fiery objection to your professor. An exigence prompts a communicative impulse, and this impulse may derive from *social situations* ("Well, Kevin, when *are* we going to get married?"), from *psychological conditions* (a feeling of loneliness stimulates you to call someone for a date), or *from nonhuman roots* (your bike hike along a polluted stream may inspire an impassioned oration from you about our ecological death wish).

There are, of course, many situations which do not constitute *communicative* exigences and hence cannot be modified by discourse. Try as hard as you will, no amount of talk can cause a chair to levitate, no matter how fervently you may wish it. Some people have great difficulty in distinguishing between communicative and noncommunicative exigences. Thus in certain severe forms of mental pathology, disturbed persons talk to inanimate objects, *as if* their discourse could effect unmediated changes in the physical world. In the more usual instances, however, the exigence will help to illuminate for us what *social constraints* we will face in a given communication situation. In Unit III of this book, we will discuss three of the most common communicative exigences which face public communicators.

the interpretive phase

Quite simply, the interpretive phase of communication tells us what the exigence "means." In interpreting an apparent exigence, a speaker either consciously or unconsciously asks himself three questions: (1) Is this a situation that demands a talking response from me? (2) What communicative expectations does the audience have of me? (3) How can I best respond to the set of social conditions I now face? The answers to such questions, quite obviously, will determine in large part how we will operate in a later phase of communication, the message-creating phase.

SPEAKER AND INTERPRETATION

Because we are not always sure of our own communicative abilities as speakers, and because listeners do not always specify their expectations of us, dealing with an exigence can often be a harrying prospect. How many of us, for example, have missed that perfect opportunity to squelch the loud-mouthed clod at the party? All the way home we kick ourselves for not thinking of that "zinger" quickly enough. Besides missing a communicative exigence altogether, we might *misinterpret* the "problem" situation. ("Well it's not my fault, Claire. How was I to know that your wink meant your contact lens was slipping?")

Perhaps the most common problem of all in communication is our seemingly endless ability to make *inappropriate responses* to the set of conditions that have demanded our talk. Because of misanalyzing the values of our audience, because we lack the facts to back up our position, or because we sequence our remarks too casually, we are often unable to respond satisfactorily to the situation we wish to change. Thus, a speaker communicates successfully when he is able to know *how* to make the appropriate response to the appropriate *person(s)* at the appropriate *time*.

LISTENER AND INTERPRETATION

The assertions made by the speaker are part of the listener's reason for responding—his exigence. When interpreting such remarks, there are at least two factors which affect what we as listeners will "take away" from what a speaker says.

One such force, which Thomas Scheidel (1972) and others call *filtering*, is the all too human procedure by which *listeners hear what they want to or are "set" to hear and discard that with which they cannot be bothered*. That is, being the efficient little computers they are, listeners are not usually interested in "storing" away things that do not interest, entertain, or motivate them. Borden, Gregg, and Grove (1969) are not quite sure what we "do" with this excess material—whether we "bury" it deeply in the mind for later use or "dismiss" it entirely. (From the practical standpoint of the speaker, such information is "gone" from listeners' minds and cannot be of assistance to him.) Thus, being the free spirit he is, a listener will "pick and choose" from the remarks made by the speaker. Consider Scheidel's description of this filtering process.

We see a fairly obvious manifestation of . . . [filtering] . . . in a listener who is slightly hard-of-hearing. He may miss some of what is said, perhaps a great portion of it. Or, again, we may see this sensory filtration at work in a listener who is foreign born and is only now acquiring the use of English as a second language. The vocabulary or syntax in some parts of what he hears will be confusing for him, and he may not receive useful sensory impressions of them at all. In a speech communication situation, the speaker may have among his listeners the man who is slightly deaf, the man of foreign birth, another listener who may be intellectually dull, another who is sleepy, and still another whose thoughts are primarily focused on a problem he must face tomorrow. For any of these reasons, large portions of the speaker's message simply may not be received by anyone in his audience.[2]

If filtering were not enough to confound the speaker, completing —the reverse of filtering—enters the game. *Completing* is the listener's tendency to "add something" of his own as he "digests" what a

---

[2]From *Speech Communication and Human Interaction* by Thomas M. Scheidel, pp. 165–166. Copyright © 1972 by Scott, Foresman and Company. Reprinted by permission of the publisher.

speaker has said. Anyone who has ever observed an imaginative classmate contemplate a Rorschach ink blot only to "see" a 7-foot Martian four-putting the sixteenth green at Coral Gables, knows what we are talking about. Scheidel's book *Speech Communication in Human Interaction* provides a good discussion of the completing phenomenon and how it affects all listeners, thereby affecting those who would address them:

Obviously, our human need to infuse perceptions of our environment with order and completion places a number of special demands on us as speech communicators. Our individual needs, expectations, and previous experiences will all influence the ways in which we will employ the principle of stimulus generalization to "round out" what we have seen and heard. In a speaking situation, if we expect "illogical ranting" from "that buffoon on the platform," we will probably hear it. If we expect cogency, we are likely to hear that. If we approve of the viewpoint of a speaker who is speaking to us from a considerable physical distance, we may see him as taller or handsomer than he really is. If he says something which— coming from another speaker—would be objectionable, we excuse the comment with the paraphrase, "When he said. . . , he meant . . ." In this interpretative manner we often add to a transmitted message. In these and similar ways we often help to fulfill our expectations.[3]

Knowing what we now know about perceptual worlds, the filtering and completing phenomena should not surprise us. As a listener listens to a speaker, he cannot help but draw upon his own roles, values, reference groups, and so on, and hence "make his own" message from the (by now) "scraps" the speaker himself has offered.

Past experiences are especially helpful to our filtering and completing. For example, say a speaker is urging us to go skiing at Sun Valley over spring vacation. As she utters her message, her listener "completes" and remembers his own enjoyable time at Aspen the year before. Because he is occupied "completing" in this fashion, the listener also "filters" (i.e., misses) much if not all of the speaker's Sun Valley pitch. Naturally, the more intimate the speaker's understanding of her listener's perceptual world, the more she can account for such addings and subtractings as she creates speech materials.

To compound even further our speaker's difficulties, researchers have also discovered the perverse fact that listeners can listen much faster than talkers can talk. With all of this "lag time," therefore, listeners are quite able to filter and complete, *and* possibly catch a bit of the speaker's message on occasion.

[3]From *Speech Communication and Human Interaction* by Thomas M. Scheidel, pp. 170–171. Copyright © 1972 by Scott, Foresman and Company. Reprinted by permission of the publisher.

the idea-generating/reconstructing phase

As you look at our model of the communication process (Figure 3), one feature that should be clear is the distinction we are trying to make between a speaker's *generation* of an idea and a listener's *reconstruction* of that idea. Ideas cannot be sent *in toto* from a speaker to a listener. Rather, drawing upon the components of his perceptual world, the listener filters, completes, and thereby *builds* his own idea of what the speaker has said. Obviously, a listener's "reconstructed" idea can sometimes approximate the speaker's "generated" thought. In fact, this rough sort of approximation is not totally uncommon and is about the best we can hope for in communication, at least until the advent of a more dependable form of mental telepathy.

One interesting set of studies was completed at Northwestern University by Roy Wood and his colleagues (1971). These studies were an attempt to discover factors that would consistently improve the fidelity of this idea-generation/reconstructing process. Wood had each of his subjects select a partner and play the game "Password," a guessing game in which the "speaker" selects an "idea" (e.g., the word "dog") and, by giving single-word clues (e.g., canine, hound, etc.), attempts to get his "listener" to respond with the original stimulus— dog. Wood and his associates were attempting to discover the types of paired communicators that would be quickest and most accurate when playing this talking game.

The results were not surprising. The researchers discovered that persons with highly similar backgrounds (e.g., same type of family, education, etc.) were much more effective "password communicators" than were persons with diverse past experiences. While this finding naturally did not hold in all cases, there was a distinct connection between the similarities of participants' perceptual worlds and their ability to communicate accurately with one another (hence, generation = reconstruction). Another study (Vick and Wood, 1969) validated the idea of a "generation gap" by discovering that persons of the same age could generally pass-words more effectively than could people of different age groups.

We cite these results to encourage you. Efficient communication *does* occur and someday research will document other factors which help improve the process. A note of caution should be added, however. Most of us do not communicate in single-word chunks. We hurl streams and streams of words at one another and simultaneously use our voices and bodies to communicate even more information. Ideas, feelings, or meanings, unlike light or sound waves, do not "travel between" communicators' perceptual worlds. Therefore, the best a speaker can hope for is to increase shared understanding between himself and his listener. Total message fidelity, in *human* communication at least, is impossible. Thus a speaker's ideal in communication is *to get a listener to reconstruct the speaker's idea as the speaker would if the speaker lived in the listener's perceptual world.*

the message-creating phase

An exigence is presented to us as speakers. After a fashion, we interpret its implied constraints as best we can. All this produces a thought, an idea, a construct, or whatever we call that "thing" that *has* to get out of us. Then the real work begins. Being humans, we must then set about to discover *ways* of making this concept clear, acceptable, and appealing to others. The idea cannot just pop out of us full blown. Rather, we must select among communicative options and create *a message, that is, ideas designed to be cast in a socially perceivable form.*

CREATING MESSAGES: AN EXAMPLE

Think, for example, of the man whose girlfriend is late for a date (thus creating for him an *exigence*). He *interprets* such shenanigans as constituting rejection, and *generates an idea*—for instance, the feeling of anger. As time passes, the anger increases: "How dare she stand me up?" "Who does she think she is anyhow?" Next, he begins thinking about "communicative revenge," and starts to calculate the message options that will let her know that *he* is not one with whom she can trifle. The alternatives come readily—the sneering, sarcastic "Well, it's about time" approach; the blasé, super-sophisticated "Oh, were you late? I didn't notice" line; or the hurt, depressed "I suppose this means that you've (gulp) rejected me" strategy. All throughout this message-creating phase, he calculates the projected effects of his message upon her, trying to select the communication option that will make her realize what a dangerous game she is playing. Then, as she rushes into his arms with a "Gosh I'm sorry" and a kiss, his idea-generator and message-creator slip a cog as he ad libs, "Oh, that's OK. Just seeing you here makes up for the waiting."

All of the tortuous calculating that our irate dater undergoes is his attempt to work through the manifold options that a communicative exigence can prompt, and to find the ideas and structural methods which will best express his feelings of anger and frustration. Why he changed his mind at the last moment is a mystery to us. It could have been the case that *he* felt incapable of "carrying off" certain of the message forms he was considering. Or, he might have reasoned that his *listener* would have been unable to respond efficiently to the types of remarks he was contemplating. It is perhaps most likely that her arrival *removed the exigence*—thus causing feelings of relief rather than those of anger to well up within him. Regardless of the reason, our young man had to go through a very speedy process of altering his intended message.

As this example shows, *message creation is the process of selecting from a set of communicative possibilities those ideational and structural "triggers" which are designed to act upon or "tap" the "potentials for response" that listeners have within themselves.* Figure 4 is an attempt to convey this definition visually.

Our definition and diagram do not imply a simple, sure, stimulus-response, action-reaction procedure. On the contrary, message-creation is surrounded by uncertainty: Can I *know* all of the "triggers" available to me to meet this exigence? Which of these "triggers" can I best *bring off* in communication? Does my listener have the *potential* for response necessary to satisfy my communicative requirements? Will I be able to successfully *tap* that potential and hence move my listener in the direction I desire? In short, doubt surrounds the search for and utilization of message options (that is, discussable ideas and ways of sequencing those ideas), as well as the listener's receptivity to these communicative forces.

In a very real sense, this entire book is designed to help you improve your chances for successful communication by adding to your ability to create effective messages. In Chapter 4 we will see how the *speaker's image itself* is often a rich source of "triggering devices" for communication. Chapter 5 will point out some of the potentials

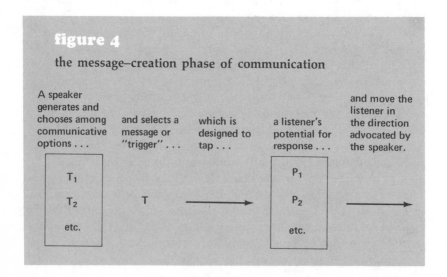

figure 4

the message–creation phase of communication

A speaker generates and chooses among communicative options . . .   and selects a message or "trigger" . . .   which is designed to tap . . .   a listener's potential for response . . .   and move the listener in the direction advocated by the speaker.

T₁

T₂   T   ⟶

etc.

P₁

P₂

etc.

for response that are imbedded within all listeners, how these "potentials" fluctuate in importance within audiences, as well as how we constantly go about the business of changing or reordering the heirarchy of potentials we have within ourselves. Chapter 7 will present an experimentally tested procedure for improving your message-creating ability, for helping you "see" a larger number of communicative options than you would have seen normally by "just thinking." Chapter 6 will attempt to point out some of the criteria we might want to apply when selecting among the message choices open to us and, finally, Chapters 7, 8, and 9 will indicate how various sorts of communicative situations and exigences expand and constrict the message options available to us in our quest for effective interaction with others.

the symbol-manipulating phase

You will remember that we have defined a message as ideas *designed to be cast* in a socially perceivable form. The symbol-manipulating phase of communication is the intellectual procedure we go through in trying to make our messages socially perceivable. Ideas, message options, persuasive appeals, communicative choices, etc., are really quite irrelevant from the standpoint of *social sharing* unless they can somehow be "released" from our perceptual worlds by means of a recognizable symbolic system. Throughout the thousands of years of his existence, man has developed only two such symbol systems— verbal and nonverbal—and for the rest of his time on this planet, he will probably continue to try and understand these systems.

Much could be said about the "translation" process whereby "created messages" become "socially perceivable" by "being cast in language." Infinitely complex in themselves, these operations are further affected by several forces and constraints. Among these are our own familiarity with the formal and informal "rules" of language usage, our listener's past experiences within his language community, and our ability as speakers to process cognitively the "thoughts" that somehow result from the verbal and nonverbal symbols we use in communication. Unfortunately, the present lack of knowledge about such complexities (as well as your authors' own limitations) makes such discussions well outside the purview of this book. We know that some *ways* of coding messages are preferable to others ("This is no time for talking, kiss me you fool"). In the following chapters we will attempt to present empirical and theoretical findings which may assist us in marshalling language resources, thereby giving our messages social visibility.

The thought with which we want to leave you at this point is simply this: Even though a speaker has discovered a message option that will successfully meet the communicative exigence he faces, and at the same time provide a suitable *form* for the idea he has generated, he still must face the agonizing series of verbal and nonverbal decisions that will give his message social impact. That such a series of procedures can be intellectually taxing is evidenced by the following vignette of a man who has a message but who also has difficulties manipulating his symbols:

"Write your own letter of recommendation," said Charlie, "and I'll sign whatever you write. I'll stop at your house on the way to the airport. . . ."

I was touched. Good old Charlie! What a friend! He had given me a blank check. All I had to do was write an unforgettable letter and my life would be changed from that of a lowly advertising copywriter to that of an exalted advertising-agency creative director. I went to my typewriter and began . . .

> This is to recommend Mr. James R. De Foe. He is a workhorse who would be an asset to any company. I have seen him work 12-hour days, 7 days a week, month in and month out. You have a winner in this gentleman who isn't afraid to roll up his sleeves and dig in. Sign him up quick whatever his price.

"You sound like a grind," my wife said. "If you get the job, they'll dump every kind of problem on top of you and expect you to live at the office."

"You're right," I said, getting myself another drink. "But I don't have much time. Only twenty minutes."

I wrote:

> This is to recommend James R. De Foe, a charming, quick-witted and talented gentleman who isn't afraid of work. In the midst of the biggest crisis, Jim will come up with a jest that will break the tension. If you want to laugh, hire him. But don't be deceived by Jovial Jim. When the chips are down, he delivers with a smile. He's worth whatever price he asks.

"That's awful," my wife said. "I wouldn't trust such a clown to carry my groceries. You're applying for a top executive position, not office jester. You need a more balanced approach."

"You're right," I said, hating her. "Please pour me a drink."

I made another try.

> This is to recommend James De Foe, a well-balanced man. He works hard; he plays hard; he's a delightful guy. Whether it's solving a problem or shooting out of a sandtrap, Jim's your man. You can't go wrong with well-balanced Jim De Foe. Meet his price, whatever it is.

"There's too much with the 'well-balanced,' " my wife said. "It sounds as if your sanity were being questioned. It also sounds fictitious. I can't picture such a person. There's no firmness, no character to the person . . ."

"This is my last try," I said in the tightly controlled voice of a man about to explode. "Whatever I write now goes into that letter." And I wrote:

It is my pleasure to recommend De Foe. He is adequate.[4]

the signaling phase

MESSAGE SIGNALS

As we leave the symbol manipulating (or final readying stage) of communication, we enter into a bewildering world of physical phenomena, of light particles, sound waves, and innumerable other sensory stimuli. One thing that we do *not* find in this "no man's land" between perceptual worlds is *meaning*. Nor do we find messages, "thoughts," exigences, or symbols. For these latter constructs are just that—constructs. Before another human can even begin to "get our drift," he must attempt to make some *sense* out of the way that we, through our speech behaviors, have changed the light and sound signals that are impinging on his physiology. That is, (mental) *symbols* differ from (physical) *signals*. Clevenger and Matthews (1971) add to our distinction of symbol and signal when they state:

You will recall that the signal is a physical event, such as a sequence of acoustic vibrations, while a message is a symbolic event representing an interpretation of the physical occurrence. Signals pass through channels in the environment, but messages occur only at source and destination. (pp. 93–94)

This talk of persons simply "shifting around" light waves and sound waves as, say, they attempt to communicate mad passionate love to one another, takes the poetry out of life. But we mention this idea of signaling to instill a measure of communicative humility in you. *If speakers assume that the meanings in their worlds must necessarily be presented to listeners via complex, little-understood, physical stimuli, then perhaps they will not assume that people can share meanings or feelings in any isomorphic (one-to-one) sense.* As we have said before, to assume that we share perceptual worlds is to stop adjusting, to stop making calculated bets, to stop being concerned with decoding the physical stimuli that others make available to us. Operating with the "my meaning = your-meaning" equation as an underlying premise, is bound to lead to interpersonal trouble. This refusal to acknowledge, to account for, and to adapt to the countless

[4]James R. De Foe, "This is to Recommend, Well . . . Me." Reprinted with permission from *The Saturday Evening Post*, January 28, 1967, p. 18. © 1967 The Curtis Publishing Company.

translations and transformations that people must make when talking and listening would appear ludicrous, if it were not so sad:

> [Professor] M. was in rare form today. He came in, stood on a chair, and said, "What do you want out of school? Why are you here?" And then when he had a fairly good discussion going, albeit one with much breast-beating about Selling Out to the System, he said, "Yes, we can understand all this by understanding Marx on use value and exchange value," and off he launched into a dull, incredibly boring reading (not a lecture, a *reading*, verbatim, from a book) on Marx. And people wonder why I'm disillusioned with school. When the New Breed profs can't even *talk* a good game, and revert to pedantry, why bother? Can't they see what they're doing? Are they really that blind?[5]

CONTEXT SIGNALS

As anyone who has ever attempted to woo a woman (or a man) in a noisy, crowded beer joint knows, speakers and listeners are not the only ones who change the physical environment and hence affect human interactions. Contextual factors, items such as the hardness of the pew in church, the music at a rock concert, and the ranting and raving of delegates to a political convention, will determine to a great extent how receptive listeners will be to the messages of God, Cat Stevens, and the Democratic Party. Knowledgeable speakers often can take advantage of such contextual signals when furthering their communicative goals. Some irreverent TV news commentators have said that when attempting to push through a platform plank at a political convention, long-time patriarch of the Democratic Party, Sam Rayburn, would often strike up the band immediately after the "aye" votes were recorded, thus drowning out any dissenting voices in the crowd.

Generally, we seem to have more *control* over our message-derived signals than we have over the physical happenstances which sur-round our talk. As mentioned in Chapter 1, members of an audience can do much to enhance, to neutralize, or to detract from the rhetorical impact of a speaker. Perhaps realizing this, Edmund Muskie was one of the first candidates in contemporary politics to turn derisive heck-ling into an advantage. When confronted with a particularly vocal demonstrator, Muskie typically invited him up to the platform so that he could attempt to rebut the Senator's position. For many onlookers, these spontaneous invitations depicted Muskie as a man with a direct, immediate sense of communication with his audience—all because he was aware of and able to adapt successfully to context events.

[5]Kate Haracz, "The Diary of Kate Haracz: Journal of an Undergraduate," *Change*, May-June, 1970, p. 16. Reprinted by permission.

This idea of context signals reemphasizes the *totally situational* nature of communication. It also points out that communication must be situational, and how the moment-to-moment changes of exigence, message-creation, and context can both challenge and frustrate a speaker who attempts to manage and to direct communicative forces. Thus, we must try to deal with situational factors in communication. Society does not smile benignly upon those who would ignore context by talking exclusively to inanimate objects, by muttering to themselves in the presence of others, or by patiently expecting verbal feedback from chairs, breadboxes, and 6-foot rabbits named Harvey. Amusing though such incidents may seem, communication pathologists have long argued that our ability to cope with and to adjust to context are, in the final event, among our most solid claims to sanity.

the feedback phase

Looking at our view of the process of communication, you should have noticed our attempt to depict the *interactions* that occur between a speaker and his listener. In our model, at least, remarks made by the speaker constitute an exigence for the listener—a need to respond in some manner, whether verbal or nonverbal. But the response can be misinterpreted. As you attempt to fire up your dozing 8:00 A.M. speech class with a rousing "Let's really support old State U at this Saturday's game" oration, your eyes fix upon the lovely, smiling, bright-eyed lass who appears to be absolutely drenched in the meaning of your speech. Little do you know from her feedback that she is just assuming her traditional and much practiced "classroom pose" and, that even as you plead your case, she is contemplating which date she will accept for the weekend.

Perhaps the most frustrating thing about these sometimes subtle, sometimes blatant "returning messages" is that they occur while you —the speaker—are creating messages and manipulating symbols yourself, thus giving you still another exigence to meet with discourse. Hence, the simultaneity and circularity of communication is difficult to envision, and definitely difficult to deal with in actual spoken interaction.

conclusion

If you find the tone of this chapter to be a bit pessimistic, you have sensed the authors' meaning. Finding effective means of communicating our thoughts and feelings is a tortuous and sometimes bleak experience, as, say, international peace talks continue to remind us. But *if we assume that listeners will misunderstand us if it is at all possible for them to do so* (and it usually is), we will then be forced into a real-life awareness of the necessity of maintaining conceptual flexibility, of seeking out the most likely basis for placing our communicative bets, of searching for the slender threads of similarity that run through our perceptual worlds, and of fighting our ways intelligently through the labyrinth of exigences, ideas, messages, and symbolic referents that constitute our communicative acts.

Past research in communication has not left us totally defenseless in our day-to-day interpersonal struggles, however. In the next three chapters, we will discover that a speaker does indeed have some draft-eligible resources to help him man the rhetorical battle stations. Our images as people, the beliefs and understandings of those to whom we talk, as well as the messages that we ourselves create are all potential allies for speakers who would prevail over those heathen listeners and bring home the fruits of communicative victory—a shared thought or two. Thus, the pessimism displayed in the following verse is perhaps not totally warranted at this stage:

When a word was a word and it meant
What it said, and the world was simple and new
A man made his words and he knew what
They meant, and his friends knew their meaning, too,
Living was easy; communication was brief;
Complexity ne'er spoiled one's view
When a word was a word and it meant
What it said, and the world was simple and new.

Now I look at the sky and I say that it's
Blue and you smile and say yes, sky is blue
But I don't know that blue, as I think of
Blue, is the same blue to me as you.
And I scream in disgust and I know
That I must make you see how blue is my blue
But I know it's but nought when I see
All I wrought was a lopsided point of blue.[6]

---

[6]From Linda Burleson McAnally, "Communication A.D.," A publication of the Interpersonal Communication Clearinghouse, Texas Tech University, Lubbock, Tex. Reprinted by permission.

UNIT II

resources for communication in public settings

UNIT II

The indoor speaker loses as many crowds as we do, but he never finds out because their bodies are still there. We of the outdoors cannot fool ourselves: if the audience is not there it is plainly not there, and talking to no one in public has more than a hint of nightmare. Its ever-present possibility forces us to study the crowd and our subject, and ourselves. I write of what I have thus learned —in Hyde Park London, Times Square New York, Franklin Park Washington, the South Side of Chicago, Sydney's Domain, on the bank of Melbourne's Yarra, and in several dozen other spots.

. . .

One way or another the crowds have taught me a vast amount—directly by reminding me of things I had not sufficiently dwelt on, indirectly by forcing me to go deeper than, but for the pressure of their questioning, I should have gone. To have everything one utters subjected to crowd scrutiny, every word liable to challenge on the spot, is very concentrative.

. . .

Crowds can be maddening—spoiling your best
effects by interjections; shouting you down
(this is true in Australia and England; I've
never had it in America); worst of all, walking
away and leaving you talking to no one. As
you grow in experience, the proportion of the
disagreeable diminishes; but it never wholly
vanishes. And, be you as experienced as you
may, there are still meetings in which the
disagreeable has a carnival. When it has, there
is no consolation in putting the blame on the
crowd. They don't invite you; you invite
them. Whether a party has been a success or
a failure, there is no appeal against the judgment of the guests.

. . .

Listeners arrive with no objections sizzling
and leaping inside their heads; their questions
arise out of what they have heard us say in
our speech. So that what we talk about is
entirely up to us; but they can still walk away
the moment they are bored. We still have to
interest them sufficiently to keep them
standing there.

. . .

But before we can make contact with men's
minds, they must be persuaded to listen. It
would be unwise to rely on the personality of
the speaker or on the natural interest of the
topic. In religion there are few topics which
make today's man feel "I must listen to
this!" The Inquisition, perhaps; it is hard to
think of another.*

*F. J. Sheed, "My Life on the Street Corner." First
appeared in Saturday Review, May 10, 1969, pp. 22, 23, 66, 67.
Copyright 1969 by Saturday Review Co. Used with permission.

These remarks were made by F. J. Sheed in his article "My Life on the Street Corner." For many years, Sheed spent much of his time as a sort of roaming religious lecturer—buttonholing people on street corners, collaring whatever large or small crowds he could, and (to complete our metaphor) losing his communicative shirt all too often!

Sheed's remarks are compelling. Here is a man who seems to have come up with a theory of how communication works—or ought to work—and has learned it from real-life experience. From his years of lecturing, Sheed seems to have concluded that public communication is very much a transactive experience, a continual giving and taking between speaker and listener, a phenomenon that continually defies any *casual* attempt to define it, regulate it, or control it. He has found that in public communication, the best option we have for determining success is that of making a series of intelligent bets. He implies that the odds of high predictability in public communication are no better than those offered by a one-arm bandit in Las Vegas. And in public communication, no IOU's are given or accepted.

implicit theories of communication

The primary value of Sheed's remarks lies not only in his acute analysis of human behavior, but in his vision of the nature of communication itself. He seems to have, as Bonnie Johnson (1972) would call it, an "implicit communication theory." Johnson has discovered that *there is oftentimes a direct relationship between how a person behaves when communicating and how he thinks human communication in general works.* Johnson defines an implicit communication theory as a set "of beliefs which non-scientists use to explain to themselves how symbols influence men. The term 'implicit' is used because the beliefs are not always plainly stated; often they are best seen in passing references" (pp. 1–2).

In her study, Johnson found a number of such implicit theories of communication operating in the minds of everyday talkers. Some persons, for example, believe that in order to communicate effectively, we must find the appropriate *weapons* to use on our auditors. Others think that communication is sort of *magical*—a process that "just happens." Still others see communication as a kind of *mechanical* procedure whereby we pull the appropriate lever in order to get the desired response—as if people were but so many cigarette machines.

According to Johnson, the important thing about implicit communication theories lies in *how they affect the individual's spoken be-*

havior. For example, if I believe that communication basically is a mechanistic process, I will live my life trying to find the appropriate "button" to push for each person with whom I come into contact—a mode of thinking that can lead to dehumanization. On the other hand, if I believe that communication is nothing more than an interpersonal magic act, I will either not treat my communication contacts seriously, or I will not try very hard to improve them. (It's all magic, after all!)

We can, of course, think of still more common implicit communication theories. Preachers often see themselves as "shepherds leading their flocks"—hence the very paternalistic tone of many contemporary sermons. Ralph Nader, as another example, seems to see his communicative job as that of *"attacking* the fortress of public opinion," a state of mind which probably does much to contribute to the hard-charging, usually negative manner in which he seems to approach those in power.

We could go on to list many other implicit theories, but shall refrain from doing so. Rather, we would like to add to Sheed's remarks by suggesting that *communication is best conceived of as a process through which people, possessed by varying levels and types of "potentials," come together (through words) by pooling their motivational, experiential, and attitudinal resources.* This "coming together" has some of Johnson's "magic" to it, but more fundamentally, such a "merging" is characterized by growth, change, unpredictability, and activity. To our way of thinking, speakers are not pinball players, nor are listeners pinball machines. Rather, speakers and their messages are the pinballs themselves and listeners are the levers, bumpers, tripping devices, and, on those especially good occasions, the multicolored lights and delicious ringings of that great pinball game of life!

Like Sheed, your authors would encourage you to view listeners as being very active creatures, persons totally capable of bringing both frustration and exaltation to even the most mundane of communicative experiences that we as speakers share with them. The implicit communication theory upon which this book is based (which we have already hinted at in Chapter 3) has been delineated many years ago by, of all people, Aesop:

The Wind and the Sun were disputing which was the stronger. Suddenly they saw a traveller coming down the road, and the Sun said: "I see a way to decide our dispute. Whichever of us can cause that traveller to take off his cloak shall be regarded as the stronger. You begin." So the Sun retired behind a cloud, and the Wind began to blow as hard as it could upon the traveller. But the harder he blew the more closely did the traveller wrap his cloak around him, till at last the Wind had to give up in despair. Then the Sun came out and shone in all his glory upon the traveller, who soon found it too hot to walk with his cloak on.*

Let us consider, for a moment, the sort of implicit "communication" theory that our two protagonists seem to have had in mind. Wind, being the rugged individualist that he is, assumes that a forceful presentation of his message will win the day. Sun, on the other hand, demonstrates his brilliance by remembering that travelers (listeners, if you will) have certain "sets of potentials" within them (e.g., body temperature tolerances) that he, as "speaker," must reckon with quite seriously. Sun also knows that (via his past interactions with Traveler) he has established a certain social image. By sensitively and insightfully attempting to manage these several resources, Sun has emerged the victor. And he has done so *because of his perception of the interaction,* not because of any gimmickery he employed. In other words, his attitude toward communication determined, in large part, his success. Who could blame Traveler for resisting the callous, overpowering messages of Wind, a communicator who treats his fellow interactants with disdain, without regard to the gifts they have brought to the communicative festivities?

the resources of public communication

In Unit II we will attempt to follow our implicit communication theory rather religiously by considering the various *resources* available to a speaker who desires to reach some accord with a public audience. We will assume that communication situations are resplendent with a number of natural resources that speakers can mine, and that the ways in which these resources are marshalled will determine the outcome of any given communication experience.

In Chapter 4 we will consider the research and theories surrounding the speaker as a communicative resource. We will talk about the credibility of the source of a communication and the images listeners have of the persons who attempt to influence them.

Chapter 5 will discuss the resources within the listeners. The types of beliefs, attitudes, and experiences listeners "bring to" an interaction, will be discussed, as well as how they help to determine the thrust and impact of the communicative experience. We will argue in this chapter that those windy speakers who are unaware of or are

*C. W. Eliot (ed.), "Aesop's Fables," *Harvard Classics,* vol. 17 (New York: Collier, 1909), pp. 35–36.

unconcerned with the intellectual and emotional make-up of their hearers are betting on long shots on which even Jimmy the Greek would not give you odds.

Finally, in Chapter 6 we will treat the communicative resource over which the speaker has the most control—that which he says. We will present what research and theory have defined as especially appropriate *attitudes* for us to incorporate when selecting among the many "ways of saying" that are open to us as communicators. In addition, we will suggest that to have significant social impact, our message-making must be especially responsive to the resources lying within the speaker and his listeners.

While necessity forces us to distinguish between speaker, audience, and message potentials, we do so unwillingly. To separate such inseparable entities belies all that we have said in Chapter 3 about the "interactingness" of communicative processes. Thus, we will, in this unit, be especially dependent upon *you* to remember the hyphens in the phrase, speaker-audience-message resources. We will depend upon you to view communicative resources as a sort of complex human lattice-work in which how you view me and what I say interacts continually and intricately with that which already exists within you. We are placing this "connecting" burden upon you, not with the authoritarian flair of the Wind, but with the warm hope that it will help you find your own intellectual place in the Sun.

the speaker
as resource

CHAPTER 4

Kay: Are you buying that magazine again? I thought you'd outgrown that stuff.

Bruce: What do you mean? *Playboy's* got a lot of good articles. You just resent the pictures, that's all. The interview is always good, and the articles are written by experts in law, automotives, and . . .

Kay: Maybe so, but then why do they fill it with the other junk? If the articles are as good as you say, they wouldn't need those pictures.

Bruce: What's wrong with the pictures? I thought you were such a liberated woman.

Kay: I'm only offended by poor taste, and those pictures are exploitive! And—admit it–that's what sells the magazine.

Bruce: Well, *some* people may buy it for the pictures, but that's not why I buy it. Besides, if you want pictures, there are other magazines with better ones. You know my interest in new cars—*Playboy* always has the latest, and I like to keep up. And just last month, they interviewed Henry Kissinger. If it were such a terrible magazine, surely a man like that wouldn't allow himself to be interviewed in it!

Kay: Maybe Kissinger used the interview to get his personal ideas out 'cuz he knows the magazine sells—not because of his great regard for it. And as far as your interest in cars—you'd probably do better to get a magazine devoted entirely to cars. Anyone who drives an Edsel shouldn't brag about his great interest in cars.

Bruce: I'll ignore the insult—the Edsel is becoming a collector's item, anyway. Anyhow, *Playboy* covers a lot of ground in many areas with ... with real experts.

Kay: Sort of a bawdy *Reader's Digest*, then?

Bruce: I'll ignore that, too. Anyway, I get a lot from *Playboy*. You may still think I buy it for the pictures, but I don't. And a lot of apparently intelligent people agree with me. It's always in my doctor's waiting room.

Kay: Yeh—and the time we stopped at Pete's Pool Parlor for cigarettes, there were all the leading minds, standing around, ogling the great articles!

Apparently Kay does not think much of Bruce's choice of reading material—at least not of the pictures that accompany it. Among other things, she accuses Bruce of being immature. The strategies that Bruce uses to counter this charge and to defend his character constitute the focal point of this chapter. Before reading on, you might want to try and list the ways in which Bruce tries to defend himself against Kay's assertion. We will discuss these strategies toward the end of this chapter.

In our society, the effectiveness of what is said depends to some extent on who says it. The young child's "Oh, yeah? Who says so?" and the adult's somewhat more subtle "Where did you hear that?" illustrate that credibility plays an important role in communication. Perhaps nowhere is this belief demonstrated more clearly (and more frequently) than in advertising. In the marketing biz, it helps to be sponsored by an indisputable source—someone held in esteem by the general public. Whether the reasons for this person's fame are related to the product being sold is irrelevant—it is assumed that the general public will make the transition necessary for, say, Olympic swimmer Mark Spitz to sell Timex watches. Thus, we have been treated to a political shoot-out between film stars John Wayne and Warren Beatty, and a presidential race in which the voices of entertainers Sammy Davis, Jr., Bill Cosby, Martha Raye, and Nancy Sinatra carried much weight. The indisputable-source gimmick can backfire, of course: One gourmet reports that he has not returned to the supposedly exclusive restaurant that served Idaho trout complete with indisputable source attached to gill—"As advertised in the *Saturday Evening Post.*" (The indisputable source had, at that time, been out of business for some years!)

Ordinarily, people will confidently purchase life insurance from Art Linkletter, cleaning products from Paul Harvey, deodorant from Dick Butkus, and shaving lotion from Joe Namath. And who really knows household plumbing problems like Josephine? Who can dispute the woman in nurse's clothing who tells how nutritious a particular chocolate drink can be? Or the 55 hospitals in the nation (only 55?) who would not clean their toilet bowls with anything else? Or the mother-in-law's personal "ok" for the see-yourself shine attained by a certain dishwashing liquid? Anything is possible. If you believe Bob Richards you can even be a champion by eating the breakfast of. . . . No doubt you can think of many additional examples of the importance of the source (persons, groups, or media) to the effectiveness of a communication experience.

However, we should not be totally facetious about this matter of credibility. After all, people were exterminated in World War II by people who claimed at the Nuremburg trials "the Führer told us to do it." Similarly, during the initial stages of the Watergate affair, Richard Nixon repeatedly asserted that he was guilty only of having *believed the wrong people* about the burglary and cover-up. Equally disturbing is the study reported by Milgram (1963) in which he discovered that people were quite willing to administer severe electrical shocks to others as long as such actions were "legitimized" by an authority figure (i.e., the experimenter).

perspectives on source credibility

Thus, contrary to the impression that some of our examples may have created, the effect of the indisputable source must be reckoned with in communication. The reasons for our dependence on such sources are perhaps best illustrated by looking at *the types of advice* we seek from them.

BELIEF TYPES AND CREDIBILITY

Milton Rokeach (1968) posits that we organize our beliefs into five classes, along a central-peripheral dimension. The most central, *primitive beliefs* (100 percent consensus), represent "basic truths" we all hold about physical reality, social reality, and the nature of the self. Since these beliefs represent the consensus of virtually everyone in a position to know, they are not subject to the power of the indisputable source. Other kinds of *primitive beliefs* (zero consensus) are also not subject to the effect of the indisputable source. While such beliefs are not the products of universal consensus, they are based on direct personal encounter. Thus, if my experiences tell me that I live in a hostile world, it will be difficult for an indisputable source to convince me otherwise.

Authority beliefs are nonprimitive beliefs developed within the context of our social structure—family, class, peer group, ethnic group, religious and political groups, and country. They are beliefs which are not a product of our direct experience—instead, we hold such beliefs because they center around a person or around institutions which we regard as "inherently" good (e.g., the Bible). Although authority beliefs are important and generally resistant to change, they too can be modified by an indisputable source. For example, during the late 1960s there was an exodus of Catholic priests from the Church. Such alterations in the position of their indisputable sources engendered kindred rejection of basic Catholic precepts for many parishioners.

Even more open to such change are *derived beliefs*, or beliefs we perceive to *emanate* from our indisputable sources. Thus, while a Catholic priest may be a part of the authority belief structures of some people, what he *says* may help form many of the derived beliefs. Thus, many old-line Catholics, while denying the wisdom of his action, might feel that a priest is still a "good man" after he leaves the Church.

Rokeach's final class of beliefs is labeled *inconsequential beliefs*. They represent more or less arbitrary matters of taste and, because they result from direct experience with the object of belief, they are seldom subject to the influence of the indisputable source. For example, the movies *Love Story* and *The Sound of Music* were box-office hits while panned by many (supposedly authoritative) critics. A previous comment by a well-known observer of moviedom seems to apply: "Nobody liked it but the audience." *In summary, then, the indisputable source operates most persuasively in a sphere where we have little or no direct personal experience with the object(s) of our belief.* In such areas, we turn to others for advice.

RESEARCH IN CREDIBILITY

Under a multitude of rubrics (ethos, prestige, source credibility, expertise, charisma, leadership, image, status, reputation, probity, personal credibility, ethical proof, personal persuasiveness, personality effects, impressions, etc.), theorists and experimenters in communication from classical to contemporary times have devoted considerable effort to the study of the indisputable source or the speaker as a resource in communication. In fact, as Andersen (1971, p. 217) points out, "more research on this topic has been reported in recent communication journals than on any other single concept specifically related to communication."

These studies largely support our common-sense observation that source credibility is an important factor in communication. For example, in an early study, Kelman and Hovland (1953) prepared a speech favoring extreme leniency in the treatment of juvenile delinquents. Students doing senior work in a summer high school were requested to listen in class to a recording of an educational radio program—ostensibly to judge its educational value. In the course of the program, three different introductions to the speech dealing with leniency were used in different classes. In one introduction the speaker was identified as a judge in a juvenile court—a highly trained, well-informed, and experienced authority on criminology and delinquency. In another (ostensibly "neutral") introduction, the speaker was said to be someone picked out of the studio audience. The third "speaker," also just chosen from the audience, revealed during the interview that he had a criminal record and had been a juvenile delinquent.

In the postexperiment questionnaire the students were asked to respond to the speech. Although the speech was the same in all cases, reactions to the total communicative experience—message *plus* speaker—varied. The audience felt that the judge's speech was much more "fair" than that of the former delinquent. The judgments for the neutral member of the audience lay somewhere in between. Opinion change results closely paralleled the evaluations of fairness of presentation.

Three weeks after listening to the speech, however, the attitudinal differences among the experimental groups *were no longer present;* there was a decrease in acceptance of the communication for those who had heard the positive communicator (judge) and a slight increase for those who had listened to the negative communicator (the juvenile delinquent). The effect of the indisputable source had thus lost some impact over a period of time.

The Kelman and Hovland results serve as a summary of the experimental research assessing the effects of source credibility on communication. Initial credibility has consistently been found to have a significant effect on *immediate* attitude change (but not on learning)—attesting to the fact that it is hard to take the human out of human communication. It appears that after a duration of time, however, audiences tend to disassociate the speaker and the message and remember only the message.

The Kelman and Hovland study can serve also as an example of the research model most frequently used to determine the effect of source credibility. The speech was held constant, the audiences were equivalent; the characteristics of the speaker were systematically varied in order to find out what factors attributable to the speaker are persuasive.

This makes effective persuasion sound simple: all you must do is find an authoritative figure who will deliver your message. Not so. In order to demonstrate why this clear and meaningful description of source credibility is deceptive in its simplicity, the remainder of this chapter reviews the source credibility literature by focusing on two questions: What is source credibility? What can a speaker do to enhance it?

the nature of source credibility

Let us begin with a formal definition. *Source credibility consists of an audience's perceptions of the speaker (independent of the speaker's intent or purpose) which vary over time and lead the audience to accept or reject the attitude, belief, and/or action the speaker proposes.*

AUDIENCE'S PERCEPTIONS OF THE SPEAKER

You are probably tired of reading that meanings are in *people*, but the concept is important enough to bear repeating. In part, an audience accepts or rejects what you say on the basis of personal characteristics they perceive in you. Obviously, if they do not know that you help little old ladies across the street and open car doors for a woman, they cannot use such data when forming their opinion of you. Even if they do possess this information, members of your audience are likely to *act* on such data differently—some will see you as a real "gentleman," while others will label you "male chauvinist pig." Members of an audience judge your credibility as a speaker on the basis of information they have about you, and how, in turn, they feel about people who possess such qualities. "Credibility" lies within *listeners'* minds. As Shelley Berman says, for a speaker "that's a stinking situation!"

CREDIBILITY VARIES OVER TIME

Communication is a *process*. Sometimes it is useful to stop the process in midstream and examine the component parts—bearing in mind that we may distort reality by so doing. For source credibility, it is sometimes profitable to examine the component phases of its maturation or decline at three stages in the process: before, during, and after a communicative act.

initial source credibility

It is all but impossible for a speaker to begin his speech with a clean slate. Somewhere along the line, members of his audience have formed judgments as to his personal credibility or to that of "people like him." Some of these perceptions—those constituting initial source credibility—could have been identified 24 hours before the speech, a week before, or even a month before. What concerns us most at this point are the ways listeners view a speaker when he begins speaking.

While the feelings that exist in hearers during this initial phase originate from a variety of sources, Andersen (1971, p. 224) identifies four factors that most frequently contribute to initial credibility: (1) *experiences* with the speaker either direct or vicarious (e.g., we were in the army together); (2) *facts* known about the speaker, particularly those that provide indication of referential class membership (e.g., he always hung around with the officers); (3) *endorsements* offered by others (e.g., Captain Dennis always liked him); and (4) *immediate stimuli* leading to the actual communication (i.e., his tone of voice on the phone seemed like he's going to hit me up for a loan).

By the time you deliver your first speech in class, you will have interacted with most of your classmates. As a result, they will have formed impressions of you, much as you have of them. This is one of many public speaking settings which do not provide the first exposure to the speaker. Even if we had not actually interacted with the speaker in person, we may have had—probably have had—*vicarious* experiences with him. Thus, mass media, for example, provides much information about newsworthy people *before* they are seen by local audiences. In addition, friends and acquaintances relate information about the speaker—again, helping us relate vicariously to the speaker or to people similar to him. Thus, it is rare to find an audience that has formed no opinion as to the credibility of the speaker prior to interacting with him or her.

The second category of information about the speaker concerns his *reference group membership*. What we know about a speaker causes us to associate him or her with a variety of stereotypes or attitudes. We may know little about that girl in class other than that she is president of her sorority, but we are imbued with numerous associations with the category "sorority president"; in the absence of other information, we utilize these associations as bases for making judgments. To hear that a person is an athlete, a veteran, a businessman, a nurse, etc., instantly conjures up sets of associations in many of us. Audience judgments of the label may vary, but the labels provide the audience with a means of associating the speaker with a class or category of people and most significantly, *applying the attitudes they hold toward that class to the speaker*.

The third source of information about the speaker is provided by *endorsements*. At some public speaking events we have little prior knowledge about a speaker aside from who sponsored or endorsed him. On this basis, we may decide to hear the "official" Democratic speaker rather than listen to the candidate endorsed by the Republican party. Evidence also indicates that the introduction of a speaker will provide a source of sponsorship and hence influence his credibility rating. A speaker who receives a favorable introduction from a well-regarded individual will be perceived as more credible than a person who receives a positive introduction from a negatively evaluated source. Credibility can be infectious.

The final source of information about the speaker consists of the speaker's *personal appearance and actions*. The dress of the speaker, his posture, physique, and manner, and his responses to things happening around him may all contribute strongly to his initial source credibility.

At this point it would be nice were we able to come out with a formula: a speaker's initial credibility is a function of two parts prior experience multiplied by sponsor and divided by waist size. Unfortunately, it is impossible to say which of the four categories contributes most to initial source credibility in which situations. What we can say is that, based on a variety of sources, audiences make judgments about the credibility of a speaker before he ever begins to speak.

process credibility

By identifying a second stage of source credibility, we are suggesting that there are shifts in credibility which occur during actual interaction. Studies have been made of factors that effect these process changes, but few were made of the spoken act in a phase-by-phase fashion. An excellent exception is a study conducted by Brooks and Scheidel (1968). Using a tape-recorded speech by Malcolm X (the late spokesman for the Black Muslims) to a predominantly white college audience, Brooks and Scheidel spliced seven 30-second silent periods into the tape at what seemed to be "natural" divisions of the speech. The speech supported the proposition that American blacks should separate themselves from white society. Counting the silent period at the end of the tape, white undergraduate students in introductory public speaking classes were asked to provide ten evaluations of the speaker —one at each of the silent periods, in addition to a pre- and post-message evaluation. On a 1–7 scale from negative to positive, the results were as follows:

Pretest	2.53	Time 5	4.39
Time 1	4.54	Time 6	4.97
Time 2	4.34	Time 7	4.02
Time 3	4.06	Time 8	3.93
Time 4	4.30	Posttest	3.82

Because Brooks and Scheidel used a tape-recorded message, the changes in credibility we see across time were probably due primarily to verbal and vocalic factors. In a live public speaking setting, stimuli arising from the source, the occasion, the audience, and the channel will also lead to changes and modification of initial source credibility. In all cases, however, it seems safe to assume that process credibility is an undulating, changeful phenomenon.

It is also possible to identify some of the elements that influence process credibility. When looking at these variables, it must be remembered that, rather than producing simple linear effects (e.g., older people are more credible than are young people), they often *interact* in very complex ways. Thus, for some members of the audience, a male may be perceived as credible when speaking on the topic of football, while a female may appear quite authoritative when addressing herself to the topic of nutrition—but not vice versa.

With this warning of "interaction effects" in mind, we can list elements that research suggests influence process credibility. Later, when we suggest how a speaker can enhance his credibility, we will incorporate findings from studies involving these variables. Thus, we present this list simply to point out *how many* factors can potentially contribute to process credibility. Whether they consistently add to or detract from credibility is not known at present:

1. *source characteristics:* attractiveness of speaker, neatness of dress, mode of dress, height, sex, race, fluency of delivery, extroverted/ introverted styles of delivery, use of dialect
2. *message characteristics:* self-reference, prestige-reference, evidence,

organization, fear appeals, opinionatedness, language intensity, audience adaptation, metaphors, analogies, obscenity
3. *channel characteristics:* visual materials; oral delivery and combination of media
4. *audience characteristics:* credibility proneness, ego-involvement, source-receiver identification, stress, observed audience response
5. *occasion characteristics:* attractiveness of setting, temperature, color, space

We provide this list of topics that have been studied while noting the danger outlined by Borden, Gregg, and Grove (1969):

... The reasons for liking or disliking, accepting or rejecting another human being are too numerous to mention without becoming simplistic and tedious. Any listing of ethos factors is incomplete, unrealistically dichotomous, arbitrary in terms of definition, and, on the whole, as useless as various listings of motivational factors have proven to be. We can fairly safely assume some connection between the acceptability of a communicator as he is perceived by his audience and those values, desires, and goals which the audience perceives as being important to them. (p. 204)

terminal source credibility

The interaction of initial credibility and process credibility results in terminal source credibility. The relative contribution of each to terminal credibility is a matter for speculation. The image a speaker will have after interacting probably depends a great deal on the *intensity* of our initial feelings about him. In other words, the more prior knowledge you have about the speaker, the more important is initial credibility to our "summed up" impressions of the speaker. For instance, since the students in Brooks and Scheidel's study did not know a great deal about Malcolm X ahead of time, process credibility (the image he created while speaking) was probably a primary determinant of his final credibility standing.

dimensions of source credibility

Thus far, we have talked as if source credibility were a unidimensional construct—as if a speaker's credibility falls at some point on a continuum ranging from complete credibility to complete incredibility. A number of studies have attempted to investigate this assumption and the evidence suggests that it is not correct. Apparently, people use a number of *independent* dimensions when making their judgments of a speaker's credibility. As Cronkhite (1969*a*, p. 177) points out, the aspects of a speaker that listeners take into consideration when assessing his credibility "include 'trust-worthiness,' 'dynamism,' 'competence,' 'sociability,' 'evaluation,' 'agreeableness,' 'extroversion,' 'emotional stability,' 'conscientiousness,' 'culture,' 'objectivity,' and probably 'identification,' depending on who did the study, what kind of subjects he used, what kinds of topics he used, what kinds of speakers he used, what kinds of test items he used, and what kinds of factor analysis he used."

Thus, while we know that source credibility is a multidimensional phenomenon, exactly what, or how many, dimensions there are remains undecided. What follows, therefore, is our interpretation of the number and types of subareas constituting source credibility. We suggest seven such independent dimensions:

1. *power.* The speaker is perceived as one who can provide significant rewards and punishments for listeners. (E.g., "Well, Kay, if I'm so immature, maybe I shouldn't be taking you to the movie tonight.")
2. *competence.* The speaker is perceived as having knowledge and experience about a topic that others do not have. (E.g., "Just look at all the well-known people who write for and write letters to *Playboy*—politicians, authors, artists, doctors, and lots of other professionals.")
3. *trustworthiness.* The speaker's present behaviors are seen as being consistent with his past behaviors. (E.g., "Have you noticed me treat you or other women with any less respect because I read *Playboy*?")
4. *good will.* The speaker is perceived as having his audience's best interest in mind. (E.g., "You've always said you're proud of the way I treat you, and *Playboy* is where I learned how to be suave.")
5. *idealism.* The speaker is perceived as possessing qualities and values his audience esteems and to which it aspires. (E.g., "You've always admired the fact that I know more about current events than you do. Where do you think I get such knowledge?")
6. *similarity.* The speaker is judged to resemble the audience in significant ways. (E.g., "Now, Kay, you know that both of us have always said that it is important to be well informed on current social issues.")
7. *dynamism.* The speaker is perceived to be aggressive, emphatic, and forceful. (E.g., "Face it! It's great! Best mag on the rack!")

Ostensibly, these seven dimensions are independent: the audience's perception of a speaker on any one dimension may have little or nothing to do with their views of this speaker on the other six. Thus, a speaker who is judged to be powerful (e.g., your favorite senator), can range from highly competent to totally incompetent on another dimension. Or, a powerful, competent speaker can be seen as being highly trustworthy or totally untrustworthy. A salesman may know his product (competent), but he cannot punish you for not buying it. A teacher is competent, but has power as well.

In other words, as with many communication variables, source credibility is a distinctly situational phenomenon. In some instances, the trustworthiness dimension of credibility may become the crucial communicative issue (e.g., President Nixon after John Dean's revelations about Watergate). At other points in time (e.g., the 1973 gasoline and food shortages), the battle will be waged between "competent" sources (Ralph Nader *vs.* the Secretary of Agriculture) who are competing for public belief. All of this has been documented by Applbaum and Anatol (1972) who discovered, among other things, that while expertness may be the most crucial dimension of credibility in a classroom speech, in other situations (e.g., sermonizing in church), trustworthiness may be the more relevant aspect of a speaker's image.

We began this portion of the chapter with the question, "What is source credibility?" Before applying this knowledge to the problem of enhancing credibility, let us summarize what we have discussed thus far: Source credibility consists of seven relatively independent types of judgments made by listeners of some speaker. Such perceptions of listeners are independent of the speaker's own intent, although they may be influenced by it. While stimuli arising from the source, the occasion, the audience, and the channel will cause source credibility to vary over time, in the short run, at least, sufficiently high source credibility will lead the audience to accept or reject the attitudes, beliefs, and/or actions the speaker endorses.

gauging source credibility

In order to enhance his credibility, a speaker must make choices surrounded by constraint and possibility. These constraints and possibilities generate out of the speaker, the audience, and the situation. Thus, the first step in discovering the "credibility choices" open to you as a speaker is to find out what the audience currently thinks of you. This process of developing self-awareness or sensitivity to your own social image is difficult. As numerous authors have pointed out (and as we implied in Chapter 3), when a speaker addresses an audience there are at least three "speakers" present:

1. *the speaker's speaker:* what he believes he is and what he believes he is not. (E.g., "Ain't I dynamic!")
2. *the audience's speaker:* what the audience believes the speaker is, what they believe he is not, and the value they attach to these beliefs; this is the image we have labeled source credibility. (E.g., "What a piece of deadwood this guy is.")

3. *the speaker's view of the audience's speaker:* what the speaker believes the audience believes about him; this is the speaker's perception of his source credibility. ("It's obvious from their closed eyes that my dynamism has put them in a trance.")

A difficult, but necessary, prelude to making choices which enhance our credibility is that of adjusting Speakers 1 and 3 to Speaker 2. In other words, the constraints under which a speaker operates are imposed by how he thinks he is doing and how his audience perceives him to be doing. Only when a speaker has accurately assessed his assets and liabilities, and only when he has carefully evaluated his audience's perceptions of himself, will he be in a position to make wise, informed choices among strategies for enhancing his source credibility.

Such an assessment might begin with a list of your assets and liabilities—as *you* see them—in relation to the seven dimensions of source credibility. To this end, a form similar to the following credibility checklist might be useful. Let us assume, for example, that you are to give a classroom speech on drug addiction. When preassessing your personal resources as a speaker for such a chore try to use the form as illustrated in Table 1.

Even if you are honest with yourself when filling out such a form, you will only be recording your perceptions of *your* speaker (Speaker 1) and *your* impression of the audience's speaker (Speaker 3). Such estimates might change, of course, as you actually engage in interaction, where moment-to-moment "credibility adaptations" are necessitated. Whenever you do your assessing, however, it is good to remember that the audience's speaker constitutes the acid measure of your credibility. While you cannot climb into the minds of your auditors and check out your social image, you might try duplicating a form such as ours and administering it to your classmates. By comparing their actual responses to your predictions of their responses, you might get some insight into your own native ability to read an audience's view of you. Also, such a procedure might point out for you those dimensions of credibility of which you are particularly aware or to which you are blind. As if you had not heard it enough by now, communication is the kingpin of trial, error, and (intelligent) guess-work.

enhancing source credibility

To this point our discussion of strategies for enhancing source credibility has been somewhat abstract. Assuming, for example, that you have decided that your best strategy is to build competence, what

table 1

credibility checklist

FACTORS	ASSETS	LIABILITIES	SUGGESTIONS
Power	Not much. I might be able to show them that my speech could save their lives.	They see me as just another person in class, with no special power to reward and punish.	Dramatize the horrors of drug addiction; back it up with plenty of painful examples.
Competence	They know from Bob's comment in class that I made the dean's list last semester.	I've never told them about my interest in drug addiction. Could be starting from scratch with most of them.	Mention early in speech about my work with the Crisis Center. Get that *Time* article.
Trustworthiness	Some of them know I really followed through on the group assign-ment. They shouldn't feel that I'd trick them.	This will be a new topic for me. Most unlike my last speech on the campus election scandal.	Don't have much to worry about here. Might remind them that I stuck with them when the professor tried to spring a quiz on us!
Good Will	My strong suit. By now the group knows that I'm major-ing in social work—who could hate a social worker?	No problem as long as I stay with hard drugs. Can't come down hard on pot.	Many of them smoke, so I'd better steer clear of the marijuana issue or they'll see me as caring more about preaching than about them.
Idealism	They know that I'm always up in the clouds and generally aspire to the same things they do.	Got to be care-ful not to get too carried away with the moral stuff. Stick to the "fully func-tioning human being" idea.	Should probably stress our com-mon goals early in the speech *before* I mention drugs.

table 1 continued

FACTORS	ASSETS	LIABILITIES	SUGGESTIONS
Similarity	I've been in class with them all semester. They know I dress and talk like most of them.	Could be a problem if I come on like Ms. Know-it-All. Have to steer clear of my religious views on the subject with these heathens!	Better tie this in with Claire's speech on legalizing pot. This should build more common ground between me and them.
Dynamism	My biggie! They know that they can't shut me up when I get committed to a topic.	No problem! (As long as I remember not to talk too fast!)	Pace yourself, baby, pace yourself.

can you do? Answering this question is difficult, for—as Cronkhite (1969b, p. 127) has pointed out—"the experimental research has not produced many practical suggestions as to how a speaker can make himself influential." Furthermore, even when specific strategies are suggested for communicative use, there is little evidence to suggest which dimension or dimensions a particular strategy will enhance. What follows, therefore, is our attempt to catalog the specific strategies a speaker might use to enhance his "credibilities." Our list does not pretend to be exhaustive—merely suggestive. It is based, in part, upon our condensations of research summaries by Andersen and Clevenger (1963) and by Littlejohn (1971).

POWER

use an overt power strategy sparingly and subtly. If you have the ability to reward and punish the audience, you will not need to mention this fact. They will be aware. It is not necessary, for example, for your teacher to remind you that his ability to grade serves as a source of power. When he overtly reminds you of his power in an attempt to get you to feel, believe, or do as he suggests, you—like most people—are likely to resent it and to rebel in some fashion. There is evidence to suggest that more attitude change will occur when an audience does not feel itself *forced* to comply with the speaker's suggestions. On the other hand, it is often helpful to show how you as a speaker can exert influence *on behalf of* an audience.

indicate that the "power balance" between speaker and audience will be maintained. By this we mean that a speaker who indicates that *both* speaker and audience will profit *equally* from the interaction is well-advised to do so. As mentioned in our prologue to Unit I, a speaker who presumes to address a public audience has, by that very action, implied that he seeks something. Thus, in most situations, a speaker is wise to acknowledge what he expects to derive from the interaction and what "power" the audience itself is likely to derive from interacting with this speaker at this point in time.

COMPETENCE

associate yourself with other highly credible individuals. For example, evidence suggests that a speaker who receives a favorable introduction from a well-regarded individual will be perceived as more credible than he would have without such a psychological link. You may not be able to make this choice, but if you can, choose Dick Allen rather than Charlie Brown's Joe Schlablotnik.

demonstrate personal acquaintance with topic (self-reference). If the topic is something with which you are personally involved (you've done it, it's part of your job, it's your hobby, etc.), an audience is more apt to believe what you say about the topic. It is important, therefore, to let the audience know why *you* have chosen to speak on *this topic*—how *you* got involved and why *you* care.

demonstrate familiarity with special vocabulary of the topic. An additional way to demonstrate competence is through the correct use of terminology related to your topic.

demonstrate familiarity with persons who are expert in the field (prestige-reference). Citing such authorities in support of a point you are making is especially important if the audience perceives you as a moderate or low credible source. When quoting experts, the more credible the source, the more it will do for your own believability. Therefore, it is wise to analyze your audience carefully to discover their indisputable sources. You may perceive Dr. Benjamin Spock to be competent and trustworthy but if your audience does not, citing him in support of your point will hinder rather than help your credibility. If you already possess high competence credibility, quoting experts will not add to it appreciably, or so says the research.

be sure that your speech is well-organized. While a well-organized message may not increase credibility, a disorganized speech will usually decrease it. Thus, it pays to spend time organizing your speech in a fashion that your audience will be able to follow. (More about this in chapter 7.)

TRUSTWORTHINESS

if at all possible, establish verbal interaction with the audience.
This is difficult at times, but a speaker who acknowledges that he is willing to open himself up in direct ways to on-going public scrutiny, often gives the impression that he is sure of himself and of his position. As will be seen in Chapter 6, a spin-off benefit of such an approach is that the audience feels complimented by a speaker's willingness to partially relinquish his "control" of the flow of discourse. Listeners oftentimes reason, in such instances, that a speaker who opens himself up to challenge in this manner is one who can be trusted to maintain his views in other communicative situations.

demonstrate that your present behavior is consistent with your past behavior. It is often good to "remind" the audience of what you have done in the past on their behalf or on behalf of the proposition you advocate. This is especially important when "trustworthiness" is at issue. Being the "comparers" they are, listeners like to see a certain amount of consistency (or excusable inconsistency) in the behaviors of persons who ask for their adherence.

show that you can be trusted by being as explicit as possible and by entertaining alternative points of view. There are times, of course, when explicitness is not very desirable in public communication situations (e.g., when treating a point that can damage you in the minds of your auditors). Still, most listeners appreciate someone who does not "beat around the bush." Also, it is often wise to treat both sides of an issue in order to build an image of "fair-mindedness." As we will see in Chapter 9, such an approach is almost mandated when listeners are highly resistant to the speaker's proposal.

make sure that your verbal and nonverbal behaviors are consistent.
Thousands of subtle, nonverbal cues can suggest that you do not really believe what you are saying. Because people believe that nonverbal cues are harder to fake, they tend to believe the nonverbal more than the verbal.

GOOD WILL

demonstrate that your proposal will benefit the audience. Show how the audience will gain important rewards by accepting your position or, at least, that they will not lose by doing so.

show that other groups of similar individuals have accepted your proposal. If other groups have perceived your good will, this one should too. With such an approach you might make your image "contagious."

communicate genuine expressions of interest and affection. The key word here is genuine. Fake expressions of interest and affection often are easily detected by listeners who have a reason to be wary.

SIMILARITY

provide an overt statement of agreement with audience on, at least, peripheral issues. If you cannot agree with the audience on major issues, at least take a positive, agreeing position on a minor point. No matter what the audience, you should be able to find some minor issue to agree on.

learn to control your nonverbal behavior. As Mortensen (1972, p. 156) points out: "The only limit to the discovery of links between impressions of similarity and nonverbal cues seems to be the time and ingenuity investigators devote to such research." Personal appearance and demeanor such as nuances of posture, body position, physical distance, eye contact, dress, grooming, and the like, all provide the audience with cues for seeing the speaker as similar or dissimilar to themselves. Many of these cues are hard to control, but others are not. For example, most of us know how to dress and groom appropriately for various social situations. The challenge for a speaker (should he decide to accept it) is to discover those nonverbal cues that communicate similarity for the *particular audience* in question.

demonstrate that you represent the "greatest common denominator" of the audience's beliefs and values. In *public* communication situations, a speaker must be especially careful not to alienate a sizeable portion of the audience. Because a *group* of listeners usually harbors diverse and sometimes opposing viewpoints, a speaker is wise to emphasize those aspects of himself and his audience that are likely to meet with the greatest amount of *collective* agreement.

disassociate yourself from ideas and institutions that are disliked by the audience. This is the obverse of the previous proposition and can be an especially important factor contributing to credibility in many situations. For example, during the 1972 presidential race, George McGovern felt it necessary to separate himself from the "radical fringe" that had brought him to a position of popularity. The need for him to do so became especially pronounced *after* he was designated as the official representative of the Democratic party, a group that contained a good number of labor unionists and old time politicos who passionately disliked McGovern's leftist followers. Obviously, he did not succeed in making this disassociation stick in the minds of most.

IDEALISM

depict yourself as being both similar to and different from your audience. This is but one of the many dilemmas associated with building credibility. Obviously, listeners admire those who share the values, attitudes, and goals to which they aspire. On the other hand, unless a person is somehow "different" from them, listeners would have little reason to "look up" to you. Thus, by demonstrating that you possess certain knowledge that the audience needs or that you embody certain of their aspirations in rather dramatic ways, you as a speaker may be able to build an alike-but-different image for yourself.

indicate what you have risked (or are willing to risk) on behalf of your proposal. Most of us, it seems, tend to believe those who have "been to the barricades" on behalf of something they strongly believe in. Martyrs, after all, take on an "idealized" image because they have given of themselves totally to some particular group or ideology. While most speakers cannot depict themselves as martyrs in the true sense of the word, they can show that they are "ideal" representatives of a particular position in that they have placed themselves "on the line" for their beliefs.

DYNAMISM

indicate exactly what behavioral commitments you have made to your position. If you can show what you have *done* on behalf of your proposal, you might be perceived as being aggressive, emphatic, and forceful. For example, one of the reasons that Gloria Steinem was able to rise to a position of influence in the women's movement may be due to the energetic manner in which she demonstrated her commitment to the women's cause. Research indicates that a highly "intense" and strongly opinionated message will be perceived as dynamic and hence build a speaker's credibility in many situations.

learn to control delivery variables. Some research indicates that nonfluencies (e.g., speech errors like "uh" and "er") can affect negatively an audience's image of a speaker's dynamism. In interpreting such findings, however, we must be cautious. Delivery variables are difficult to control for, and excessive concentration on *our* bodies may distract us from the more important job of watching for and adapting to listeners' feedback.

As you can see, source credibility is a complex and dilemma-ridden phenomenon. We have posited that seven relatively distinctive dimensions contribute to credibility and have tried to suggest how each dimension might be successfully tapped in situations of public influence. Still, contradictions abound. For example, when attempting to be dynamic, a speaker can get so carried away with himself that he fails to demonstrate good will toward his audience. There is no easy resolution to such a quandary, but perhaps by being aware of the communicative options for building credibility, you can pick and choose among them and hence find techniques appropriate to your individual tastes and needs.

PUTTING SOURCE CREDIBILITY TO WORK: AN EXAMPLE

Some people *do* build credibility, however! Consider the case of Senator Edward Kennedy who, in July of 1969, faced one of the most tearing and frightening communication situations he has experienced to date. As you probably know, Senator Kennedy and Miss Mary Jo Kopechne were driving along a dimly lit road on Chappaquiddick Island, off the coast of Massachusetts. While driving, Kennedy's car went off the road and into a pond, whereupon Miss Kopechne met with a tragic death. Kennedy was held legally (and more important for our purposes) morally responsible for her death.

Seven days after the incident, Kennedy appeared on television to explain his plight to the people of Massachusetts (his home state) and to ask for their continued support. Because commentary in the press had been mixed, and because many throughout the country now doubted Kennedy's veracity, he found himself in a communication situation uniquely fueled by matters pertaining to his credibility as a source of information.

Because *credibility was distinctively at issue* in this situation, we felt that it would be profitable to analyze Kennedy's speech with the tools made available by our discussion of the methods for enhancing credibility. As you read the following remarks by Kennedy, note especially how he attempts to salvage a sagging image of trustworthiness and good will, how he implies that he is still "ideal" in some ways, and how he demonstrates that his power, competence, and similarity to the people of Massachusetts had not been diluted by the events of the preceding week. While some of his language may help you see the dynamism he attempted to muster, only a videotaped version of the speech would show you the emphasis and force connoted by his nonverbal cues. Consider, then, our example of credibility in crisis as analyzed in Table 2.

table 2

analysis of Senator Kennedy's speech*

COMMENTARY	SAMPLE MESSAGE
Demonstrates personal acquaintance with topic through self-references	My fellow citizens: I have requested this opportunity to talk to the people of Massachusetts about the tragedy which happened last Friday evening. This morning I entered a plea of guilty to the charge of leaving the scene of an accident. Prior to my appearance in court it would have been improper for me to comment on these matters. But tonight I am free to tell you what happened and to say what it means to me.
Shows that an explicit discussion of events is possible and desired by this speaker	On the weekend of July 18 I was on Martha's Vineyard Island participating with my nephew, Joe Kennedy—as for 30 years my family has participated—in the annual Edgartown Sailing Regatta. Only reasons of health prevented my wife from accompanying me. On Chappaquiddick Island, off Martha's Vineyard, I attended on Friday evening, July 18, a cook-out I had encouraged and helped sponsor for a devoted group of Kennedy campaign secretaries. When I left the party, around 11:15 p.m., I was accompanied by one of these girls, Miss Mary Jo Kopechne. Mary Jo was one of the most devoted members of the staff of Senator Robert Kennedy. She worked for him for four years and was broken up over his death. For this reason, and because she was such a gentle, kind and idealistic person, all of us tried to help her feel that she still had a home with the Kennedy family.
Carefully chooses language which indicates an awareness of audience's sense of morality	There is no truth, no truth whatever, to the widely circulated suspicions of immoral conduct that have been leveled at my behavior and hers regarding that evening. There has never been a private relationship between us of any kind.

*Edward Kennedy, "Address on the Mary Jo Kopechne Incident," July 25, 1969.

table 2 continued

COMMENTARY	SAMPLE MESSAGE
Disassociates himself from ideas and actions disliked by the audience	I know of nothing of Mary Jo's conduct on that or any other occasion—the same is true of the other girls at that party—that would lend any substance to such ugly speculation about their character. Nor was I driving under the influence of liquor. Little over one mile away, the car that I was driving on an unlit road went off a narrow bridge which had no guard rails and was built on a left angle to the road.
Gives a dynamic (vivid) presentation of the events	The car overturned in a deep pond and immediately filled with water. I remember thinking as the cold water rushed in around my head that I was for certain drowning. Then water entered my lungs and I actually felt the sensation of drowning. But somehow I struggled to the surface alive. I made immediate and repeated efforts to save Mary Jo by diving into the strong and murky current but succeeded only in increasing my state of utter exhaustion and alarm. My conduct and conversations during the next several hours, to the extent that I can remember them, make no sense to me at all.
Indicates that he is willing to entertain alternative points of view	Although my doctors informed me that I suffered a cerebral concussion as well as shock, I do not seek to escape responsibility for my actions by placing the blame either on the physical, emotional trauma brought on by the accident or on anyone else. I regard as indefensible the fact that I did not report the accident to the police immediately.
Uses chronological pattern of development so that listeners can follow along easily. This depicts him as being methodical and well organized.	Instead of looking directly for a telephone after lying exhausted in the grass for an undetermined time, I walked to the cottage where the party was being held and requested the help of two friends, my cousin, Joseph Gargan, and Phil Markham, and directed them to return immediately to the scene with me—this was some time after

table 2 continued

COMMENTARY	SAMPLE MESSAGE
	midnight—in order to undertake a new effort to dive down and locate Miss Kopechne.
	Their strenuous efforts, undertaken at some risks to their own lives, also proved futile.
Asserts that present behaviors are excusably inconsistent with past behaviors	All kinds of scrambled thoughts—all of them confused, some of them irrational, many of them which I cannot recall and some of which I would not have seriously entertained under normal circumstances—went through my mind during this period.
Associates himself with other highly credible individuals	They were reflected in the various inexplicable, inconsistent and inconclusive things I said and did, including such questions as whether the girl might still be alive somewhere out of that immediate area, *whether some awful curse did actually hang over all the Kennedys*, whether there was some justifiable reason for me to doubt what had happened and to delay my report, whether somehow the awful weight of this incredible incident might in some way pass from my shoulders.
Attempts to show that his feelings (verbalizations) and (nonverbal) behaviors coincide and are mutually reinforcing	I was overcome, I'm frank to say, by a jumble of emotions, grief, fear, doubt, exhaustion, panic, confusion, and shock.
	Instructing Gargan and Markham not to alarm Mary Jo's friends that night, I had them take me to the ferry crossing. The ferry having shut down for the night, I suddenly jumped into the water and impulsively swam across, nearly drowning once again in the effort, and returned to my hotel about 2 a.m., and collapsed in my room.
	I remember going out at one point and saying something to the room clerk.
	In the morning, with my mind somewhat more lucid, I made an effort to call a family legal adviser, Burk Marshall, from a public telephone on the Chappaquiddick side of the ferry and belatedly reported the accident to the Martha's Vineyard police.

table 2 continued

COMMENTARY	SAMPLE MESSAGE
Depicts himself as having certain idealized attitudes toward religion and morality	Today, as I mentioned, I felt morally obligated to plead guilty to the charge of leaving the scene of an accident. No words on my part can possibly express the terrible pain and suffering I feel over this tragic incident. This last week has been an agonizing one for me and the members of my family and the grief we feel over the loss of a wonderful friend will remain with us the rest of our lives.
Subtly and self-effacingly reminds audience of his own position of political power	These events, the publicity, innuendo and whispers which have surrounded them and my admission of guilt this morning— raises the question in my mind of whether my standing among the people of my state has been so impaired that I should resign my seat in the United States Senate. If at any time the citizens of Massachusetts should lack confidence in their Senator's character or his ability, with or without justification, he could not in my opinion adequately perform his duty and should not continue in office.
Demonstrates familiarity with persons who are "expert" in the field	The people of this state, the state which sent John Quincy Adams and Daniel Webster and Charles Sumner and Henry Cabot Lodge and John Kennedy to the United States Senate, are entitled to representation in that body by men who inspire their utmost confidence.
Shows agreement with audience's sense of right and wrong	For this reason, I would understand full well why some might think it right for me to resign. For me this will be a difficult decision to make.
Reminds the audience of favorable past ties they have shared	It has been seven years since my first election to the Senate. You and I share many memories—some of them have been glorious, some have been very sad. The opportunity to work with you and serve Massachusetts has made my life worthwhile.

table 2 continued

COMMENTARY	SAMPLE MESSAGE
Suggests that speaker–audience interaction on this issue is possible and desirable	And so I ask you tonight, people of Massachusetts, to think this through with me. In facing this decision, I seek your advice and opinion. In making it, I seek your prayers. For this is a decision that I will have finally to make on my own. It has been written a man does what he must in spite of personal consequences, in spite of obstacles and dangers and pressures, and that is the basis of all human morality.
Indicates what he can potentially risk on behalf of his proposal	Whatever may be the sacrifices he faces, if he follows his conscience—the loss of his friends, his fortune, his contentment, even the esteem of his fellow man—each man must decide for himself the course he will follow. The stories of the past courage cannot supply courage itself. For this, each man must look into his own soul.
Holds out the hope that both speaker and audience can profit from the interaction	I pray that I can have the courage to make the right decision. Whatever is decided and whatever the future holds for me, I hope that I shall be able to put this most recent tragedy behind me and make some further contribution to our state and mankind, whether it be in public or private life. Thank you and good night.

conclusion

Naturally, most of us need not attempt to pull out all of the credibility stops in our usual interactions with others. We feel, however, that Kennedy's speech indicates that many of the credibility principles we have discussed in this chapter can be put into practice in efficient and meaningful ways. That Kennedy's speech encouraged an outpouring of affection and support from his Massachusetts constituents does indicate that public communication can be a highly effective vehicle for extracting oneself from very undesirable credibility circumstances. Still, the fact that many others in the country remained unconvinced of Kennedy's role as moral exemplar, indicates that one man's credibility is another man's foolishness.

As we have seen in Chapter 2, and as we will again consider in Chapter 9, a speaker's credibility is always a potentially important force in *oral* communication. Because we as people always go with the words we speak, the student communicator can hardly avoid pondering the various components of source credibility. To dismiss the *human* dimension of communicative encounters is to ignore the single most important element that makes human communication human and which makes such encounters so variegated, unpredictable, and sometimes, even delightful.

the audience as resource

CHAPTER 5

Greg: Hi, Dad! Did you have a good day at the office? I'll bet you're glad it's Friday, huh?

Mr. B: You bet I am! All that traffic–I was late for the sales meeting, and some of those fellows down there just can't seem to follow orders. What a week!

Greg: Wow! You must be glad it's over. And wait till you see the fantastic dinner Mom prepared! She's been working on it ever since she got home from the play rehearsal.

Mr. B: Well, then—how about relaxing at a movie or something tonight—we could ask the Scotts to go along.

Greg: That's a great idea! You deserve a night out, and Scotty was just telling me about the neat car his folks just bought. Have you seen it? They'll probably want to drive and show it off a little. I guess it really is nice.

Mr. B: Not a bad idea, a movie. But—I don't know —maybe after such a rough week you'd rather just go alone so we could really relax.

Mrs. B: That does sound nice. And we can see the
Scotts' new car when they come for dinner
tomorrow night.

Greg: Gosh—I'd ask the Scotts anyway. Even
though you'll get to see the car tomorrow
night, you wouldn't have a chance to ride
in it—and I hear it has everything, including
the latest stereo setup—and even a bar. And
hearing what kind of day you've both had. . .

Mr. B: Well, let's see how we feel after dinner, OK?

Greg: If I were you, I wouldn't wait. They may
make last-minute plans and you could miss
them.

Mr. B: That reminds me—what are *your* plans
for tonight, Greg?

Greg: Oh, uh . . . I'm not really sure yet. Scotty and
I were sort of thinking about going to a movie
or something.

Mrs. B: Gee. Too bad Scotty can't get the car. You
can have him over here, though, if you want
to pick him up before we go to the movie.

Greg: Thanks, Mom. You really think of everything. But actually, we sort of told Debbie
and Katie that we'd take them to the movie,
and they'd probably be disappointed—and
mad—if we cancelled out this late.

Mr. B: Uh-huh.

A master of persuasion, Greg has pulled out all the stops in
his can-I-have-the-car-tonight campaign. Always alert for
feedback while, at the same time, choosing his responses carefully so
as to get his "main points" in, he settles finally on a cornering tactic
—and his father is well aware of it.

We all learn rather early in life that audience analysis and adaptation is at the very heart of the communication process. While some
of us may be better at applying this knowledge than others, most of
us come to know that the communicative strategies that work on
our parents will not work necessarily on our sisters or brothers, our
friends, or our friend's parents. Thus, consciously or unconsciously,

we learn to accommodate our messages to the people with whom we communicate. When, as in Greg's case, the situation appears to warrant it, we devote considerable time and effort to planning our approaches well in advance. Who among you, for example, would attempt to "explain" your absence from the last quiz without giving some thought as to how to approach your instructor most effectively?

What we will be saying in this chapter, therefore, should not be completely foreign to you. By this point in your life, you have already analyzed and adapted to thousands of "audiences." Hence, this chapter will perhaps just reassist you in organizing your past insights into a systematic framework for use in analyzing and adapting to audiences *in public communication settings.*

In the language of Chapter 3, we will be looking here at the types of "potentials" that reside within listeners when they join together to become a public audience. Our chapter is thus divided into the following areas: (1) dimensions of audience analysis, (2) the nature of *public* audiences, (3) audience effects on public communication, and (4) the potentials for response which reside within listeners.

As we have said and will say throughout this book, the listener is the ultimate arbiter of our communicative success. In addition, if we believe that communication is an interactive process—a sort of mutual blending of (at least) two complex human elements—then we must give careful consideration to the fellow at the other end of the string. That the listener can have tremendous impact upon what we as speakers say and do is well documented in the following anecdote:

It was in the lobby of the Martin Beck Theatre, during the first intermission of the performance of *The Lake,* that Dorothy Parker made one of her most celebrated remarks.

Someone said to Mrs. Parker (referring to Katherine Hepburn), "Kate's wonderful, isn't she?"

"Oh, yes," agreed Mrs. Parker. "She runs the gamut of emotion all the way from A to *B!*"

The crack is remembered better than the play.

It should be noted that by this time Mrs. Parker had married Alan Campbell, who had been one of Kate's many beaux.

Some years later, I (Garson Kanin) was working on a film with Dorothy Parker. In the course of a casting discussion, she began to sell Katherine Hepburn. I was astonished.

"I thought you didn't like her," I said.

Those great brown eyes became greater and browner.

"Me?" said Dottie. "I don't think there's a finer actress anywhere."

"But what about 'all the way from A to B'?" I reminded her. "Or didn't you say it? Or do you think she's improved?"

Dottie sighed. "Oh, I said it all right. You know how it is. A joke."

She looked distressed. She shrugged and swallowed. *"When people expect you to say things, you say things. Isn't that the way it is?"* **(italics added)**[1]

dimensions of audience analysis

In a sense, this entire chapter will discuss matters pertaining to analyzing (and subsequently adapting to) an audience. In this section, we would like to give you an overview of our *sequential* options for assessing the potentials for response that lay buried within those cantankerous listeners with whom we must transact so much of our social business.

While the goal of audience analysis and adaptation is similar for all communication situations (How can knowledge about the people I will be talking with be used to increase the probability of achieving my ends?), approaches for achieving this goal must vary from setting to setting. As stated in Chapter 1, public settings differ from other communicative circumstances in a variety of ways. Let us relist just a few of these public communication "distinctives":

1. The public communicator must attempt to analyze and adapt to *many* diverse people simultaneously.
2. In doing so, the on-going feedback he receives is more restricted and subtle, and, hence, more likely to be misinterpreted.
3. Therefore, public communication requires a higher degree of *advanced* speech preparation than is required by more private settings.

Given what we know about such settings, then, how can a public communicator cope with the formidable task of analyzing and adapting to the many diverse people that compose his audience?

When thinking about audience analysis, we can profitably arrest the process at three points in time: (1) *prior to communication*—where the public communicator is most concerned with discovering in advance those characteristics of his auditors which will predispose them to accept or reject his message, (2) *during communication*—where he is most concerned with monitoring audience feedback so as to discover whether his previously selected communicative options need modification, and (3) *after communication*—where he attempts to discover whether or not his message actually achieved the goals he had specified ahead of time. Let us consider each stage of the process separately.

[1]From *Tracy and Hepburn* by Garson Kanin (New York: Bantam, 1972), p. 17. Copyright © 1970, 1971 by T. F. T. Corporation. Reprinted by permission of the Viking Press, Inc.

PRIOR AUDIENCE ANALYSIS

Because public communication usually demands that a speaker bear the brunt of the talking burden, advanced preparation is the key to analyzing and adapting to all those different people out there. To start such a process, you could simply get a list of the audience members and strive to learn every conceivable thing about each of them. But the people making up your audience are so multifaceted that you could not possibly hope to *use* such volumes of data (which would be incomplete under any circumstances) even if you did manage to compile it before speech time. Thus, another option would be to look at the *whole* audience. For example, you determine that they all belong to the Lions Club and are male. Satisfactory? Not really, since we can seldom treat an audience as if it were a single entity. Even though people behave distinctively when brought together (e.g., because of group pressures), they still retain much of their individuality: "When we become members of audiences, we all trim the sails of our behavior to the winds of group opinion and practice; yet each sails his own vessel, however much he likes to keep the fleet in sight" (Wilson and Arnold, 1968, p. 77).

Thus, the speaker must effect a compromise between conducting a psychiatric interview and a shot-in-the-dark foray. If we think about the members of the audience in such a way as to *cluster* them in terms of similarities and differences related to how they will respond in this situation, we might generate useful data. A happy medium would be to regard neither *one*, nor *all*—but small clusters of people (overlapping, possibly) who have something(s) in common. Figure 5 depicts our necessary compromise in conducting prior audience analysis.

Helpful as such an approach to prior audience analysis might be, we are still left with a more burning question: What do you look for in such "clusters" of people? One answer lies in an attempt to understand some aspects of the psychological make-up of people in general and then to use such "search lights" to discover relevant aspects of the actual audience we will be dealing with in communication. Later in this chapter, we will attempt to lay out some of these pertinent resources residing within most all listeners. As a sort of preview to that section, we might list four of the most common questions a speaker might ask when speculating about his intended auditors: (1) What information do I have about their *attitudes* and *values*? (2) What *kinds* of beliefs will I be addressing myself to in this communication situation? (3) What sorts of *experiences* have these listeners had that may add to or subtract from my communicative impact? and (4) What kinds of general listeners' *needs* will be brought to bear on this speaking situation? Modest though this "starter's list" is, answers to such

figure 5

audience analysis in public communication

Options	Analyze each individual in audience.	Treat audience as "clusters" of listeners.	Analyze audience as if it were a single listener.
Example	"That lady in the gray hat looks uncomfortable with my last statement."	"I've got to remember that the audience is composed of both young people *and* their parents."	"They're all white Protestants and hence should respond similarly to my remarks."
Commentary	Audience analysis becomes an exercise in futility.	Audience analysis becomes both precise and manageable.	Audience analysis provides little data to guide us in creating appropriate messages.

questions can do much to direct a speaker's mind in his search for things sayable.

PROCESS AUDIENCE ANALYSIS

Prior audience analysis always is a gamble since the speaker can never be certain that his inferences about the audience are correct. As a result, public communicators must necessarily consider how their listeners are responding from moment to moment during the speech. In its literal sense, of course, this is impossible. Still, speakers need to know whether their audiences are, in some fashion, interested, understanding, and accepting of the messages with which they are presented. If an audience does not so respond, the speaker will need to modify his or her original strategy in order to produce the desired results.

But again, the question appears, What is it that the speaker should observe? Moreover, how can he immediately *interpret* what he notices? How does he incorporate this feedback while making intelligent adaptations to his auditors? Unfortunately, perhaps even more so than in the case of prior analysis, there are no easy answers.

Oftentimes, all a speaker has to work with are the nonverbal responses of his audience. Thus, what the speaker must do is to maintain close visual contact with his audience as he attempts to monitor and interpret their behavior. In so doing, he must strike a balance between ignoring important feedback and becoming overly sensitive to the negative or positive feedback of one or two individuals. The *public* communicator must be concerned with the *major* trends he sees in his audience.

While such bromides may be obvious to you, it should be stressed that when process-analyzing our listeners, we are making inferences about their internal states. Sometimes such inferences may prove to be incorrect, but more often they are right. Research would suggest that most speakers can identify reliably the following cues as being either positive or negative.

positive audience feedback
> Constant eye contact
> Smiling
> Positive head nods
> Comfortable, but erect posture
> Note taking
> Little or no movement of the body or limbs

negative audience feedback
> No eye contact (or eyes rolled up)
> Slouched posture
> Manipulating or examining objects or parts of the body
> Looking around the room at others
> Doodling
> Shaking head
> Yawns
> Tapping fingers
> Eyebrow movements (down and together)
> Questioning facial expression

Thus, if the speaker focuses on major trends in his audience, he should be in a position to adjust his behavior in order to modify or to intensify the feelings of the majority of his listeners and not to concentrate excessively on the kibitzing moron in the third row. That such "process feedback" can be of great import to the speaker seems undeniable. If, for example, listeners' responses indicate that they do not accept or understand the point the speaker is making, he may have to provide additional clarification or even move back to a pre-established point of mutual agreement. The success or failure of public communication depends to a great extent on our ability to "read" an audience and to modify our behavior to account for on-the-spot exigences. We perhaps should apologize for making such obvious comments, but each time we encounter a college lecturer who has not peered past his podium in 30 years, we feel compelled to renew such preaching.

POST-AUDIENCE ANALYSIS

After the speech is over, most speakers would like to know the effect their message had before they prepare to steal out of town. If they specified their goals in a meaningful way ahead of time, they are well on the road to discovering their impact. A meaningful goal statement might ask: How will I know when my speech has been successful? or What would I like to observe my audience doing in what situations? Post-audience analysis, therefore, consists of gathering evidence that relates to goals that have been specified in advance.

The public communicator has a variety of tools for gathering such data. Audience behavior during and immediately following the speech can provide many clues as to its effectiveness. Applause, questions, compliments, and wholesale criticism may indicate which points were not understood, which points needed greater support, and to what extent members of the audience favored or understood his remarks.

Questionnaires, interviews with audience members, and follow-up conversations can sometimes provide the speaker with a precise assessment of his effectiveness. For some speeches, very precise measures are available: Did they sign up for the proposed project? Did they contribute to the Will Rogers Clinic? Did they vote for Barney Hinkle?

When you know that you will be addressing the same audience several times—as you would in a speech communication class—post-audience analysis may suggest communicative options for use in future presentations. If approached dispassionately, feedback from the instructor, from friends and class members, and from audio- and videotape recordings can lead to an accurate assessment of our strengths and weaknesses as public communicators.

the nature of public audiences

In this section, and in the two that follow, we would like to point up some of the things worth knowing about listeners and audiences in general. We believe that *by knowing what to look for* when analyzing an audience through time, certain *adaptive potentialities* may present themselves to you. We want you to fully exploit the *adaptive* nature of communication and feel it would be helpful if you became a bit more familiar with the adaptees.

As we implied in Chapter 1, public audiences are a mottled collection of animals indeed. There they sit, seemingly ready to assault your messages with a Pandora's box full of experiences, goals, attitudes, expectations, and 28 other flavors of communicative surprises. No matter how much you have preplanned, rehearsed, organized, and analyzed, it always seems that you miss an important bet or two. And so it must be in public communication, where you cannot reach all of the people all of the time. The demands made by *public* audiences are often complex and conflicting.

To dramatize the heterogeneity of assembled listeners, let us consider a "public audience" that you are probably most familiar with—the college lecture audience. Let us further assume that you are taking an introductory psychology course at the University of Michigan with 103 other students. You look around the room, and your classmates all look about the same—about an equal number of straights and freaks, men and women, sleepers and awakers. But look more closely. If this is the "average" class that Ringwald, Mann, and their colleagues (1971) studied, there are many surprises lurking within this ostensibly similar group of students. In fact, this public audience apparently is comprised of eight distinct "clusters" of individuals, each of whom places very different communicative demands on the professor. See if you can find yourself in this mob-turned-audience:

1. *the compliant students.* **Five men, seven women. The typical students of the traditional classroom. Conventional, contented, trusting of authorities, willing to go along with what the teacher wants. Focus on understanding material rather than criticizing it or formulating own ideas. Somewhat younger than average (mostly freshpersons), may not have begun Eriksonian identity crisis.**
2. *the anxious-dependent students.* **Twelve men, sixteen women. Very concerned about and dependent on what authorities think of them. Low self-esteem, doubtful of own intellectual competence, anxious about exams and grades. Class comments hesitant and tentative.**
3. *the discouraged workers.* **Three men, one woman. Intelligent, hard-working, intellectually involved, but chronically depressed and personally distraught. Afraid their destructive impulses will lead them to hurt others.**
4. *the independent students.* **Nine men, three women. Self-confident, interested, involved; tend to identify with teacher and see him as colleague. Older than average (mostly juniors or seniors); seem to have achieved firmer identity than students in other clusters.**
5. *the heroes.* **Ten men, no women. Intelligent, creative, involved; resentful of authorities, rebellious. Introspective; struggling to establish identity. Ambivalent toward teacher, erratic in performance.**

6. *the snipers.* **Seven men, three women. As rebellious as the people in the previous group, but more defensive and less creative. Low self-esteem, afraid of introspection, attracted to authoritarian class structure. Uninvolved and indifferent toward class; stress fact that they were required to take course. In class, tend to lash out and quickly withdraw.**
7. *the attention-seekers.* **Five men, six women. Orientation social rather than intellectual. Want to be liked, to please, to get good grades. Women flirt, men show off and joke. Not introspective; both self-esteem and control depend on periodic reinforcement from others.**
8. *the silent students.* **Eight men, twelve women. Speak in class only when sure teacher will approve. Feel helpless, vulnerable, threatened in relation to teacher; fear engulfment by him but long hopelessly for his affection.**[2]

If we can assume that Ringwald's psychology classes represent the usual range of attitudes and motivations that inflict groups of listeners, we can draw some general conclusions about the natures of public audiences. Such a list might start like this:

1. Public listeners will have *a host of motivations for interacting* with the speaker. Some listeners may have come to carp, others to learn, and still others have come because there was not much else going on.
2. Public audiences will contain a wide *range of attitudes toward the speaker and his topic.* For example, depending on the political climate of your own campus, a speaker from the John Birch Society may address fellow extremists, left-wing anarchists, and a collection of middle-of-the-roaders—all of whom go to make up "an" audience.
3. Public audiences are uniquely *susceptible to forces existing within the group* itself. As mentioned in Chapter 1, intra-audience effects can do much to reinforce or to counteract remarks made by a speaker. Thus, in our psych class example, it is possible that the snipers (Group 6) may further discourage the discouraged workers (Group 3), thus cutting into the teacher's own communicative goals.

We could undoubtedly list still more characteristics of public audiences, but even these three points are enough to give us a flavor for

---

[2]B. E. Ringwald, "Conflict and Style in the College Classroom," excerpted from *Psychology Today* magazine, February, 1971. Copyright © by Communications/Research/Machines, Inc.

"collected" listeners. Because they present themselves to speakers in groups and subgroups, public auditors raise *special* communicative problems for the harried speaker.

For example, you have probably noticed that public talk "sounds different" from your more usual, two-person interactions. The very language you use when whispering to your classmate before it's "your turn," seems to undergo a strange metamorphosis when you stand up and stare out at that sea of faces in your speech class. Thereafter, you seem to talk in more *general* terms. You use more "we's" than "I's." You search for examples with which *your listeners* can identify. These alterations are but a few of the accommodations forced upon us as speakers addressing groups of listeners.

Consider the following speech. See if you can tell where it was given, what types of listeners it was designed for, and who the speaker might be:

It is a pleasure and a privilege to be here with you today. These great annual meetings are always an inspiration to me, and doubly so today. But we're in the midst of trying times. So you'll pardon me if I cast aside the glib reverberations of glittering generalities and the soothing syrup of sugar-coated platitudes and put it to you the only way I can, straight English.

We're losing the battle!

From every corner the people are being weaned away from the doctrine of the Founding Fathers. They are being detoured from the high-speed highways of progress by the utopian highwaymen.

Now let me say that I do not wish to turn the clock back. None of us do. All forward-looking businessmen see themselves as partners on a team in which the worker is a full-fledged member. I regard our employees as our greatest business asset, and I am sure, mindful as I am of the towering potentials of purposeful energy in this group of clear-sighted leaders, that, in the final analysis, it is the rock foundation of your policies, too.

But the team can't put the ball across for a first down just by pushing it. The guards and the tackles can't do their job if the quarterback doesn't let them in on the play. And we, the quarterbacks, are muffing the ball.

How are we to go over for a touchdown? My friends, this is the 64-dollar question. I don't know the answers. I am just a plain-spoken businessman. I am not a soothsayer. I have no secret crystal ball. But I do know one thing: before we round the curve into the homestretch we have a job to do. It will not be easy. I offer no panaceas or nostrums. Instead I would like to suggest that the real key to our problem lies in the application of the three Es. What are the three Es? Enterprise! Endeavor! Effort!

Much has been done already. But let's not fool ourselves: the surface has hardly been scratched. The program is still in its infancy. So let me give it to you straight from the shoulder. The full implication, gentlemen, depends on us.

We have the know-how.
With sights set high, let's go over the top![3]

Over the top, indeed! If you are having trouble sorting out the meaning, let alone the impact, of this rhetorical foolishness, you have read carefully! It really is just a "nonspeech," a put-on that was concocted by a humorist in order to dramatize the usual fare served up at the annual business meeting of Anycompany, Inc. But it makes a delightful point about public audiences—they force us, as speakers, to climb the ladder of abstraction a bit; they demand that we find ideas and language that will fall within the range of tastes they embody collectively. Of course, they demand more than the above inspecific piece of verbal tripe. Still, the fact that this speech does not sound all that abnormal should indicate that talk designed for *public* audiences has imposed upon it certain communicative constraints not found in our more private, *targeted* exchanges.

audience effects on public communication

Because they come packaged in public sizes, audiences produce other adaptive demands for the speaker. Here, we will treat factors that the communicator might want to take into consideration when analyzing and preparing messages for public audiences. From among the many effects produced on a speaker's messages by an audience's "groupness," we have selected the following to treat briefly: (1) the results produced by multiple audiences, (2) the effects engendered by an audience's polarization, (3) the implications resulting from the size of an audience, (4) the effects produced by an audience's expectations, and (5) the impact of reference groups on public communicative experiences.

THE EFFECTS OF MULTIPLE AUDIENCES

For any number of reasons, the audience sitting in front of the public communicator and the audience which he wishes to influence may not be identical. An important distinction the public communicator must make, therefore, is between his immediate—physically present —audience and his peripheral listeners (those physically removed from the interaction).

A peripheral audience may be of two general kinds: those exposed to the message via the mass media simultaneously with the immedi-

---

[3]"The Language of Business," *Fortune*, November, 1950, p. 114. Reprinted by permission of *Fortune* magazine.

ate audience's exposure, and those receiving the message later by word of mouth. In the former case, the public communicator may or may not have to account for the demands made by both of his audiences. For example, Joe McGinniss, in *The Selling of the President 1968*, describes a case where the main concern was with the peripheral (mass) audience:

There was to be a studio audience—three hundred people—recruited by the local Republican organization. Just enough Negroes so the press could not write "all-white" stories but not enough so it would look like a ballpark. The audience, of course, would applaud every answer Richard Nixon gave, boosting his confidence and giving the impression to a viewer that Nixon certainly did have charisma, and whatever other qualities he wanted his President to have. . . .

. . .

"One problem you're going to have here, Roger," a local man said, "is the size of the studio. You've been working with an audience of three hundred, I understand, but we can only fit two hundred and forty."

"That's all right. I can get as much applause out of two hundred and forty as three hundred, if it's done right, and that's all they are—an applause machine." He paused. "That and a couple of reaction shots. . . ."

. . .

"Now, when Mr. Nixon comes in," Jack Rourke was saying, "I want you to tear the place apart. Sound like ten thousand people. I'm sure, of course, that you'll also want to stand up at that point. So what do you say we try it now. Come on, stand up. And let me hear it."[4]

Obviously, such a blatant disregard for the immediate audience is unwise in most cases. Usually, the public communicator must balance the demands of both his immediate and peripheral audiences. This may mean, for example, that the local joke that goes over so well with the home congregation may not work as well when Billy Graham addresses *both* the folks back home and the unseen millions watching him over national television. It was his failure to account for this multiplicity of respondents that created so many problems for Barry Goldwater in his 1964 campaign for the presidency. By focusing almost completely on his immediate audience, Senator Goldwater repeatedly found himself in situations such as this one:

At an early-morning press conference at Laconia he [Goldwater] was asked whether he would campaign on a promise to lead the United States out of the United Nations if Communist China were admitted to the UN.

"I would be inclined to do so," he said.

The wire-service and network reporters were still phoning this story

[4]From Joe McGinniss, *The Selling of the President, 1968* (New York: Simon & Schuster, 1970), pp. 61, 98, and 106. Reprinted by permission.

to their offices when Goldwater took off for the nearby town of Meredith. I wasn't on deadline so I tagged along. He made his appearance there on a curb in front of a tiny crowd. One man said, "My wife wants to know what you would do about the United Nations."

Goldwater said earnestly: "We must stay in the United Nations, but we must improve it."

"You never opposed the UN then?" the man asked.

"No," said Goldwater.

A little later he appeared at the local high school and said that if China were admitted, "I think it blows the whole thing to pieces."

That evening at Colby Junior College for girls, he said, "I've never said let's get out of the UN. I don't know how that rumor ever got started."

On still another occasion he said that he didn't think the world was ready for an organization like the UN.[5]

The second type of peripheral audience may be of more immediate concern to the average speaker. In a pioneering study, Lazarsfeld and others (1944) discovered that, after presenting a message over one of the mass media and then measuring the impact of that message, there was little or no immediate effect. When they repeated the measurement some weeks later, however, they discovered that significant changes in beliefs had occurred. In trying to explain their findings, they suggested "that ideas often *flow* from radio and print *to* opinion leaders and *from* these to the less active sections of the population" (p. 151). A sort of Tinker-to-Evans-to-Chance of the communication biz!

Numerous studies have since confirmed this "two-step flow hypothesis" and have indicated that certain individuals (variously labeled fashion leaders, gatekeepers, influencers, information leaders, key communicators, sparkplugs, style setters, or tastemakers) have the ability to influence other peoples' behavior in important ways. For this reason (as we saw in Chapter 1) they are most frequently called *opinion leaders.* When a public communicator knows that his audience is inhabited by a few of these influential individuals, he is obviously wise to focus much of his communication on them. Isolating such individuals is the hard part. Berelson and Steiner (1964) summarize the characteristics of the typical opinion leader thus:

By and large, opinion leaders are like the rank and file of their associates but of slightly higher educational or social status; they give much greater attention to the mass media on the topics of their opinion leadership; they are better informed, more partisan, and more active than their associates. Opinion leaders differ for different topics—sports as against politics, for example—but they have in common their channeling of the impersonal

[5]Charles Mohr, "Requiem for a Lightweight," *Esquire,* August, 1965, p. 68. Reprinted by permission. © 1965 by Esquire, Inc.

content of mass communications into the personal stream of influence ("the two-step flow of communications"). Opinion leaders are effective, not only because they are personally trusted, but because they can adjust the argument to the individual case, because they can personally and immediately reward agreement, and because they allow for compliance without persuasion.[6]

The point we wish to make in this section, then, is that the public communicator must make a decision as to whom he desires to influence. Is it the majority of his immediate audience? Just a few? None? Does he wish to reach some peripheral audience? Which one? Must he balance his strategies to meet the demands of *both* types of audiences? An intelligent unfolding of communicative options will hinge on responses to questions such as these.

THE EFFECTS OF POLARIZATION

One useful dimension along which audiences may be classified is the degree of similarity or "togetherness" imbedded within them in a communication setting. A useful classification of this sort (provided by Hollingworth, 1935) groups audiences into five types ranging from the pedestrian to the organized.

The audience with the least common polarization—the *pedestrian* audience—is typified by those who stop to watch the person selling vegetable slicers in a supermarket. Except for the fact that each listener has interrupted what he or she was doing for the moment, the individual auditors have no obvious ties with the speaker or with other members of the audience. The salesperson's first task, therefore, must be to capture attention or at least divert it from the other marvels of the supermarket.

With a *passive* audience, the speaker has already claimed attention. Such audiences are most frequently "captive" listeners: for example, students who inhabit lecture halls because they want to pass a course which requires attendance. Since the audience has already directed their attention toward the speaker, his main task is to sustain and direct *their* interests.

The third type of audience—*selected*—shares with the speaker a common and known purpose, but may not be in agreement as to how to achieve certain goals. For example, all members of the PTA audience might agree that a problem exists, but may not be in agreement as to how to solve the problem. Since the audience has chosen to at-

---

[6]Bernard Berelson and Gary A. Steiner, *Human Behavior: An Inventory of Scientific Findings* (New York: Harcourt Brace Jovanovich, 1964), p. 550. Reprinted by permission.

tend the speech on the basis of their inherent interest in the topic, the first task of the speaker in such situations is to take sources of motivation and channel them in some preconceived direction.

Similar to the selected audience is the *concerted* audience. Its members share a pressing, active need to achieve some end, oftentimes accompanied by sympathetic interest in the topic and speaker. Usually, however, no clear division of labor or rigid organization of authority is embodied in such audiences. While the inclination of such an audience normally is to go along with the suggestions of the speaker, they must be convinced. The difference between the selected and concerted audiences may be explained by the following comparison. While the delegates to the World Council of Churches Convention (selected audience) may agree on their combined purpose for convening, each represented denomination (concerted subaudience) brings individual concerns to bear on the communicative situation.

The final type of audience—*organized*—is typified by military gatherings and many extremist political groups. Such audiences are oftentimes completely devoted to the speaker and to his purpose. The "doctrine" is known and accepted. The lines of authority are clear. The speaker's main job in such situations is to specify and help implement the action to be taken.

Although no research has yet been done on the question, it is probably true that communication itself helps to create and to disband such audience types. Thus, speakers launched the women's movement in situations involving pedestrian and passive audiences, and, through persuasion, eventually built and sustained concerted, and later, organized audiences. While much of your classroom speaking will be done in the face of passive (maybe, on some issues, selected) audiences, there is much reason to be aware of the communicative options and demands residing within such collections of individuals. More than one speaker has failed to win the day because he has misperceived the motivations and orientations of his assembled hearers. The Bible-toting Campus Crusader who talks to all others *as if* they were "one of us," and succeeds only in insulting his *passive* audience, is but one example of the failure to adapt to the types of audiences we as speakers attempt to merge with daily.

THE EFFECTS OF SIZE AND DENSITY

Many social psychologists, rhetoricians, and practitioners in the field of public communication allege that audience size—both absolute and relative—has an impact on the choosing of communicating options. Obviously, as the absolute size of an audience increases, the necessity for using mechanical devices such as microphones, amplifiers, and projected visual aids also increases. Thus, the public communicator who faces a large audience must be prepared to master the workings—and failings—of public address systems and other devices made necessary by a large audience. Psychologically, such mechanical mediators can sometimes adversely affect attempts to create perceptions of human intimacy in the public setting.

More importantly, however, as size increases, the transactional nature of communication is made less obvious, physical remoteness and psychological distance (oftentimes) increases, and the feedback received is less useful because it is prodigious, yet subtle, in so many cases. Thus, for example, while an instructor of a small class may allow his students almost complete freedom to ask questions, to interrupt his remarks, and to make comments of their own, as the class size increases, such behaviors become less possible. As a result, with large classes the materials must be prepared more thoroughly in advance, the instructor must accept the major portion of the speaking burden, and the amount of task-related interaction that any one class member may have with the instructor or with fellow students is reduced. The public communicator, therefore, must attempt to anticipate and adapt to the demands placed upon him by the size of his immediate audience.

Concomitant with audience size is the matter of audience *density*, which is said to have impact on the suggestibility of listeners. The few studies that have investigated this phenomenon of "packed-togetherness" have been inconclusive, but there is reason enough to suspect that the speaker cannot afford to ignore the potential import of audience density. As Minnick states:

A communicator who wishes to attain maximum suggestibility and strong emotional response often tries to seat his audience elbow to elbow and to fill clusters of vacant seats or vacant rows between the audience and the rostrum. Since a person's emotional responses are heightened and facilitated by awareness of the response of others, a communicator who assures crowded seating provides a condition of maximum effectiveness.

A standing audience is superior in this respect to a seated audience, since the members of it can be more tightly compressed and thus exposed to an even greater number of facilitating stimulations. It was no accident that the audiences of Adolph Hitler and Benito Mussolini invariably stood packed shoulder to shoulder in an arena or public square. Nor was it an accident that these audiences were notably noisy and demonstrative.[7]

Naturally, this matter of density does not always work in favor of the speaker. A person addressing a tightly-packed, *hostile* audience may be undone by the intimate interactions of his assembled hearers.

[7]Wayne C. Minnick, *The Art of Persuasion*, 2nd ed. (Boston: Houghton Mifflin, 1968), p. 70. Reprinted by permission.

THE EFFECTS OF SITUATIONAL EXPECTATIONS

That audiences come to a public communication setting with certain expectations is attested to by the fact that so many speakers find it necessary to acknowledge special merit in speaking to members of their audiences and to announce points of agreement and identification with their listeners. These expectations of listeners, of course, vary with their attitudes toward the speaker, his topic, and the speaking situation. Thus, for example, an audience member has different "sets" depending on whether he is attending a revival meeting, an acceptance speech by a Nobel Prize winner, a keynote address at a political convention, or a lecture in Physics 101. The important point here is that audience members *do* have expectations in *all* cases, and the public communicator must try to calculate before he talks what expectancies the majority of his audience will share. While it is not always necessary to meet each and every expectancy, it is necessary to acknowledge the importance of most of them.

For our purposes, it is not necessary to concern ourselves with the complex question of how these expectations are established. It is sufficient to acknowledge that (1) expectations are a function of an individual's values, experiences, personality, and attitudes; (2) like any other audience variable, expectations differ from individual to individual within an audience; and (3) certain expectancies are shared by the majority of an audience and these must be seized upon and accounted for (directly or indirectly) by the speaker. As we will see in the Epilogue to this book, a speaker who refuses to acknowledge and adapt to such implicit demands may thereby exclude the possibility of having impact in the ways he desires.

Other environmental factors that may influence audience expectations include the time of day or the month of the year, attractiveness and comfort of the room, the use of music, and the display of objects and symbols. A Fourth of July audience in the heartland of America, for example, may be disappointed and confused if they do not meet in a scenic location, hear the familiar strains of marches and patriotic melodies, while being surrounded by red, white, and blue bunting. Along these same lines, in fact, Jesus groups have finally gotten the message of Woodstock, so that when they tour college campuses, they unpack both their Bibles *and* their twelve-strings and amplifiers. All of this is done on the assumption that "since they're looking for rock, we can slip in a little old-time religion on the side!"

Both situational and attitudinal variables, then, lead the audience to expect certain things of the public communicator. In our attempts to locate these shared audience expectations, we as speakers might ask such questions as:

1. Why did the members of the audience select to be here?
2. What do they usually expect to hear in a situation like this one?
3. What previous knowledge (and hence expectations) do they have of me?
4. What do they expect to hear someone like me say about the topic in question?
5. How will the local environment affect my audience's expectations?

There are many situations, of course, where we as speakers might find it wise *not* to meet audience expectations. For example, when you announce to your classmates that you will be speaking on capital punishment, you should not be surprised to hear a few groans, so common is the topic in speech communication classrooms. These negative "sets" can do much to undermine your own potential impact. Thus, you might want to make it clear in the beginning of your speech that you will be approaching the topic in a *novel* manner, that their *previous biases* toward the topic might not be operational here, and that your commitment to the topic is such that this will not be just another speech given by just another student for the sake of a B and a pat on the head.

THE EFFECTS OF REFERENCE GROUPS

As we mentioned in Chapter 3, reference groups, composed of those persons we respect and admire, can exert significant force on our potentials-for-response as listeners. Reference groups can be classified in terms of demographic groups and voluntary groups. The former is defined by variables such as age, sex, and ethnic origin—qualities over which the individual has no control; the latter includes associations such as religious, political, and social groups to which an individual actually belongs (Black Cultural Center) or aspires to (the Jet Set). Reference groups set standards or norms of behavior which determine "acceptable" behavior for members of the group especially when there is no alternative, tangible set of standards by which to guide our choices.

Reference groups are important to the public communicator because, if correctly identified, they provide a handy set of "clustered values" which can be used to bolster a speaker's arguments. Obviously, an individual listener belongs to or selects among many reference groups which are not always relevant to the public communicator's topic or purpose for speaking. Thus, in analyzing an audience, we should look for only those reference groups that appear to embody knowledge and beliefs relevant to the demands of the situation.

The identification of such groups serves two important functions for us as speakers. First, because reference groups can determine behavior for group members, a knowledge of an audience's relevant membership groups allows us to improve our predictions about *salient* audience beliefs and hence to better adapt to them. On a small scale, for example, if you are trying to make a favorable impression on your friend's parents (who are Catholic, Republican, and certainly older), it is rather unlikely that a pro-abortion speech from you will yield the desired results if approached with the usual "zero population growth" set of assertions.

Second, knowledge of reference groups allows the speaker to select from among his own role repertoire the one or ones most appropriate for the task at hand. It's a wise corporation attorney, for example, who plays down his lawyer's role in negotiations with the union and emphasizes instead his history as a union member or leader.

Most of us rarely take the time to conduct such a role inventory, but if we did, we would find that the number of roles we can potentially bring to bear on a communication situation is much larger than expected. One of your writers attempted to take such a role inventory and found that, from time to time, he was a: child, sibling, spouse, parent, neighbor, taxpayer, consumer, voter, student, teacher, client, patient, card player, employee, employer, advisor, committee member, writer, photographer, swimmer, bicyclist, tennis player, subscriber, contributor, insuree, driver, pedestrian, and a Minnesotan. A knowledge of such potential reference group identifications allows us to determine the roles which members of an audience share with us and then to capitalize on such commonalities when speaking.

In attempting to locate such relevant reference groups within yourself and your audience, you might keep in mind that you are searching for answers to two types of questions: (1) What will such information tell me about my audience's attitude and knowledge concerning both me and my topic? (2) What will such information tell me about how I might best adapt my message to this particular audience?

Information about an audience's salient reference groups can often be obtained informally, through casual observation and inference. Sometimes the person who invites you to speak can provide much important information about the composition of your audience. Occasionally, the local mass media will give you clues as to likely reference group identification imbedded within your audience's belief structures (e.g., as a check on your own perspicacity in such matters, you might try to identify the relevant reference groups of the various people who write letters to the editor in the campus newspaper).

While knowledge about your audience's reference groups will add immeasurably in your selection of communicative options, you must be wary of stereotyping. Not everyone fits the mold that popular opinion may ascribe to certain groups. (E.g., would a "freak" or a "straight" be more likely to contribute to the United Fund?)

Another caution to keep in mind is that *public* audiences will usually identify with a great number of oftentimes competing reference groups. Thus, your job as public communicator is to focus again on the "largest common denominator" and to appeal to those reference-group based ideas that will get 51 percent of the vote. In *public* communication, you cannot reach all of the people's groups all of the time.

potentials for response in public audiences

Before moving on to our last substantive discussion in this chapter, let's recap a bit. We began with the bald-faced assertion that it is desirable for a speaker to know something about his audience before talking to them. We then looked at three rather arbitrary points in time that seemed to be especially good moments for getting such readings on the motivations and potential responses of a group of listeners. Then came the tough question: what does one read?

We responded by suggesting that it was first necessary for speakers to come to grips with the heterogeneity of public audiences, and with all that this confrontation implies for the communicator. More recently, we suggested that our audience analysis also should be informed as to matters pertaining to the multiplicity of the audiences we address, and to the polarization, size, density, and collective expectations of such assembled listeners. Lastly, we attempted to stress the importance of knowing the kinds of reference groups, or sources of identification, that our listeners have within them.

So far, however, we have only talked in general about the "things" that individual listeners bring to bear when assessing a speaker's remarks. We have talked rather obliquely about such mavericks as beliefs, attitudes, motivations, and needs. In this section, we hope to remedy that situation a bit.

BELIEF SYSTEMS

Have you ever stopped to ask youself *how* you know what someone else believes? Why, anyone knows that you find out what someone believes by . . . by . . . well, you just have to. . . . Actually, there is a very simple response to the question—you guess!

Not a very telling answer, but about all we have to go on in normal, everyday communicative experiences. This is not to say that our bets cannot be precise and sophisticated. While we cannot "really know" what someone else believes, we can make some intelligent guesses. And we do have *data* upon which to make our rather fragile assessments of the insides of someone else's perceptual world. We *can* get an inkling of the shape and magnitude of another's belief system (here defined as a person's sum total of predispositions to act in a particular way). As we are using the term here, *a "belief system" is a hypothetical construct which indicates what we would do (if the opportunity presents itself) about a certain object, person, or idea.* As such, a belief system has a number of components, all of which are depicted in Figure 6.

You will note immediately that we actually "see" about half of what makes up a person's belief system—we guess about the other half. All we have to go on when assessing another's attitudes and values is what he says he believes (opinions) and what he actually does (physical behavior). In order to have tools for exploring this question, let us consider some definitions.

Attitudes are beliefs that are target-specific—that is, oriented to a *specific* object, person, or idea. Thus, "Richard Nixon is truthful," or *"Last Tango in Paris* is a great movie" are both attitudes. *Values* are beliefs that represent general, abstract, idealized conceptions of objectives, people, or ideas. For example, "People should be truthful" or "Man is inherently bad." Another's attitudes and values are not directly observable by us and thus can only be inferred on the basis of others' opinions or physical behaviors.

Opinions are verbalized beliefs (observable by others) which may

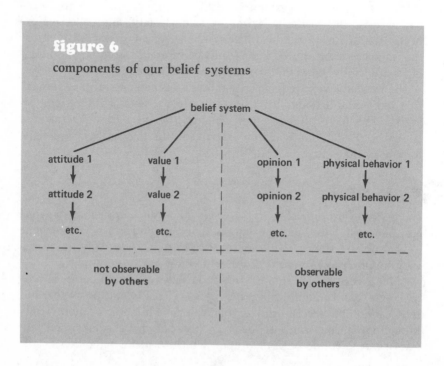

figure 6

components of our belief systems

or may not represent attitudes or values. Thus, I can say "I like Don" (opinion), even if my "real" attitude is quite the opposite. The same holds true for *physical behavior*—actions or artifacts that may or may not represent attitudes or values. I may, for example, drink beer at a party (physical behavior) even though I find beer distasteful or go to church each week even though I no longer believe in organized religion.

When viewed from this perspective, then, *audience analysis is a process of making inferences about the internal states of a group of auditors and then using such information to guide us in our thinking about responses to the communication situation.*

We have rather consciously used the word "system" when discussing the nature of an audience's beliefs, because the word *system* implies that multiple and complex interactions take place between the forces that make up our beliefs. In trying to find out what a person believes, what his "potentials for response" might be, we have a number of directions in which to go. We can, for example, use:

1. **opinion 1** to predict **opinion 2** ("You say you love me. I suppose that next you're going to say you want to marry me.") or **physical behavior 1** ("He said he loves me. Maybe he's going to try to kiss me.")
2. **physical behavior 1** to predict **physical behavior 2** ("Oh, no, the boss didn't smile at me today. Maybe he's going to bawl me out.") or **opinion 1** ("He kissed me! Will he now tell me he loves me?")
3. **opinion 1** to predict **attitude 1** ("He says he voted for Nixon. That means he must like the dope.") which may, in turn, predict **attitude 2** ("If he likes Nixon, he probably also likes Agnew.") or **value 1** ("Anybody who likes Nixon probably believes in superpatriotism.")
4. **physical behavior 1** to predict **attitude 1** ("He's reading the newspaper at the table. He must not love me.") which may, in turn, predict **attitude 2** ("If he doesn't love me, he must want a divorce.") or **value 1** ("Anyone who doesn't love me must be a homosexual.")
5. **opinions or physical behaviors** to predict **value 1** ("Anybody who talks and acts like that must be a Fascist.") which may, in turn, predict **value 2** ("Anyone who believes like that must also be an isolationist.") or **attitude 1** ("One who believes in superpatriotism probably thinks Agnew is great.")

Complex though this "systems" view of beliefs may be, a public communicator who does not seriously reckon with such complexity when analyzing and adapting to an audience might find himself or herself in serious trouble. Thus, the following quasipractical implications of the notion of belief systems might apply to the public speaker:

1. Obtaining a sufficient *amount* of information about your audience is desirable since, by understanding the *overall* structure of a belief system, we are then in a position to speculate about the specific beliefs relevant to our proposition.
2. Observing opinions and physical behaviors which are *relevant* to our communicative purpose is important. Obviously, listeners do and say many things which may shed little light on the *particular* attitudes and values we are primarily interested in assessing.
3. Noting *consistent* modes of behavior and opinion-giving is important since *patterned* responses of this sort tend to give us the most important information about a person's *basic* attitudes and values.
4. By especially assessing those opinions and physical behaviors which are exhibited under *stress* by listeners, we may be able to determine the attitudes and values that are consistently salient to them. After all, it is what we do and say when the "chips are down" that often reveal our gut beliefs and motivations.

In short, then, a speaker need not know everything about a particular group of listeners. By knowing enough of his audience's consistent beliefs, especially those beliefs that are made manifest in important situations relevant to the speaker's communicative purposes, we can at least make intelligent satellite probes into the perceptual worlds of listeners.

MOTIVATING NEEDS

We can cut across the forces which guide and direct an audience's responses from still another direction, by envisioning public audiences as embodying certain specific needs. These needs (some of which have been suggested by Maslow, 1962, and Steele and Redding, 1962, among others) are the basic forces which motivate us to accept or reject the predications of a particular speaker. Such a perspective views man (in part) as a need-fulfiller, one who sees the fulfillment of certain needs as being basic to his survival, other needs as being especially pertinent to his happiness, and still other needs as being irrelevant to both his survival and his happiness at certain points in time.

We all have needs. You might have a need at the moment to skip to another chapter. You might have a need for a coke. You might have a need to throw a beer can at your roommate. While interesting, these are not the needs with which we are most concerned in this section of the chapter. Rather, we will focus here on the needs that groups of people share, for it is only GROUP *needs and aspirations* that are of prime relevance to the public communicator. You can be sure, however, that if chapter-skipping, coke-drinking and can-throwing were shared *consistently* by a *significantly large number* of people, they would be included in Figure 7. But to include them would be to mislead you as a public communicator—one who is looking for safe ways to lay his bets about the majority of his listeners. Take a look at Figure 7 which depicts *some* of the needs relevant to speakers interested in affecting "publics."

As you can see, we have grouped the needs of people-in-general into five levels. Level 1, Basic Physiological Needs, includes those things we require in order to live a life of any sort. We cannot get along very well unless our basic needs for shelter, health, etc., are satisfied in some fashion. Next, we are told that life would not be

figure 7

a hierarchy of needs for public audiences

6. subgroup and individual needs							
5. group-determined needs	feminity virility youthfulness scientism creativity cleanliness cultural activity exploration etc.		escapism convenience mystery social mobility decorum luxury entertainment social dominance etc.			less motivating for all	
4. culture-specific needs	religion intelligence privacy thrift modernism tradition efficiency		employment ownership education patriotism government				
3. cross-cultural needs	relaxation physical attraction physical comfort independence		authority economic stability family leadership heterosexuality social stability				
2. basic social needs	personal identity		social companionship				
1. basic physiological needs	food	sex	health	safety	space	extremely motivating for all	

worth living unless our Level 2 Basic Social Needs are attended to in some fashion. Unless we have some inkling of "who we are" (personal identity) and someone else to explain ourselves to (social companionship), life does not promise to be very satisfying.

The public communicator usually can count on the existence of other needs in his auditors, and, if perceptive, can draw upon such needs when asking for an audience's adherence. Level 3, Cross-Cultural Needs are those requirements which persons of all societies crave to have satisfied. If anthropologists are right, *some sort* of need for physical comfort (above and beyond the satisfaction of our basic physiological needs), independence (not to be confused with democracy), economic stability (not capitalism), family ties, and the like, are common to most people of most cultures.

We are obviously motivated by even more. Level 4 needs, those that are Culture-Specific, must also be satisfied in some fashion. Here we have listed needs especially relevant to modern, westernized society. The American values of privacy, thrift, ownership, education, religion, and a curious combination of modernism and tradition (among others), have become the stock in trade of countless public communicators in our culture. Appeals made to needs at this level are often strongly motivating and hence provide a handy body of resources from which a speaker may draw when asking for the attention and assent of a public audience.

Finally, Level 5, Group-Determined Needs, are also included in our diagram since they probably constitute the body of needs most frequently tapped in public communication situations. Here we find needs that are held strongly by certain sizeable *segments* of our society; we find the forces which motivate us to accept or reject women's liberation, the space program, the middle-class ethic of social dominance, and the prospects of a Majorcan vacation. Here we see the needs that impinge most directly on our day-to-day experiences with public communication. Here we see the beautiful blonde selling Right Guard via a perverse combination of femininity, youthfulness, cleanliness, and even social mobility!

We were not able to include beer-can throwing in our chart, although such a need would probably fall in among the thousands of Subgroup and Individual Needs which motivate *some* of us quite strongly. To include them, however, would be to detract from our emphasis on the needs of which *public* audiences find themselves desirous. So we leave it to you to fill in the blanks in Level 6 with your own preferences for pepperoni pizza, Jack Nicklaus, and *brief* books on public communication.

Undoubtedly, there is much to quibble with in our categorization of specific needs. Some of you, for example, may feel that religion is much more a cross-cultural need than we have given it credit for here. Indeed, you may be right, since needs often "move" from level to level as societies grow and *express* their own aspirations and desires. Hopefully, however, you will not allow your quibbling to offset the essential points we are trying to make here:

1. Public audiences have imbedded within them certain needs which vary significantly in motivating power.
2. Persons agree to engage in public communication in order to assure themselves that these needs can be fulfilled more fully than they are at present or that valued needs will continue to be satisfied at their present levels.
3. Public audiences place demands on a speaker to show how his information or proposal can meet the needs that they feel are of immediate importance to them at the moment of interaction.
4. Public audiences are generally distrustful of speakers who urge the abandonment of *basic* needs in favor of desires that only a few of them share.
5. The speaker's own individual and subgroup needs may not be appropriate for introduction into a *public* communicative environment.
6. These varying sorts of needs can provide for the speaker *sources of insight and argument* upon which to draw when he searches for materials with which to motivate groups of listeners.

As sort of a summary to our discussion of public needs, and in order to convince you that all of this *does make a difference* in communication, Table 3 offers you the following piece of discourse. It is just a rather ordinary public message, one that you would find in almost any popular magazine you might happen to pick up. Still, when viewed from the standpoint of motivation, interesting and important insights abound. As you read this selection, note the remarks we have made in the left column, remarks which indicate how we feel the "speaker" is attempting to analyze and to *direct* the motivating forces residing within her intended audience.

conclusion

We have covered a lot of territory in this chapter, and, yet, still not enough. We have not mentioned, for example, that listeners' *experiences* (actual, vicarious, and projected) also help to determine what responses they will make to a piece of public discourse. We have not discussed the important concept of *latitudes of acceptance and rejection*, a construct which implies that most listeners have within them

table 3

appealing to listeners' needs: an example*

COMMENTARY	SAMPLE MESSAGE
Taps real or vicarious experiences; appeals to personal identity and "familial" needs	Ever go to a company picnic and find you've got competition? I did. I looked at those petite girls my husband works with and I suddenly saw myself: the fat wife. That's when I turned into 160 pounds of fear and jealousy.
Taps real-life experience of audience; builds rationale for exploring unknown product	I had always loved to cook and bake and my Larry could put it away without even gaining. Some husbands are like that. But me? I just blossomed out—on submarine sandwiches, pizzas, cakes and pies. Why, that fellow on television who said, " I ate the whole thing!" had nothing on me.
Reinforces personal identity and heterosexuality needs; introduces appeals to physical attraction and femininity	Sometimes Larry and I would even get up in the middle of the night and go out for ice cream. Next day, though, I'd hate myself. Larry never said anything about my gaining. He didn't want to hurt me, I guess. But I got the message another way. When he saw me in the cow-size clothes I had to buy, he just stopped giving me compliments. That crushed me. But it really took those slender, attractive women at the picnic to convince me that a wife can't sit back and get fat.
Eliminates conflict between need for habit and need for physical attractiveness	I had tried to reduce a number of times with liquid meals, grapefruit diets, reducing pills. But they didn't work for me, especially the liquids. I needed something to chew on.
Reassures audience that need for health will be satisfied; "proves" the scientific validity of the product	Thank goodness I'd read those stories of people who had taken those reducing-plan candies, Ayds. I finally decided to try them so I went to the drugstore and bought the plain chocolate fudge kind. I carefully read the direction folder in the box and learned that Ayds contained vitamins and minerals but no drugs. That made me feel even better about starting the Ayds plan.

*"I didn't want to lose him, so I lost 59 pounds," by Shirley Gallagher (as told to Ruth McCarthy), *Family Circle* August, 1972. Reprinted by courtesy of Ayds.

table 3 continued

COMMENTARY	SAMPLE MESSAGE
Asserts that pattern and stability can be preserved with product; introduces appeal to efficiency	At breakfast, I took a couple of Ayds with tea—you can have any hot drink—about 15 minutes before eating. Cereal or an egg and toast for me. At lunch, I'd take my Ayds and tea again and have soup, sometimes a sandwich or salad. Then at dinner, Ayds and tea again and a small portion of whatever the family was having.
Reinforces efficacy and health arguments	I'll tell you, those Ayds really helped me curb my appetite. They're so good, I'd eat a couple between meals, too. They contain only 26 calories apiece, which was much better than a slice of my own chocolate frosted "Wacky" cake.
Begins to satisfy need for distinctive personal identity; introduces fulfillment of social dominance need	The plan worked beautifully for me. I lost pound after pound. Each time I went down, I'd run out of the bathroom and say: "Come look, I've lost again!" When I hit 101 pounds, everybody in my home town, York, Pa., was looking. That's when the truth really comes out. Like this friend of mine. I used to complain about being fat. But she'd say: "Oh, you're not heavy." Now she introduces me this way: "Would you believe that Shirley was once pudgy?"
Summarizes satisfaction of family, heterosexual, and physical attractiveness needs	Larry of course, is just as proud as he can be. Picks me up these days like I'm one of the kids. I'd never let him attempt it when I was fat.
Encapsulates the fulfillment of social dominance need; final reinforcement of femininity need	The company picnic changed for me this year, too. Thanks to the Ayds plan, I heard someone say: "Wow! Here comes Larry and his 'new' wife."

a *range* of beliefs about any given object, person, or idea. Some of us, for example, are quite willing to vote for Charles Percy for president, yet are not willing to canvas the neighborhood on his behalf. Thus, it is not merely a case of our believing or not believing in someone or something—rather, we believe in degrees.

Another undiscussed but important conditioner of our potentials for response as listeners deals with our attitudes toward *consistency*.

A wide body of literature dealing with what has come to be called *consistency theory* has not been treated here. Yet, for a full appreciation of the nature of public listeners, such perspectives are necessary. What would happen to Oral Roberts' adherents, for example, should he announce that he has decided to sell love beads for a living? Will his former adherents give up religion and join him in the love-bead business? Will they tell the good reverend to get lost? Or will they "make believe" that the whole thing never happened, and instead invent a host of reasons to explain this public mirage? The answers to such questions do not come readily or simply, and hence a detailed discussion of such matters lies outside of the purview of an introductory book of this sort, although they will be treated briefly in Chapter 8.

Still, we have discussed much. We have seen that a public communicator must know and adapt to the *major* potentials for response that lie within his auditors. Hence, audience analysis becomes a primary and indispensable concern to any public talker. To inform such an analysis, we have seen that an appreciation of an audience's heterogeneity is necessary as is a realization of the many potential effects produced by the coming-together of a body of listeners. We have also been concerned with how a knowledge of the attitudes, values, and needs of his auditors can direct a speaker's search for appropriately adapted sayables.

In the following chapter we will be discussing some of the more practical implications of our discussion of audience potentials. When doing so, we will argue that a consideration of audience must always accompany the attempt to create effective messages. Thus, we thought that one way to bridge the gap between Chapters 5 and 6 would be to quote from the maverick actor, George C. Scott, a professional "message-maker" and "audience analyzer." Despite his militaristic theory of communication, Scott directs our focus well when he says:

One of the most important attributes for an actor to cultivate is a sense of analysis of himself and his audience. The audience is a dark thing, a peculiar animal, an enemy that must be assaulted and won. That's the big competition right there—not between you and the other actors but you and the audience. The only measurement of fine acting is so simple, yet so many actors get fouled up about it. It's this: Does the audience feel it? *It doesn't matter a damn what the actor does or does not feel—it's what the lady with the blue hat down there is feeling.* You as an actor can suffer the agonies of the damned, but unless that's communicated to the people who paid $9.90 to see it, you've failed.[8]

[8]"Scott on Some Aspects of Acting," *Time*, March 22, 1971, p. 66. Reprinted by permission from TIME, The Weekly Newsmagazine; Copyright Time Inc.

the message as resource

CHAPTER 6

Knowing something about the other persons in the class is good because I can at least try to gear my speeches toward them, talking about something they will understand. I can also somewhat anticipate their reactions. However, I will never know exactly what they will do or say. No one can. There's always some element of a person that we don't know. That's what makes people so interesting.

. . .

I have found that in the future I will have to be more explicit in order to get people to understand me. This assignment really showed me how differently people think and interpret ideas.

. . .

The speakers who made the biggest impact on me were the ones who shared parts of their own lives. Telling stories of one's own experiences, especially if they are personal like Debby's, gives me the feeling that they trust me. If people trust me enough to think I will not attack their innermost feelings, I will give them my best attention. I really hate to hear some-

one talk about something that they are either bored
with or don't know anything about.

. . .

I was more confident than last time. I was able to look
everybody in the eye. I glanced around the room
continually. I had more confidence in myself and
more confidence in my subject. I also had more
confidence in everyone listening. They all know
what it's like to talk in front of the class and how
they all like everyone else to listen.

. . .

The feedback cards showed that most of the people
knew what my main idea was, but I felt as if they
weren't very interested, or if they were interested,
they didn't show any response.

. . .

When the speech started, I experienced about the
same type of tension a person might experience while
waiting in a doctor's office for a shot. The shot
doesn't hurt as much as the anticipation of what's going
to happen leads you to believe. Surprisingly enough,
I became very relaxed during the speech itself. Being
fairly well-versed in the subject, the tensions were
kept to a minimum.

. . .

I found out that it's easy to sound good to yourself
and for the rest of the class to be totally indifferent.

The remarks you have just read were made by students who
had just completed classroom speaking exercises. We do not
present these observations because they are theoretically trenchant
(though some are), nor because they open new vistas in the study of
communication (though some might), and certainly not because they
are dramatic, earth-shaking, statements about speaking and listening.
Rather, we have included them here because they speak to some of
the essential, very human issues that many of us are concerned with
when conversing with others.

There are, perhaps, no startling insights to be found in these written "debriefings" of speech experiences, but lurking beneath the sur-

face of these casual remarks are a host of intriguing observations on the contingencies of human communication. For example, in these short excerpts we find echoes of both the "highs" and the "lows" of talking. Some of the students reflect a growing confidence in their ability to manage successfully the demands placed upon them by their own ambitions, by their ability to construct intelligent messages, and by their listeners' often irascible modes of responding. We also see the frustration that an apathetic or confused audience can generate in a speaker, as well as the continual struggle that speakers wage when attempting to assess the effect they are having on their hearers. In other words, it is easy to sound good to yourself while the class is totally indifferent.

In this chapter, we hope to probe in some depth the underlying issues about communication that we find so conscientiously raised by these students' comments. We would like to focus on the elemental, or essential, demands that all communicative situations place upon the messages we construct for others. In the following pages, we will address ourselves to the *basic* hurdles that the speaker must overcome, whether he addresses one person or many. As we go about our discussion, it might be interesting for you to return from time to time to the student reactions included above—they have a way of getting to the heart of the matter.

basic demands of message-making

If asked, most of us could probably come up with an intuitive list of communication basics—you must have something to say, some way of saying it, and someone to whom to say it. Needless to say, this triad of necessities leaves something to be (practically) desired. So too does the oft-quoted, but rather vacuous, set of communicative prescriptions we have all heard countless of times—"tell 'em, tell 'em what you said, sit down!" On the assumption that something intelligent can be said about the essential demands that all communication situations place upon our message-making, we hope in this chapter to illuminate the following requirements that attending listeners place upon those who would dare to engage them in discourse:

1. In some fashion, a speaker must demonstrate his commitment to his *message*.
2. Through some means, a speaker must demonstrate his commitment to his *audience*.
3. Somehow, a speaker must attempt to *balance* these "commitments."

4. Ultimately, a speaker must gain some type of *self-clarity* about his own resources as a speaker as well as about his listeners' capacities for response.

We are not suggesting that these four mandates are all we need observe in winning friends and influencing people. But, if pressed, we might be so bold as to assert that friends are rarely won and people are seldom influenced by a speaker who disregards these ABC's of communication. Or to put it another way, these principles of effective speaking constitute necessary, but not sufficient, conditions for profitable interaction with others.

demonstrating commitment to the message

My fellow Americans. It is with great pride and a sense of gentle humility that this speaker stands before this magnificent convention audience with a message of welcome and a clarion warning to this great nation, to our children, and to our children's children, that this political party will henceforth take its place in the sunlit and glorious future that is our party's rightful destiny, a destiny replete with the splendor of governmental accomplishment, with the blessings of our distinguished political ancestors, and with a burning sense of national purpose that will serve this country in good stead in the days that lie beyond.

Even the kindest among us will recognize this passage as unadulterated nonsense! Yet it is just this sort of thing to which many speakers at political conventions have treated us since time immemorial. Such speakers seem to feel duty-bound to eschew their personal feelings, to search for the most abstract of metaphors, in short, *to divorce themselves from their messages.* In the fictitious (but painfully familiar) passage cited above, we see the verbal rantings of a man bent on treating his audience to a kind of speech-by-formula. The speaker makes no reference to himself nor to those he is addressing; he does not detail *his* personal convictions or *his* reasons for speaking. In short, our imaginary speaker seems to be compromising his medium— human speech—for, as we observed in Chapter 2, speech by its nature is a phenomenon attended by me-ness.

Perhaps we should pity rather than censure this convention speaker, who is probably the product of years of the abstract, formulary, impersonal discourse that is the conventioneer's stock-in-trade. Nevertheless, there are those who object to this emasculation of human speech and who insist on *making the medium work for them.*

Consider the case of Lawton Chiles, then a first-term senator from Florida, who was called upon to give one of the welcoming addresses at the 1972 Democratic National Convention. From a national standpoint, Chiles was unknown, and he knew it. Apparently, he perceived his main communicative challenge at the convention to be one of explaining why *he* was talking to the assembled delegates and why *he* was worthy of having their attention. In attempting to satisfy such rhetorical demands, Chiles attempts to *demonstrate his commitment to his message by revealing his personal stake in the interaction.* In so doing, he steers well away from the communicative claptrap that was his "rightful destiny:"

Since I learned I'd been selected to make the welcoming talk on behalf
of the great State of Florida, I've been thinking about how it happened that
I was given this opportunity.

Two years ago I was just half-way through my walk from one end
of Florida to the other. The first statewide poll showed only 5 percent of the
people recognized my name. I had no money in a race that required a
million-dollar stake and I was running against two millionaires. . . .

Before my walk ended, I met thousands and thousands of others who
never had had a chance to see or talk to an office-holder or a candidate
running for office. They had only seen them on TV.

Because I was out there where people could see me and talk to me,
they hoped that I would be different—that I would listen—so they elected
me. That's how I happen to be here to welcome you.

But it's not quite that simple because the people that I listened to
got to me. I found they love this country—that they were way ahead of
their leaders—that they wanted to have a part in solving problems. They
looked at me in the eye and asked me:

Will you come back—will you be different—will you listen?

So because of how I got elected, I carry a burden of how to keep
faith with the people and that burden has only increased since I have been
in the Senate. Because of that burden I do welcome you as delegates to
this Convention—but with the same challenge that the people gave me—

Will you listen? Will you be different?[1]

Now some might argue that Senator Chiles has gone beyond the limits of demonstrating personal involvement in his message here and has, in effect, merely produced an egocentric speech, unfit for the occasion or the audience. This may well be the case but many would judge otherwise.

For instance, Chiles does not continue on in this very personal vein, and later in the speech focuses on national and international matters. In doing so, however, he never strays far away from explaining why these issues are important to *him*. When a speaker (like Chiles) attempts to demonstrate commitment to his message, he really says two things—*I know what I'm talking about and I mean what I*

[1]Lawton Chiles, "Address at the 1972 Democratic National Convention," July, 1972. Reprinted by permission of Lawton Chiles.

say. Chiles' command of the "facts" in the passage cited above as well as his attempt to say "I know because I've been there—I've made an investment" are, in the language of Chapter 4, his attempts to demonstrate competence and trustworthiness, *to show that he stands with his message.*

Any number of everyday examples will serve to point up how interested we as listeners are in assessing a speaker's commitment to his message. We are generally intolerant, for example, of one who pays lip service to an idea, but who fails to indicate what he *has done, is doing, or will do* on behalf of the proposition he advocates. In a similar vein, many TV buffs are especially annoyed by "lip-syncing," the process by which a popular singer on a variety show simply "mouths" the words to her current hit, while her previously recorded voice wails plaintively in the background. Upon seeing such antics, the TV watcher might mutter, "Doesn't she care enough about that song to make a real-life, here-and-now investment in her message?" On still another front, some of us are especially bothered by persons who frantically search for million-dollar words, only to wind up mispronouncing them badly. Ostensibly, we feel that such a person is "making someone else's message" and would be better off to "say it in *his own* words."

In this era of ghost-written speeches, dubbed foreign films, and the televised college lecture, there appears to be a growing cynicism in connection with this concept of commitment-to-message. In some sense, listeners have been inundated by the Ford salesman who drives a Chevrolet; hence listeners seem to hold speakers "guilty" of non-commitment to their messages until they can prove themselves "innocent." A wary speaker, therefore, is often wise to demonstrate initially what he perceives to be his stake in the interaction and what behavior he has engaged in on behalf of his proposal. Perhaps this is why the introduction to Senator Chiles' speech was so heavily laden with demonstrations of his personal commitment to the message he was carrying to the convention.

As we have seen in Chapter 4, a speaker has a number of resources to draw upon when attempting to build credibility. When striving to demonstrate commitment to his message, however, a speaker's options seem to be somewhat limited. We can envision two traditional means by which a speaker can indicate that he knows what he is talking about and means what he says: first, by revealing the self and second, by presenting "the facts."

PERSONAL REVELATION AS MESSAGE COMMITMENT

If the audience and occasion permit it, one of the most dramatic ways of displaying that we have a stake in the message we are presenting is to recount what we have done on behalf of the proposition we are advocating. Listeners seem to treat a speaker's *personal experiences* as one of the best indicators of message commitment. Thus, speakers are wise to demonstrate that their personal experiences are accurate and relevant to the proposition they are advocating.

Naturally, demonstrating the authenticity of our personal experiences can be problematic at times as, say, the fisherman's "one that got away" stories continue to remind us. Likewise, the sociology professor who "goes off on tangents" about his summer vacation will probably not be perceived as providing *relevant* data to support his point on the sociological impact of Marx's theories of collectivism. Personal revelation has its communicative liabilities.

personal revelation and situation

Using personal revelation in an attempt to demonstrate commitment to a message seems most appropriate *when the audience views the speaker favorably*. After all, why should a respected speaker attempt to marshall a mass of facts when he simply can draw upon the very basis of his credibility—his audience's perceptions of his past accomplishments? Thus, the speaker who uses personal revelation should do so knowing that the wisdom of such an approach rests entirely upon the audience's previous evaluation of him as well as their estimates of the verifiability and appropriateness of the speaker's experiences to the topic under discussion.

Let us consider an example. Several years ago, a man by the name of James Snavely gave what might have been the first and only public speech he had ever given. He addressed the Philadelphia chapter of the American Civil Liberties Union in order to thank the membership for their assistance in a series of court battles he had been fighting. He did not come to the meeting armed with statistics or lawyers' briefs. He came only to tell of the rather painful series of events he had experienced over the previous six years. Needless to say, he was facing a friendly audience, one that had no reason to suspect him of dishonesty or irrelevance. Perhaps knowingly, then, he chose a very wise rhetorical course—the simple and direct presentation of his personal experiences:

Approximately 5 1/2 years ago, I sent my oldest child for her first day to school; my child was given, by the teacher, a card for my signature. This card was for my permission to attend religious training in a nearby fire hall under the guidance of Child Evangelism Inc. Needless to say, I made the un-christian move of not signing it. Several days later I received a letter on school stationery, signed by the principal, that explained why I should sign the card. The letter proceeded to tell me how last year 500 and some odd children, out of 500 and some, had attended regularly every Wednesday, and of the work that was being done by this training, that the school fully endorsed and supported this Bible study, and further told me of the large financial contribution made by these children last year to the missionaries overseas. On the second Wednesday of this Bible study, I asked my child how many of the 37 in her class attended. She told me, all but her. I naturally became worried. I asked my child what she and the teacher do while Bible study is in progress. She told me the teacher goes to the fire hall to teach Bible study while she stays alone in her room and plays blocks. The following Wednesday I went to the school and verified this with my own eyes. I was now becoming disturbed. . . . I then contacted the superintendent of the jointure, and after much argument he promised me that the teacher would not leave my child alone again. Several Wednesdays later I checked with my child to see if this situation had been corrected. She told me it had. I asked her what she and teacher do while the other children are at Bible study. She told me, her teacher reads her Bible stories.[2]

Snavely goes on to tell of the social and financial persecutions he and his family suffered at the hands of his community and concludes his speech by urging the group to continue to work for greater human tolerance.

values of personal revelation

Snavely's speech is not an oratorical masterpiece, but it is a good example of the kind of communicative impact that the detailing of personal experiences can bring about. Besides revealing a very intense commitment to his message, Snavely's tale has a number of additional benefits:

1. *removing impersonality.* Many communicative situations, especially public ones, tend to foster "third person speech," in which the speaker refers neither to himself nor to the audience. Mentioning personal experiences helps to break through this wall of estrangement by depicting the speaker as a real-life, definable individual.
2. *flattering to the audience.* Especially for a private man like James Snavely, revealing personal experiences can be quite threatening. But by such personal presentations, a speaker can tell the audience that they are somehow "special" and worth his risking his "privacy." Perhaps this aspect of risk is what accounted for the outpouring of affection that Senator Edward Kennedy received from some after presenting his version of the much-discussed Mary Jo Kopechne incident.
3. *intensifying the message.* Whenever we open our personal lives to another, there is some element of risk involved, even if our pre-

[2]James Snavely, "Address at the Philadelphia Branch, American Civil Liberties Union," December 12, 1964. Reprinted by permission of the American Civil Liberties Union of Pennsylvania.

sentation is not as personally painful as Snavely's or Kennedy's. Thus, when a man digs deep into his own life for supporting material, he is, in effect, telling his audience that *his message* is more important than any discomfort or embarrassment he might suffer.

4. *tapping readily available resources.* From the standpoint of searching for things to say, our life experiences obviously provide us with an efficient source of information-retrieval. *We* are the "experts" on our own lives and hence our experiences present a handy body of materials from which to draw in communication. It is for this reason that speech teachers since time immemorial have urged student speakers to speak on topics with which the students have had *experience*.

FACTUAL PRESENTATION AS MESSAGE COMMITMENT

Despite the many dividends to be derived from using our personal experiences in order to demonstrate commitment to our messages, there are a number of liabilities to this approach. As many cynics have observed, personal experiences are fine, as long as they are *our* experiences! Thus, speakers rarely find themselves in a position where the presentation of their life-events are *alone* sufficient for effective communication. Someone, somewhere, always seems to want the "facts." Often, these "someones" are members of a skeptical or hostile audience. Sometimes, these "someones" are simply people who have little sympathy for a speaker who sees *himself* as the only body of resource material available for communication.

necessities of factual presentation

Empirical research in communication has documented again and again that a presentation of cold, hard evidence is often helpful in speaking situations. James McCroskey (1969) of West Virginia University found one dominant theme in the research literature: when the speaker is unknown or held in questionable regard by an audience, a presentation of factual evidence is mandatory.

Intuition itself would probably force us to this conclusion. For example, who would be naive enough to doubt that it was Ralph Nader's *command of the facts* that allowed him to launch and sustain the consumer movement? As long as lethargic bureaucrats could dismiss Nader's assertions as *his opinions* or as the product of only *his experiences*, they could hardly be expected to take action on his proposals. Perhaps because he appreciates the *universality* connoted by factual evidence, Nader has stocked his "Raiders" almost exclusively with lawyers and scientists—persons capable of gathering and intelligently disseminating the "facts."

In the handbook *Action for a Change*, Nader and Ross are careful to urge even campus consumer groups to speak primarily from something other than a uniquely experiential basis when directing their persuasion at hostile audiences:

Take for example the corporate polluter. Sit-ins and marches will not clean up the rivers and the air that he fouls. He is too powerful and there are too many like him. Yet the student has unique access to the resources that can be effective in confronting the polluter. University and college campuses have the means of detecting the precise nature of the industrial effluent, through chemical or biological research. Through *research* **such as they perform every day in the classroom, students can show the effect of the effluent on an entire watershed, and thus alert the community** *to real and demonstrable* **dangers to public health—a far more powerful way to arouse public support for a clean environment—than a sit-in. (italics added)[3]**

In the less dramatic world of the speech class, there is *nothing inherently valuable* in showing up for your speech with an armful of note cards. Factual knowledgeability is simply *one way* of demonstrating that you have made a *special* commitment to your message— that you mean what you say and know what you are talking about. Still, whereas the Vietnam vet in your class can easily draw upon his past experiences when speaking on the ravages of war, you, who have spent most of your life in school, must search for other ways of signaling to the audience that you have made a full-scale investment in your message of peace. Opinions are fine, but some audiences demand more.

Our remarks in this section are tempered by the inevitable caution —all communicative approaches should be situationally determined. Commitment to the message can be shown in a number of ways— through personal history, through factual presentation, and sometimes even through the simple expedient of taking a firm stand on the issue in question. But all such communicative choices must "pass through the filter" of audience expectation.

demonstrating commitment to the audience

If you are a particularly hardy person, you might want to try a little experiment. The next time you walk through the dorm, take a tape recorder with you. Find four or five of your friends engaged in a rap

[3]From *Action for a Change* by Ralph Nader and Donald Ross with Joseph Highland, pp. 25–26. Copyright © 1971, 1972 by Ralph Nader. Reprinted by permission of the Viking Press, Inc.

session. Enter the room, sit down, and simply turn on the tape recorder. What happens? The first thing you will probably notice is the
silence or "shock" stage, which is quickly followed by the "outrage"
phase—"What the hell are you tape-recording us for?" That's your
cue to leave—quickly!

the demands of adaptation
Now why would a bunch of adults get so up-tight about a tape recorder? After all, they were undoubtedly committed to their messages—they knew what they were talking about and meant what they
said. They were probably generating great thoughts that were just
meant to be recorded for posterity, weren't they? Of course they were
not. Your friends were simply engaging in speech-for-pleasure and
were doing so for each other—not for parents, steadies, teachers, or
other "foreign elements."

By invading the group with your tape recorder, you have introduced a potentially new and unknown audience into the dynamics of
their conversation. As humans, we seem to have a built-in desire to
adapt our messages to *particular* others, not to anyone who happens
by and observes our "captured" words on tape. One need go back no
further into history than to the Watergate affair to verify such a doctrine. Presidents, like all of us, want to know "who out there" will be
listening to their taped remarks.

In communication, commitment to our messages is simply not
enough. We can know all the facts in the case, but if this information
cannot be efficiently adapted to *particular* others, it will have little
social impact. Similarly, your revealed personal experiences and gut
feelings can possess both richness and depth, but if others do not perceive such qualities in your remarks, your feelings and experiences
are of little *social* value.

In an elementary sense, commitment to an audience involves two
things: (1) demonstrating that we are making messages for the *particular* audience we are addressing and (2) demonstrating in some
fashion that our audience's attention and adherence is important to
us. Actually carrying off these gyrations in everyday communication
is difficult, especially when we are attempting to affect *group* attitudes, values, and levels of information. But anyone who has ever
been invited to have "an old fashioned heart-to-heart talk" with their
father, only to be "lectured at," knows how much we like to be ca-
tered to *individually* in communication.

A recent study has documented how important *particularizing our
communication* can be in helping us achieve effective social interaction. An authority on communication patterns in the family, J. G.
Stachowiak (1968) discovered that fathers of well-adjusted children

sent "targeted communications" (i.e., messages aimed at particular persons—"Good job, *Johnny*") to their children while fathers of disturbed children sent more "general" messages. This does not imply that a failure to adapt to particular others will engender mental illness in our listeners; it should infer that all listeners in any context desire to have their *immediate* worlds dealt with in communication.

Perhaps this "demand of adaptation" explains why Richard Nixon visited each and every state in the U.S. during his 1960 presidential election bid. Apparently, he reasoned that by demonstrating a *willingness to engage in interaction with particular others*, he would be making the kind of adaptive responses necessary to show his commitment to his various audiences. By actually setting foot in each state, and targeting his communications for particular segments of society, he hoped to "be with" his audience both physically and psychologically. However, as writer Theodore White notes, this tactic caused him to spread himself too thin in the campaign and may have cost him the election. Despite this, it was a good *communicative* thought.

commitment to public audiences

In public speech settings, the problems of adaptation become paramount. As we have observed in Chapter 1, the public communicator must make essentially "one" message work for great numbers of people—each person with his or her own attitudes, expectations, and interpersonal needs. *In public communication, segments of a given audience must be adapted to individually, but such adaptations occur in the presence of and are observed by other sectors of that same audience.* To resolve such a dilemma, many speakers adopt the "smorgasbord" approach, including a little something for everyone. Such a strategy has its drawbacks, since a speaker using it might be perceived as having no real message of his own.

However, problems of adaptation in public speech settings get solved. Let us consider for a moment the communicative techniques of the Reverend Jesse Jackson, one of the most intense spokesmen of today's black movement and one who many contemporary observers judge as being perhaps the most "situationally sensitive" speaker for the black community.

In July of 1971, Jackson was called upon to speak to a group of Operation Breadbasket workers in Milwaukee. While the audience consisted of many older, long-time civil-rights workers, there were also a good number of youthful activists present; similarly, blacks and whites were almost equally represented, as were men and women. To compound Jackson's problems, his audience was also composed of both well-educated (rather wealthy) citizens, as well as unskilled members of the poverty class. Jackson had to adjust *simultaneously* to all these situational demands, while conveying a forthright message. In many senses, he did remarkably well. Consider, for example, the following passages from his speech.

There was a farmer in South Carolina who had an old wood stove, and he finally got a new range—Tappan—so he moved the old wood stove out in the barn. He put some hay under it, and the dog took up residence under the stove, and the cat took up residence in the oven. So anyhow, the cat had some kittens (by some other cat). But just because they were born in the oven didn't make them biscuits! (laughter and applause) And just 'cause black folks are born in the American oven don't make them American, 'cause Americans can live all over Milwaukee, and black people can't. (applause)

Everytime some newsman asks me about the question of welfare, I always get the impression they're asking me what I think the nation's going to do about black folks? And it immediately becomes my obligation to let them know something about the history of welfare. The first thing is that welfare came into existence for white people. Black folks came out of slavery and were promised 40 acres and a mule, which amounted to an economic base at that time, but that never did come forth. And black folks had to struggle with no state support. Whereas when the depression came in the late twenties and early thirties—when the whites were unemployed—emergency acts were passed as depressionary measures. So welfare came into existence for white people. There are numerically in America more poor whites on welfare tonight than poor blacks. . . .[4]

In reading these passages, did you recognize that they both essentially carry the same message? Yet note how the supporting material and especially the language of the two passages are markedly different. Apparently, Jackson was attempting to meet the communicative demands placed upon him by subsections of his audience.

operationalizing commitment to the audience

If you can stand a bit of cultural shock, let us turn our attention away from the public platform of civil rights to consider some of the options open to the student speaker when he or she attempts to demonstrate some sort of commitment to their listening classmates. Unlike Jackson, most of us do not have the *native* intellectual and linguistic capacities necessary to make on-the-spot adaptations necessary to "particularize" an audience. But modes of public adaptation *can be learned*, and we have probably already learned some of these modes

[4]Jesse Jackson ,"Address at the Milwaukee Chapter of the Southern Christian Leadership Conference," July, 1971.

in our everyday, "private" conversations. A list of methods for demonstrating audience-commitment might include:

1. *acknowledge the interactive potential of the audience.* As far as we know, there is no heavenly ordained reason for listeners not to dialogue with a speaker. Many contemporary speakers are now beginning to realize that *some* verbal participation by an audience can produce highly favorable intra-audience effects for a speaker. Naturally, it is difficult for a speaker to "channel" dialogue in a public speech setting. Still, there are many cases in which a question directly asked of an audience can instill in listeners the feeling *that their worlds are being dealt with at the time of the interaction.* What greater way is there to inculcate a feeling of particularity than to ask a person what he or she thinks?

2. *adjust to the subtle responses of the audience.* It is not always feasible or even wise to encourage actual responses from a group of listeners. After all, there is always the chance that an ambitious listener might "hog the stage" and divert attention from the speaker's proposal. We can, however, notice, and, more importantly, *adapt to,* the subtle (often nonverbal) information with which an audience always supplies the speaker. The *attempt* to adjust for feedback is often judged by an audience as a sign of commitment to them ("You look a bit confused. Let me put it another way . . .").

3. *indicate that the audience can affect you.* In a sense, both (1) and (2) suggest to an audience that their attitudes and behaviors can and will affect the attitudes and behaviors of the speaker. Yet there are more dramatic ways of indicating that *mutual* influence will occur in a public speech situation. For example, when attempting to clear himself of charges of immorality and duplicity in connection with the Mary Jo Kopechne incident, Senator Edward Kennedy openly suggested to the people of Massachusetts that their responses to his speech would decide irrevocably whether or not he would continue to be their senator. The thousands of supportive telegrams he received at the conclusion of his address attest both to the audience's regard of him and to their receptiveness of his persuasive strategy.

4. *openly acknowledge speaker-audience similarities.* This may appear to be a totally commonsensical proposition. Yet, often, communicators only *imply* elements of speaker-audience commonality instead of making them explicit. For a speaker, public speech settings are difficult enough to manage without the added resistance created by his failure to make *obvious* the information and attitudes he and his audience potentially have in common. Even such elemen-

tary communicative devices as analogies and examples drawn from the experiences of the audience can indicate the presence of a speaker who is seeking to individuate his audience.

5. *adjust to situational changes.* Again we happen on a straightforward but oftentimes elusive rhetorical device. Being the ever-changing phenomena they are, spoken interactions involve moment-to-moment alterations in both the psychological and physical forces that surround them—the audience tires, the room gets hotter, the speaker loses his place. All such factors impinge on the consciousness of an audience and create on-the-spot exigences to be dealt with by the speaker. Situational changes *are noticed* by the audience and such happenings are oftentimes psychologically *proximate* to them. It is perhaps for this reason that students often are disgusted with the college lecturer who *reads* his notes from ever-yellowing papers. Such total disregard of audience and situation earmark a speaker who is not the least concerned with committing himself to his listeners and to their immediate existence.

6. *urge the continuity of the speaker-audience relationship.* Perhaps the subtlest of all, this proposition may well be the most important feature in signalling commitment to an audience. In essence, it encourages a speaker to regard his spoken interaction as part of the over-arching relationship he has with his audience. Because they have been bombarded with fly-by-night salesmen, contemporary listeners seem especially worried about being "used" by a speaker for his own *momentary* communicative purposes. Thus, the speaker who rushes through the interaction, fails to connect his proposal to the future well-being of the audience, or neglects to mention his own future intentions, might well signal to an audience that the interaction in which they are presently engaged with the speaker has the lasting power of a cheap brand of underarm deodorant. As Ray Bradbury says in *Fahrenheit 451,* "The difference between the man who just cuts lawns and a real gardener is in the touching. . . . The lawn-cutter might just as well have not been there at all; the gardener will be there a life-time."

balancing message and audience commitment

If you are like some students, you were perhaps a bit disturbed by the general tone of our remarks in the last section. "What's with all this adapting business?" you might ask angrily. "I'm my own man. I say what I feel. I'm not going to 'make strategies' and 'put on a mask.' " While we do applaud the rough-hewn quality of these remarks, we would like to stop for a moment and ponder a question that all of us have asked of ourselves countless times: If forced to make a decision, should I "tell it like it is" and "speak from the gut," or should I "look before I leap" and "size up the situation?"

INSTRUMENTAL COMMUNICATION

While this is an intriguing question, your authors are bothered by the "or" in this query. We do not feel that communicative situations generally force us to choose between adapting and not adapting but rather that there are, in any given situation, innumerable ways of sticking to our basic philosophical principles and still finding a way of making those views palatable to others. We do not believe that communication forces us to sacrifice deeply held beliefs in order to placate others nor do we feel that our only choices in social interaction are between being an egocentric, rugged individualist and a manipulative, weathervane chameleon.

We feel that there is a *range* of options open to us as adaptive communicators and that commitment to our message and commitment to our audience can and must be *balanced* if social interaction is to be profitable for either speaker or listener. In other words, we are advocating an *instrumental* approach to human speech, one which sees audience adaptation, audience analysis, and choosing among communicative options as being central to making effective interpersonal contacts.

As you probably already know, there is another way of approaching spoken interactions. The *expressive* view of communication sees adapting as antagonistic to individuality and views the *speaker's* feelings as the only important judge of what should be said in a given encounter. Let us pursue these two communicative styles a bit further.

components of instrumental communication

In a handbook written for door-to-door peace workers (a group of young people who at the time were striving mightily to end the war in Vietnam) Ralph K. White (1970) compares the expressive and instrumental approaches to persuasion:

To be an effective persuader, it is often useful to make a conscious choice between the "expressive" and the "instrumental" approach. *In the expressive style, the purpose is to vent or express one's own feelings; in the instrumental, it is to achieve or move toward a goal. In the present context, the distinction is between the "expressive" gratification of putting your own strongest feelings into words, getting them off your chest, and the "instrumental" satisfaction of actually communicating, and perhaps influencing them.* **This is instrumental in that it considers communication as a means to an end, the end being effective persuasion.**

There may be a paradox here, particularly for the student involved in peace work. While the life-style most characteristic of the present student generation is highly expressive, a considerable segment of that generation is now undertaking a task of persuasion that is, by its very nature, instrumental. It may be a difficult thing for some of those who do so to face up to the nature of the conflict that it involves.

Probably the chief difficulty lies in the feeling that an instrumental approach means insincerity. Actually, it does not need to mean that at all. A wholly sincere, candid person can set out deliberately to persuade others when something as important as peace is at stake, and can consider rationally what kind of appearance and manner and style of argument will best serve that end, within limits set by his willingness never to say or do anything that he does not consider authentic.[5]

Hart and Burks (1972) have recently attempted to specify further the characteristics of instrumental communication. From their rather detailed analysis, we might extract the following propositions as being perhaps most crucial to instrumental discourse:

1. *adaptation to others is vital in communication.* Because people are so extraordinarily complex and because each of us is unique, communicators simply *must* adjust to the constraints placed upon them by individual listeners. This implies that our actual remarks in communication are often quite different from what we might have said on impulse and from what we might have said to another person in the same situation.

   This does not imply that we must make endless adaptations to others. Some people, after all, have a capacity to push us to the brink of exasperation. However, in instrumental communication, the speaker is charged to consider making adaptations *before* the interaction is broken off. Adapting is difficult, as, say, our kid brother's questions continually remind us, but it is rare to find a prosperous society where the *mutual adaptation* of its members was not present.

2. *some things are best left unsaid in communication.* Who among us has not at one time had the impulse to tell a particularly obnoxious person to get lost? Sometimes we do, of course. But often-times we swallow our invective and avoid future contacts with that person. In other words, we operate instrumentally, reasoning that probably little good could be derived from a hot-and-heavy spoken confrontation at that point in time.

   When deciding what to say, instrumental communication gives

[5]Ralph K. White, "A Postscript for Peace Workers: Some Concrete Advice," in *Vietnam and the Silent Majority: The Dove's Guide*, M. Rosenberg, S. Verba, and P. Converse, eds. (New York: Harper & Row, 1970), pp. 140–141. Reprinted by permission.

us two guidelines: (1) What would I like to say? and (2) What can my listeners handle? Some persons, of course, never go beyond stage one—if they feel it, they say it. As Ralph White notes, *when something as important as peace is at stake,* it is often wise to think twice (Stage 1 *plus* Stage 2) before "telling off" the arch-conservative whose home we are visiting. Assuming, however, that a particular feeling just "has to get out" of us, that we are totally incapable of leaving it unsaid, then proposition three might be considered.

3. *the same idea can be communicated in countless ways.* Just as human beings are complex, so too are their abilities to phrase the same fundamental conception in a variety of ways. Needless to say, some ways of saying things are better than others. For example, it is oftentimes not difficult to determine if we are attracted to the girl in our Psych 212 class. After much cogitation, we decide that something must be said. Then comes the hard part. *How* do you express your attraction without appearing trite, conceited, super-cool, too reserved, etc.? While the tenets of instrumental communication are not going to tell you how to pick up girls, they do suggest that human encounters usually present us with a *range* of communicative choices. Jesse Jackson knows, as you know, that his *fundamental idea* of black solidarity *must be argued for differently* when he speaks to a black caucus of young activists and when he addresses the old-guard of the Democratic party.

We do not present the tenets of instrumental communication as a panacea to all your communicative ills. What we are arguing for here is a way of thinking about communication which suggests that commitment to our messages and commitment to our audiences need not be antagonistic forces in our day-to-day encounters with others.

THE PRACTICAL NECESSITY OF BALANCING OUR "COMMITMENTS"

Admittedly, the preceding remarks have been preachy. Let us now turn our attention to the *practical* reasons for attempting to maintain "balance" between our perceived commitment to the message and our commitment to our listeners.

What would you say is the "ultimate" barrier to effective communication—Too much talk? Not enough talk? No empathy? Too much empathy? We would like to suggest that the problem that may lie at the bottom of most of our difficulties in communication is that set of conditions which results when our message-commitment and audience-commitment are perceived to be "out of sync." In other words, when our listeners perceive that we as speakers are more concerned with appearing firm and knowledgeable than we are with adapting to their values, they turn us off. Likewise, when listeners see us as having no real stake in what we are saying, but only as trying to curry favor with them, they are equally put out by us.

Psychologist Haim Ginott made much the same points in two passages from his book, *Between Parent and Teenager:*

The phrase, "When I was your age" brings instant deafness to teenagers. They defend themselves against our moralistic monologues by not listening. They do not want to hear how good we were, and how bad they are by comparison.

.   .   .

Says Belinda, age sixteen: "My mother tries hard to be a teenager. She dresses in mini-skirts, wears beads, and talks hip. When my friends come visiting, she asks them to "ooze her some skin" (shake hands) and to tell her some "groovy" news. It makes me sick to see her act so foolish. My friends pretend that she is one of us, but they laugh at her behind her back, and they make fun of me.[6]

In the first passage we see a very common problem—that of regarding the *production* of "our" message as being of greater concern than our listeners' favorable *reception* of that message. When a teenager complains that he is being treated paternalistically by a parent, he says, in effect, two things—that his father is engaging in *self-gratification in his son's presence* and that he, the teenage listener, is being treated as an abstraction of members of his class, not as the unique individual he is. To regard our messages as more important than the people to whom they are addressed is to erect a communicative barrier that can prove insurmountable in later interactions with those same listeners.

If we dislike the arrogance and self-righteousness of the speaker who gives little regard to his audience, so too do we distrust the pandering speaker who seems to have no message of his own and is willing to tend whichever way the wind blows. Ginott's second passage is a rather poignant example of a woman who has sacrificed her "messages" in order to reach a very fragile sort of rapport with her "audience." Similarly, the baseball umpire who declares, "Well, it's a strike, but I don't want you to be mad at me so I'll call it a ball," is also allowing his commitments to be "out of phase."

Sacrificing message-commitment is really quite naive when you think about it, for listeners know full well when they enter into a situation of public discourse that they are there to be influenced, that the speaker is desirous of changing their attitudes, values, or levels

[6]Haim Ginott, *Between Parent and Teenager* (New York: Avon Books, 1969), pp. 33, 41. Reprinted by permission of Haim Ginott.

of information in some fashion. For a speaker patently to deny any personal communicative intent is to forsake the very rationale behind communication—that of mediating our and others' world through talk. Thus, we become suspicous of the car salesman who reverently asserts, "I'll probably lose my job for this, but OK, you can have it for your price and I'll sacrifice my commission." In this rough-and-ready world, listeners who enter into a public interaction realize, implicitly at least, that they have thereby entered into a pragmatic situation of *mutual influence and risk,* a situation in which both they and the speaker are attempting to accrue dividends.

The speaker then is constantly in a "double-bind" situation. He must attempt to particularize his listeners, often by demonstrating how their lives will be affected advantageously by his discourse. Equally, he must show that he has made an investment in his message by appearing knowledgeable and forthright in his remarks. Any other set of conditions would present interminable problems, problems which an *instrumental* communicator should not have to face.

Perhaps the best method of ending this section is to quote from *Canvassing for Peace* by Robert Abelson and Philip Zimbardo (1970, pp. 13–14.) In the following passage we find a set of suggestions for demonstrating our "balanced commitments":

Individuate the person, **by using names (with Mr. or Mrs. or titles when there is an age or status discrepancy). One of the many advantages of working from voting lists is that you will be able to match names with addresses. Names will of course often appear on doorbells or mailboxes and in any case exchanging introductions is the best way to begin your contact. Make the person feel you are reacting to his uniqueness and individuality—which you should be—and are not responding in a programmed way to your stereotyped conception of a housewife, blue collar worker, etc. Similarly, help the other person respond personally to you, to break through the categorization and pigeon-holing process which makes you just an anonymous canvasser. At some point, describe something personal or unique about your feelings, background, interests, etc. (which you expect will be acceptable).[7]**

gaining self-clarity in message preparation

If you are of the "expressive" school of communication, this section of the book is not for you. For here we would like to present a kind of autosuggestive format to help you ready yourself for public communicative contacts. The expressivists would see such pedantry

---

[7]Reprinted by permission of the Society for the Psychological Study of Social Issues.

as a waste of time and would instead wish to rush headlong into communication, saying whatever came to mind in whatever way seemed
handy at the moment. As you are well aware by now, your authors
feel differently.

We believe that, when creating public messages, communicators
should *consciously engage in feed-forward.* This is a process by which
humans "program" their responses *prior* to communication by hypo-
thetically "bouncing" messages off their intended listeners, thereby
attempting to assess the probable impact of their verbalizations. All
of this takes time and patience, of course. But, as Hart and Burks
(1972, p. 90) have suggested, "the rising amount of conflict and dis-
order in emotionally-torn families, in racially turbulent cities, and on
philosophically distraught college campuses" suggests that all too
often we fail to think through our message-making prior to engaging
others in communication.

PREPARING FOR COMMUNICATION

There are, of course, many ways to think through a communication
situation beforehand, but we have selected a kind of "question-
checklist" approach. As we see it, the preparation format presented
below can constitute a record of your pre-communicative thoughts.
We are not suggesting that the format be used while speaking. Rather,
our format may be a way of assuring yourself that you have "got the
bases covered" *prior* to speaking.

The primary purpose of such a checklist is to help you *clarify to
yourself* what ends you will be seeking in a given communication experience, as well as what means are available to you to reach these
ends. Unlike outlining procedures (which oftentimes focus on *you*), the
steps of the preparation format are intended to focus you on yourself
in relation to your audience. The preparation format can act as a kind
of "reminder," a reminder of some of the demands placed upon your
communicative behaviors by subject, audience, situation, and even by
yourself.

Perhaps the most basic value of the preparation format is that it
helps you get the "stuff" of your message together *before you engage
in talk,* so that *while talking,* you will be free to adapt to the situational demands that speaking always entails. The rationale here is not
complex. Why not get much of your communicative "homework"
done before speaking, so that when the "heat of interaction" hits, you
will have one thing less to worry about? Thus, instead of being a way
of preparing *a* communication, the format is a means of preparing *for*
communication.

In a sense, the preparation format will pull together many of the topics we have been discussing in this chapter. It will also preview some of the things we will be discussing in Unit III. Hopefully, the format will be helpful to you in preparing for communicative situations similar to those dealt with in the last three chapters of the book. Let us, then, look at our checklist approach to message preparation, as it appears in Table 4.

table 4

the preparation format: a checklist of considerations

QUESTIONS	COMMENTARY
1. Audience ——How much does the audience *know* about my subject? ——How *interested* in the subject are they at present? ——What attitudes of their's might create resistance in them to my proposal? ——Is there any significant common ground now existing between me and them? ——How will I demonstrate my commitment to the audience?	Naturally, many of these questions will not be of crucial concern in some communicative situations. If the audience knows very little about the topic, for example, their attitudes and prejudices may not present significant obstacles to a speaker. Still, the answers to these questions could suggest message options to a speaker that he may have not considered otherwise.
2. Speaker ——What does the audience currently think of me in general? ——Do they see me as having made any special commitment to this subject and proposal? ——To what extent can I rely on my own thoughts and experiences when preparing my message? ——Will I have to "borrow" from other sources in order to establish or reinforce my credibility?	Obviously, self-analysis is very difficult. We never know for sure what others think about us, but we do "make bets" about their perceptions of us each time we engage others in spoken interaction. Thus, the answers to these questions may help you to better lay your bets about your social image and make use of that image in communication.
3. Subject ——What constraints are placed upon me by the nature of the topic being discussed? ——Does the topic itself prescribe any appeals or strategies that might be used effectively?	Some topics seem to have built-in communicative limitations but only detailed inspection of the topic as it relates to the audience will substantiate this. For example, who could

table 4 continued

QUESTIONS	COMMENTARY
——Are there certain aspects of this topic that must be discussed above all else? ——Are there certain aspects of this topic that should be precluded from discussion?	wax eloquently about garbage? Ralph Nader can. In addition, some themes seem to "jump out" of a subject (e.g., Who could discuss leukemia without mentioning its effects on children?), but certain aspects of a topic are sometimes best left unmentioned.
4. Situation ——Are there any existing psychological aspects of the situation which may impinge on the interaction? ——Are there any existing physical aspects of the situation which may affect my communicative strategies? ——Will alterations in the physical or psychological setting be required for me to achieve the effect I desire? ——Will my own nonverbal behavior be a significant force in this inter-action?	This potpourri of factors can have great impact on our inter-actions. Aspects of time, space, and physiology may advance or retard our communicative efforts. Oftentimes, simple alterations in a seating arrange-ment can create a feeling of intimacy. Similarly, visual aids can add much to the clarity and impact of a spoken message.
5. Projected response What specific response would I like the audience to make to me? —————————————— —————————————— —————————————— —————————————— —————————————— —————————————— —————————————— —————————————— ——————————————	Naturally, listeners have a way of frustrating your intentions, but if you have some idea of what you would like them to know or feel as a result of your speech, you are a bit ahead of the game. Knowing what re-sponse you would like the audience to make will give you some basis for gauging your impact on them.
6. Central idea What one central idea would I like them to remember after they have forgotten the details of the message? —————————————— —————————————— —————————————— ——————————————	Nichols and Stevens (1957) have estimated that after a short time listeners retain no more than 25 percent of what they hear from a speaker. Thus, our assumption here is that if information can be "packaged"

table 4 continued

QUESTIONS	COMMENTARY
———————————— ———————————— ———————————— ———————————— ————————————	by means of *one* main thought, the post-speech "residue" in a listener's mind will stand a chance of being a fair representation of the speaker's proposal. Listeners will rarely provide such focus themselves; thus a clearly articulated central idea may assist them in "putting the pieces" of the speech together. Also, a clearly understood central idea will give the speaker a focal point to "fall back on" when the pressures of give-and-take interaction become pronounced.
7. Subpoints ——What subpoints will be necessary to reinforce the central idea and add clarity and force to the message? A. ————————————— B. ————————————— C. ————————————— D. ————————————— E. ————————————— ——What unique communicative function is being served by each of these subpoints?	The obvious thing to remember about subpoints is that they should not "cloud out" the central idea. Some listeners are so enamored by details that the speaker must take pains to insure that the subpoints *refocus listeners on the essential information* he would like them to take away from the communication situation. Speculating about the *functions* of the subpoints will help to *refocus you*, the speaker, on the essentials of communication (e.g., Does the subpoint reinforce your credibility, summarize previous remarks, reorient the listener, add concreteness, demonstrate message or audience commitment, etc?).
8. Supporting material ——What methods of demonstration will be necessary to clarify, vivify, and reinforce the main and subcontentions?	As we will see in Chapter 7, some methods of clarification are better than others for vivifying (e.g., the extended

table 4 continued

QUESTIONS	COMMENTARY
——Do I have any reason to believe that these devices will be effective for this particular audience? ——How, specifically, will I use such supporting material?	example) while still others are effective in adding a substantial tone (e.g., testimony) to a speaker's remarks. One basic tenet that must be remembered in regard to supporting materials is that such materials must not be stressed to the extent that listeners fail to focus on the central idea being argued for.
9. Structure ——Is there any specific plan to the ordering of the message components? ——Have I chosen my opening and closing remarks for the best of communicative reasons? ——Am I ready to reorient and summarize when the necessity arises?	Most research in message structuring reiterates the fact that the sequence of our verbalizations can have dramatic consequences on listeners' adherence. Randomly structured speech elements tend to foster confusion. Since listeners themselves *will* structure message stimuli in some fashion (a fashion not always favorable to the speaker's purposes), it behooves the speaker to assist listeners in structuring materials in ways that will continually refocus them on the residual message the speaker wishes to impart.
10. Language ——Should any connotative or denotative problems arise in regard to the types of terms I plan to use? ——Are there any terms I plan to use that need to be defined in order to prevent confusion from arising? ——Are there any verbal images available for use that will add depth or clarity to my remarks?	Since listeners often respond signally to language (e.g., the word "term paper" often provokes instantaneous, negative reactions in students) the speaker is advised to think ahead of time which terms might be troublesome to listeners. Similarly, a clear, concise piece of verbal imagery can often provide linguistic economy and obviate the necessity of having to go into great detail on peripheral issues.

table 4 continued

QUESTIONS	COMMENTARY
11. Attention ——What specific factors of attention are necessary to employ in order to channel listeners' perceptions? ——How, specifically, will I make use of these attention factors? ——Do I have any reason to believe that these factors will serve to *focus* attention on the central idea or subpoints? ——Will I have any trouble in *sustaining* attention for the duration of the interaction?	Attention is easy to get, but often difficult to maintain. Also, a listener's attention has a tendency to "scatter" and thus the speaker must constantly be on guard that his factors of attention (e.g., humor) are serving to "constrict" the attentive powers of listeners so that they are forced back, again and again, to give the speaker and his proposal due consideration.
12. Motivation ——How will I demonstrate an awareness of and tolerance for the listeners' value systems? ——What needs and desires of the audience's can be tapped in order to win their adherence to my proposal? ——How, specifically, will I attempt to motivate them to move to the position I am advocating? ——How will I overcome possible apathy or hostility to me or my proposal? ——How will I demonstrate that my message is worth listening to?	Listeners often do not possess an inherent motivation to listen. Before a listener is about to open his mind to a new body of information or attitudes, he must be satisfied that his life can be materially improved by the speaker's assertions. Above all, a speaker must *demonstrate* to listeners that the "gift" of their attention and adherence will be rewarded with important and interesting discourse and, ideally, with substantive gain.

conclusion

Our preparation format is detailed, yet the detail of the format is but a drop in the bucket when compared to the inordinately detailed complexities that result when speaker and audience come together in communication. We can, of course, just "wing it" in communication, desperately hoping that somehow, someway, the right words and strategies will pop into our heads at the moment a communicative impulse strikes us. But the basic message of our preparation format is simple: Why risk blowing the whole deal when a few minutes of

thought prior to communication can suggest, test, and resuggest strategies that may not have occurred to you when "just thinking"?

Your authors see the preparation format as a heuristic device, a
method you can use to teach or remind yourself that there are many
rhetorical avenues open to you when preparing your message. Many
of the questions in the format will become more crucial than others at
times and some of the issues might seem more relevant to your own
communicative needs than might others.

Thus, the preparation format has a number of purposes, and can
be used efficiently in many ways. But its ultimate purpose, at least
from our point of view, is to provide you with some sort of systematic
method of *clarifying to yourself* exactly what communicative hurdles
you will have to overcome in a given situation. It may also tell you
in what areas your own peculiar communicative assets may uniquely
lie. Hopefully, after your speech course is over and you have forgotten the details of the preparation format, you will be left with the
thought that to think out carefully our thoughts prior to utterance is
to pay the first premium on an insurance policy for meaningful human interaction. To us, that seems to be a Piece of the Rock worth
having.

UNIT III

problems of communication in public settings

UNIT III

My fellow citizens, it is an honor and a pleasure to be here today. My opponent has openly admitted he feels an affinity toward your city, but I happen to like this area. It might be a salubrious place to him, but to me it is one of the nation's most delightful garden spots.

When I embarked upon this political campaign I hoped that it could be conducted on a high level and that my opponent would be willing to stick to the issues. Unfortunately, he has decided to be tractable instead—to indulge in unequivocal language, to eschew the use of outright lies in his speeches, and even to make repeated veracious statements about me.

At first I tried to ignore these scrupulous, unvarnished fidelities. Now I will do so no longer. If my opponent wants a fight, he's going to get one! . . .

My opponent's second cousin is a Mormon. His uncle was a flagrant heterosexual.

His sister, who has always been obsessed by sects, once worked as a proselyte outside a church.

His father was secretly chagrined at least a dozen times by matters of a pecuniary nature.

His youngest brother wrote an essay extolling the virtues of being a Homo sapiens.

His great-aunt expired from a degenerative disease.

His nephew subscribed to a phonographic magazine.

His wife was a thespian before their marriage and even performed the act in front of paying customers.

And his own mother had to resign from a woman's organization in her later years because she was an admitted sexagenarian.

Now what shall we say of the man himself?

I can tell you in solemn truth that he is the very antithesis of political radicalism, economic irresponsibility, and personal depravity. His own record proves that he has frequently discountenanced treasonable, un-American philosophies and has perpetrated many overt acts as well.

He perambulated his infant son on the street.

He practiced nepotism with his uncle and first cousin.

He attempted to interest a 13-year-old girl in philately.

He participated in a seance at a private residence where, among other odd goings-on, there was incense.

He has declared himself in favor of more homogeneity on college campuses.

He has advocated social intercourse in mixed company— and has taken part in such gatherings himself.

He has been deliberately averse to crime in our streets.

He has urged our Protestant and Jewish citizens to develop more catholic tastes.

Last summer he committed a piscatorial act on a boat that was flying the American flag.

Finally, at a time when we must be on our guard against all foreign isms, he has coolly announced his belief in altruism—and his fervent hope that some day this entire nation will be altruistic!

I beg you, my friends, to oppose this man whose life and work and ideas are so openly, avowedly compatible with our American way of life. A vote for him would be a vote for the perpetuation of everything we hold dear.

The facts are clear; the record speaks for itself.

Do your duty.*

What kind of a speech is this? Persuasive? Entertaining? Informative? Do not turn to the back of the book for the answers—there are none. In fact, the questions themselves are probably misguided. It's simply a speech. Maybe a political campaign speech, maybe a public character assassination, maybe a put-on. If you had not read it before, it probably made you chuckle. If you had, it might have bored you. Perhaps it "did" nothing to you at all. What

*Bill Garvin, "*Mad's* Guaranteed Effective All-occasion Non-slanderous Political Smear Speech," *Mad*, December, 1970. Reprinted by permission. © 1970 by E. C. Publications, Inc.

we call this speech will depend upon the perspective we assume when looking at it. Each speech is a coat of many colors.

approaches to speech types

Now, for many experts in the field of speech communication, our preceding remark will sound a bit heretical. After all, "types of speeches" have been the ready recipients of much discussion as we look back at the 2000 years (or more) during which human communication has been studied seriously. Aristotle, knowing that in his time speeches were most often given in legislative, legal, and ceremonial settings, argued that the "types of speeches" were three—deliberative, forensic, and epideictic. Years later, various persons commonsensically reasoned that "types of speeches" could be delineated by considering the subjects being discussed. Thus, we were told that there were religious speeches, political speeches, speeches dealing with money matters, and so forth. How such scholars would have characterized a speech by Billy Graham remains a mystery to these authors.

In this century, scholars have suggested that speeches can be "typed" by considering the purpose the communicator had in mind when talking. Thus, if a speaker wanted to inform, he gave an informative speech. The speaker who wanted to persuade gave a persuasive speech. Nothing complex about that, except that the two types could not coexist in one speech. Thus, the poor student who got up to give his "informative" speech in class and wound up "persuading" his peers that life existed on other planets, was chastised, given a D, and exiled forever to the place where things go bump in the night.

Obviously, each speech acts upon hearers in a unique way. Also obvious is the fact that speeches "say" different things, are constructed in different ways, and created in numerous and complex motivational atmospheres. But exactly how they vary from one another is not known at present. Your authors do not propose to develop a "new" system for classifying speeches here. Instead, we will tacitly assume that the "same" speech given by a Bible-belt preacher can *simultaneously* inform some of his listeners that God is in the sky, make others aware that the preacher speaks in a strange dialect, and induce some auditors to believe that repentance is the road to salvation. Still others in the audience may be persuaded to give up their earthly possessions and follow the Word immediately, while those languishing against the back wall of the church may be simply "entertained" by the religious goings-on. To "type" a speech that produces such diverse effects is, to our way of thinking, an exercise in futility.

approaches to communication problems

Unit III will approach communicative types in a way different from those which appeared in previous writings on public communication. We will not attempt to tell you that there are certain heavenly ordained types of speeches, but rather that there are various sorts of *communicative problems* that the public communicator frequently faces. From among the many "archetypal" communicative problems conceivable, we have selected three to treat in detail here. You should not be misled into thinking that these three problems are mutually exclusive, or that the strategies presented for dealing with one sort of problem would not work equally well in other types of communicative situations. We do want you to be aware, however, that no matter what purpose *you* have in mind for your speech, and no matter *where* you choose to deliver your oration, that it is (1) the type of problem that you perceive as existing, (2) the type of response that you make to that problem, and (3) the type of "potentials" that listeners have within them that will determine your eventual communicative success.

Hearkening back just briefly to our discussions of Chapter 3, you will remember that we suggested that the "exigence" or problem we perceive as speakers is an important conditioner of our success in making sense to one another. In Figure 8, we have listed three common types of *communicative* exigences and have contrasted them with *noncommunicative* situations—situations that cannot or need not be dealt with by discourse. In addition, we have added in the "gray areas" that must be part and parcel of anything as complex and unfathomable as human behavior.

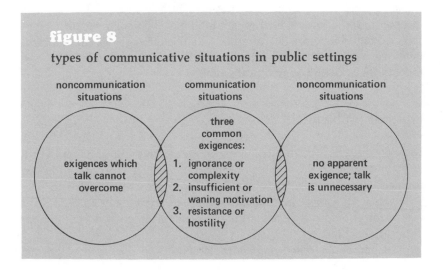

figure 8

types of communicative situations in public settings

You will note that we have depicted two sorts of noncommunication situations. By this we mean that in one case, no matter how much or how effectively we talk, the problem is not likely to be overcome by our words alone. Such a set of conditions might result when, say, your instructor asked you to count all of the occurrences of the letter "e" to be found in this book. Unless you are a masochist (or are failing the course), it is unlikely that you would engage in such behavior *no matter what* appeals, promises, or threats your instructor employed. Hence, when the requested change lies outside of the listeners' boundaries of knowledge, experience, or feeling, it is likely that one sort of noncommunication situation is rearing its ugly head.

On the other hand, there are probably many situations in which talk simply is not necessary, so strong are the informational or attitudinal bonds connecting speakers and listeners. We do not need to be reminded, for example, that our neighbor's rusty Boy Scout knife is probably not the most appropriate implement for use in open-heart surgery. And it is also unlikely that the Pope needs to be persuaded to go to church on Sundays.

The "gray areas" present special problems, however. Is it possible to get George Wallace to join the NAACP? Is it conceivable that a hard-nosed drug pusher can be influenced (with words) to give up his trade and to teach Sunday school instead? Is it necessary to remind a harried Dean of Women that some coeds have *not* contemplated suicide? Does a busy father need to be encouraged to express his love for his children on occasion? In addressing ourselves to such questions, two vexing factors should be kept in mind: (1) If we decide that talk is unnecessary in a given situation, we might inadvertently begin a process of attitudinal or informational erosion in our presumably accepting listeners. (2) If, on the other hand, we decide ahead of time that it is impossible for talk to alter a particular set of circumstances, and hence do not attempt to effect change via communication, we might very well end up fulfilling our own prophecy and making the situation a good deal worse.

types of problem situations

Despite all of these complexities, communicative life goes on. Thus, we have chosen in this book to concentrate on three common types of problem-situations. In Chapters 7, 8, and 9 we will attempt to provide you with some communicative tools to enable you to fight your way through these three sometimes-similar, oftentimes-different communicative situations.

In Chapter 7 we will discuss the resources available to you when attempting to communicate with persons who know very little about you or your ideas. There are "special" armaments available to a speaker whose job it is to reduce the complexity of a certain body of ideas for an interested but confused audience. Any of us who have attempted to explain to a five-year-old what a "President of the United States" is (and is not), knows that such situations require of us adaptations and communicative strategies not built-in at birth. "Sesame Street," a modern-day communicative phenomenon, is a brilliant example of rhetorical resources being used, day in and day out, to meet the forces of confusion and complexity that inhabit the crania of the sandbox set.

A more desirable situation would exist when "knowledgeable friends" come together to discuss matters of mutual concern. Consider, for example, the annual convention of NOW (National Organization for Women). When addressing such an assemblage, the national chairperson probably need not worry about facing angry dissent or collective ignorance of the vicissitudes affecting the contemporary woman in America. The problem or exigence she faces is created by the potential sagging of motivation for the cause of women's rights that the intervening year may have brought about in her listeners. As we will see in Chapter 8, the chairperson's job is one of giving the movement a perennial shot in the attitudinal arm so that an appropriate amount of concern and drive will sustain organizational members in the forthcoming year.

Finally, in Chapter 9, we will discuss what is perhaps the most difficult challenge of all—that of overcoming resistance to the ideas, opinions, and sometimes the personhood, of the speaker. We will discuss some of the principles of the arcane science (or social art) of persuasion, so as to help you generate and use appropriate communicative resources in situations in which you will be surrounded by collective distrust or suspicion.

These three chapters, it is hoped, will provide you with a perspective for addressing yourself to some of the most common obstacles tackled by public communicators. Unfortunately, we will not be able to provide you with ten easy methods for achieving communicative glory. We would do so, of course, if such were possible. We simply do not know enough about communication and its permutations to do so at this point, however. Yet, we do feel that if one understands the genesis and *raison d'être* of such communication problems, that one can at least approach such situations intelligently. Success in communication comes not from reading a textbook, but from dealing with real communication situations on your own terms. You must present the terms. We will discuss the situations.

reducing the complexity of information

CHAPTER 7

Ms. Dole: Now, I don't want anything too fancy or
           complicated. Just a safe little car to get me
           around town. I'm retired, you know.

Slick Sam: Got just the thing for you, little lady.
            Just feast your eyes on this little gem.
            Why I had a family with four kids in here
            yesterday who bought one just like it.

Ms. Dole: Yes, it is nice. But I think it's a bit too
           big for me.

Slick Sam: Too big? Why you need a car this size,
            what with our super-highways and 70-
            mile-an-hour speed limits and . . .

Ms. Dole: Yes, I'm sure it's very nice, but I just need
           something to get me to my bridge club
           and church and . . .

Slick Sam: Then this is just the little baby for you.
            Hop in, and you'll be the first one to arrive
            at your meetings—even if you left late!
            This model won the Daytona 500!

Ms. Dole: Yes . . . but I just want something simple.

Slick Sam: Simple? Why what could be more simple
            than this little honey? It's got a nice little

	synchromesh transmission, dual intake valves, a power-glide six and . . .
Ms. Dole:	Huh?
Slick Sam:	Well, never mind, just remember that a 318 goes from 0 to 60 in under 10, unless, of course, you've got an 8, which cuts down on your RPM's. Which, of course, helped it win the Daytona 500.
Ms. Dole:	Yes . . . Well, uh, I, uh, was hoping for something that would give me good mileage. I'm on a pension, you know, and it's difficult to make ends meet these days, what with inflation and . . .
Slick Sam:	Inflation? Why this little honey is a hall-mark of frugality, a beacon of hope to the struggling millions, a veritable boon to this great nation of ours, from the mountains to the valleys to the oceans white with . . . oh, and it *did* win the Daytona 500!
Ms. Dole:	Does all this mean I can afford it?
Slick Sam:	Afford it? Why we'll fix you up with our GMAC plan with basic 27 1/2 percent finance charge compounded semiquarterly with a downpayment equal to no less than one-half but no more than three-quarters of the unpaid balance after the standard 10 percent is deducted for our cost accounting procedures, which will leave you just enough to go to next year's Daytona 500.
Ms. Dole:	Mr. Sam, I haven't understood a word you've said and I'm leaving.
Slick Sam:	Where are you going?
Ms. Dole:	To the Daytona 500.

While our dialogue might be a trifle exaggerated, most of us have heard conversations roughly similar to this one (or even participated in a few ourselves). While Ms. Dole and Slick Sam are communicatively interdependent—that is "in the presence of each other"—the interaction would not have gone as badly had Slick Sam been more interested in communicating than in "just talking." Ms. Dole does what most of us would do, given the opportunity—she leaves.

communication and information

While our vignette illustrates a variety of points concerning communication, we included it here to highlight the importance of comprehension in any attempt to communicate effectively. In fact, in many important situations (presenting financial reports, giving lectures, teaching someone to golf, etc.), achieving comprehension is our most important product. Colin Cherry (1966) has gone so far as to suggest that today the accumulation, storage, and retrieval of information may be looked upon as a new kind of capitalism. Thus, in this chapter, reducing complexity through communication will be looked upon as the coin of the realm.

One need not look far to discover the importance of reducing complexity. As the world grows increasingly convoluted, there seems to be an ever-increasing need to know more and more, and to be able to do more and more. The amount of information generated to meet these needs is staggering. As Louis Martin (1970) points out, "If an average reader tried to catch up with one year's output of learned publications in the sciences, it would take him about 50 years of reading at 24 hours a day for seven days a week."

An illustration of the ever-increasing possibilities of the "explosion" of knowledge (and hence of complexity) is contained in Neil Postman and Charles Weingartner's (1969) temporal metaphor:

Imagine a clock face with 60 minutes on it. Let the clock stand for the time men have had access to writing systems. Our clock would thus represent something like 3000 years, and each minute on our clock 50 years. On this scale, there were no significant media changes until about nine minutes ago. At that time, the printing press came into use in Western culture. About three minutes ago, the telegraph, photograph, and locomotive arrived. Two minutes ago: the telephone, rotary press, motion pictures, automobile, airplane, and radio. One minute ago, the talking picture. Television has appeared in the last ten seconds, the computer in the last five, and communications satellites in the last second. The laser beam— perhaps the most potent medium of communication of all—appeared only a fraction of a second ago.

It would be possible to place almost any area of life on our clock face and get roughly the same measurements. For example, in medicine, you would have almost no significant changes until about one minute ago. In fact, until one minute ago, as Jerome Frank has said, almost the whole history of medicine is the history of the placebo effect. About a minute ago, antibiotics arrived. About ten seconds ago, open-heart surgery. In fact, within the past ten seconds there probably have been more changes in medicine than is represented by all the rest of the time on our clock. This is what some people call the "knowledge explosion." It is happening in every field of knowledge susceptible to scientific inquiry.[1]

As a result of the "information explosion," the communication of new and complex information is an important feature of a modern technological society. Since "to do more" requires that we "know more," and since *we cannot hope to acquire all of the information we seem to need through firsthand experience,* today more than ever we must rely on other, human sources to educate us.

In this chapter, we will examine a number of situations which require the communicating of new or complex information, explore barriers to such communication, and suggest a number of principles for increasing the audience's comprehension of a speaker's message. When doing so, we are hopeful that we will decrease, rather than add to, the complexity of the ideas we present.

It should not be surprising to you to learn that there are a number of methods available for communicating information efficiently. Even a person unversed in the area would realize that old Slick Sam missed a basketful of communicative bets. He presented factual information so quickly as to becloud the point he was attempting to make. He continually opted for terms and referred to ideas that fell outside of Ms. Dole's linguistic experience. He switched from the concrete to the abstract with little or no warning.

What he *failed* to do is equally revealing. Sam did not choose to sequence his remarks in a way that would make *patterned* sense to his listener. He chose not to imbed "comprehension checks" into his spiel, nor did he assure himself that the repetitions he included *ad nauseam* ("Remember the Daytona 500!") were sufficiently varied in content so as to reinforce, rather than detract from, his main point. We would probably have to search far and wide for a worse example of information sharing.

INFORMATION DEFINED

To this point, we have been somewhat ambiguous in our use of the term information. We will define information as *knowledge that an audience accepts as true or plausible.* So defined, information (in the

---

[1] Excerpted from *Teaching as a Subversive Activity* by Neil Postman & Charles Weingartner, p. 10. Copyright © 1969 by Neil Postman and Charles Weingartner. Reprinted by permission of Delacorte Press.

context of communication) may take the form of conclusions concerning characteristics of and relations among phenomena. Such phenomena can be classified into two categories—*observables* and *constructs*. Observable phenomena are those which, if someone were to ask "How did you know it was such-and-such?", we might well reply, "I saw it," or "I could tell just by looking at it." Constructs are not directly observable by the senses but are, in fact, derived from observables. While we do not, for example, *observe* "government in action," the behaviors of the President, of members of Congress, or of the Justices of the Supreme Court provide a basis for inferring that the government is "doing something." Somehow, we reason, what the officials do *is* the "government in action."

An exact specification of the procedure by which the abstraction "government in action" comes to be defined by the concrete actions of these various individuals is not possible, given our present understanding of such matters. Suffice it to say that, in a rough-and-ready sense, "coming to know" *involves generating constructs from observables and, in turn, using constructs to interpret still other observables.* Following such a lead, then, communication can be seen as a procedure by which the speaker helps the listener "come to know" what he, the speaker, has come to know.

Communication can also be seen as a process by which we as speakers help listeners to generate in their own minds—and on their own terms—that which *we* have observed and that which we would have *them* observe. In addition, communication is used to encourage an audience to "gather together their observables" so as to form constructs that will roughly approximate those that the speaker himself had in mind. (For example, a baseball player who hits an uncaught ball, and then circumnavigates the bases in counter-clockwise fashion without being tagged with the ball, has achieved what we can call an "inside-the-park home run.") From this vantage point, we can speculate that the difficulty of sharing information is increased when: (1) listeners deal with a fund of "observables" which differ from those perceived by the speaker; (2) listeners and speakers "share" observables but generate differing "constructs" from such data; (3) listeners and speakers "share" observables and constructs but are variously motivated by them (e.g., "OK, so he made an inside-the-park home run, Daddy. Can I have a hot dog?").

It is in the context of communication acting as a *mediator* of information that this chapter has been written. More specifically, we will try to suggest some viable methods by which the complexity of information can be reduced to a level which can be shared by speaker and audience. *When reducing the complexity of information, the speaker is, in a sense, making constructs "observable" and "observables" comprehensible.*

barriers to communicating information

Former Secretary of Commerce Luther H. Hodges used to tell the story of a plumber who discovered that hydrochloric acid opened clogged drains quickly and effectively. Not quite sure of what to make of his discovery, the plumber wrote a letter to the Bureau of Standards in Washington, D.C., describing his findings and asking whether hydrochloric acid was a good thing to use.

A short time later, he received a reply from a Bureau scientist: "The efficacy of hydrochloric acid is indisputable, but the corrosive residue is incompatible with metallic permanence."

The plumber promptly replied—thanking the Bureau scientist for letting him know that it was all right to use hydrochloric acid.

The scientist got worried and showed the letter to his boss. The boss wrote a second letter to the plumber saying: "We cannot assume responsibility for the production of toxic and noxious residue with hydrochloric acid and suggest that you use an alternative procedure."

By this time the plumber figured that somebody in Washington really liked him, so he wrote back again thanking them and reassured them that the acid was still working just dandy.

This last letter was passed on to the boss's boss, who broke off the correspondence with a terse note: "Don't use hydrochloric acid. It eats hell out of the pipes."

As this story illustrates, the communication of information is a dilemma-ridden enterprise: the communicator has a "body of material" to communicate—ideas that are involving to him and that motivate him—*but* he must present such material to listeners with varying amounts of sophistication, experience, and aptitude. Many public communicators, of course, choose not to worry about such exigences, and simply adopt a "take it or leave it" attitude in the preparation and presentation of their messages. While such a mind-set may be comforting to the speaker involved, it is hardly the best approach for presenting information to *pattern-seeking* listeners.

This portion of the chapter will present a number of information-based problems that confront the communicator as he prepares and delivers a public message. We include these dilemmas on the assumption that to be *aware* of a problem is, in a sense, to be in a position to solve that problem. The following problems and remedies are all well documented by a large body of research in speech communication, education, and psychology. Thus, it stands to (our) reason that the speaker should be aware of these communicative barriers, all of which deal with the audience's loss of information—the bugaboo of much public communication. Hopefully, the solutions we suggest to these problems will allow you to hurdle such barriers and cross the communicative finish line well ahead of the pack.

generating information

Perhaps the first and most basic issue that each public communicator must come to grips with is a kind of a two-edged sword: (1) How do I come up with a sufficient number of communicable ideas and (2) how may I assure myself that I won't come up with too much? While too many ideas will lead to "information overload" (and, hence, audience frustration), too little information may portend "information underload" (hence, listener boredom). Parents, for example, are often accused of pouring too much information into the system. Instead of simply stating the rule—"You must be in by midnight"—they embellish their remarks with so much information that you simply stop listening. Often, the rule may be so enmeshed in the "lecture" that it is not heard at all—"Let's see—the movie is over by 10:00. I don't want you out on the streets after midnight. The tires are not in good condition. You have to get up early tomorrow. . . ."

GENERATING ENOUGH INFORMATION

Obviously, before there can be "too much" information available for communication, there has to be "some." Yet, where do these speakable thoughts come from? How can a speaker assure himself that he has pulled together a sufficient amount of information for public presentation? Now, if he "just thought about his topic" for awhile, he might come up with an appropriate number of ideas. But we would like to encourage the use of another method for generating communicable ideas, a procedure that operates somewhat systematically.

Opposed to the "Method of Just Thinking" is what has been called a Topical System for Generating Thoughts. Now while this system is no press-a-button-get-a-thought twentieth century monster, it is, according to its chief promulgators (Wilson and Arnold, 1968), a system for recalling information that a speaker may not have thought of otherwise. Their approach is an elaboration of Roget's system for categorizing human knowledge: by thinking of his particular subject matter in terms of universal topics, a speaker can "retrieve" information he has previously "stored" within him. Thus, the topical system works in an autosuggestive manner—the aspiring speaker becomes his own *conscious* computer. Research has documented that more and better ideas can be generated with its use than without it. For example, an interesting study by William Nelson (1970) indicated that students using such a system generated, on the average, 17 percent more ideas than did other students who "just thought" (or in academic parlance, who used free recall).

Though initially appearing scary, the system is not all that complicated and it just might help you to answer that nagging question: "Well how the heck am I going to come up with something to say in speech class on Tuesday?" The "topical system" includes the following themes which can be developed in any speech:

1. *Existence or nonexistence* of things
2. *Degree* or quantity of things, forces, etc.
3. *Spatial* attributes, including adjacency, distribution, place
4. Attributes of *time*
5. *Motion* or activity
6. *Form*, either physical or abstract
7. *Substance:* physical, abstract, or psychophysical
8. *Capacity to change*, including predictability
9. *Potency:* power or energy, including capacity to further or hinder anything
10. *Desirability* in terms of rewards or punishments
11. *Feasibility:* workability or practicability
12. *Causality:* the relation of causes to effects, effects to causes, effects to effects, adequacy of causes, etc.
13. *Correlation:* coexistence or coordination of things, forces, etc.
14. *Genus-species relationships*
15. *Similarity or dissimilarity*
16. *Possibility or impossibility*[2]

To illustrate the use of the system, consider the speech pathology major who decides to present an address on hearing disorders. She is aware of the facts, understands the theories, is familiar with the research, but really is not sure of what to say and what not to say in a speech on the subject. By using the categories in the topical system, our speaker may be "reminded" of the essential features of hearing disorders and can then develop these features by making recourse to more specific research material. Let us consider each of the "generators," and see how they might work to remind our speaker of the salient features of hearing disorders:

1. *existence:* over 50 percent of the elderly have hearing disorders, workers in a noisy environment are especially prone to hearing problems
2. *degree:* mild ringing in ears, total deafness, death
3. *space:* intimate connection between brain and ear, ear covers only small area
4. *time:* can lose hearing overnight, many middle-ear infections occur between four and seven years of age

2John F. Wilson and Carroll A. Arnold, *Public Speaking as a Liberal Art*, 2nd ed. (Boston: Allyn & Bacon, 1968), p. 115. Reprinted by permission of Allyn & Bacon, Inc.

5. *motion:* fast movement can cause dizziness because of inner-ear problems, rapidly moving sound waves can cause temporary loss
6. *form:* some hearing losses are surgically correctable, some can be helped by hearing aids
7. *substance:* roots of hearing loss can be physical, psychological, psychophysical
8. *capacity to change:* inner ear can improve itself, surgery can correct middle-ear damage
9. *potency:* can cause death, inability to discriminate any sort of speech
10. *desirability:* hinders social interactions, can adversely affect employment opportunities
11. *feasibility:* auditory training for those with residual hearing problems, lip reading training
12. *causality:* abnormal growths in ear cause problems, high fever and infection can also cause damage
13. *correlation:* related to disease, psychological problems
14. *genus-species:* types of hearing losses are middle-ear infection, vertigo, partial deafness.
15. *similarity:* distinction between middle-ear and inner-ear problems, middle- versus outer-ear maladies.
16. *possibility:* inner ear cannot be corrected by surgery, hearing aid can help those with inner ear damage

There is every reason to suspect that our speaker would have come up with these ideas had she sat down and "contemplated" the subject of hearing disorders. The value of this system, however, is that it efficiently systematizes the search for discussable thoughts and hence may relieve the speaker of searching through old notes, reference books, and so on. If used conscientiously, the system can save the speaker time, effort, and very possibly might add to the inclusiveness and impact of the speech itself.

Naturally, in any given setting, some of the topics will be more helpful "generators" than will others. For example, one speaker might get more "mileage" out of time, space, form, and feasibility in preparing for a speech on bridge stresses, while another speaker may be assisted more by desirability, similarity, and possibility when discussing the plays of Molière. Thus, when using the system, we must keep in mind the words of its developers, Wilson and Arnold: "Every speaker does not develop all of these topics in any particular speech, nor is every imaginable thought suggested as soon as one asks himself whether he needs to talk about one or another of these [sixteen topics]. Nonetheless, this simple list of topics can be easily mastered and used to generate ideas possible for use in any speech" (1968, pp. 115–116).

Having gone through this general procedure of generating (or re-generating) thoughts, the public communicator is confronted with a variety of material that could be used in his speech. With only a limited amount of speaking time, however, he must now narrow down the material. This "sifting procedure" is often painful—after all, everything you have thought could be said, should be said! Realizing that this is impossible, however, you might then pass your thoughts through a number of mental "filters" in order to arrive at material that can be explained accurately, completely, and interestingly in a given amount of time. Throughout this process of winnowing, the speaker must constantly remind himself of his goal: what is it that I want my audience members to know or to be able to do when I get done? Before coming to any final decisions about what to say, then, the speaker should carefully consider each of the following variables previously mentioned in Chapter 6:

1. *audience.* At present, how much does the audience know about my subject? How interested are they in the material? Do they have any past experiences, attitudes, or information that I can use as common ground between them and the materials I will be discussing?
2. *speaker.* To what extent can I rely on my own thoughts and experiences while speaking? Will I have to "borrow" the thoughts or research of others in order to make my remarks clear and meaningful? Has my past behavior with this audience opened up any options that I might profitably use in this particular speech?
3. *subject matter.* Does the topic itself suggest any speaking strategies that might be useful? Are there certain aspects of the topic that should be discussed above all else? Are there certain features of the subject matter that are best not mentioned in this speech?
4. *situation.* Are there any physical or psychological aspects of this setting that may enhance or retard the clarity and vivacity of the material? Will visual aids be helpful in getting the material across? Have my past interactions with this audience suggested anything that must (or should not) be said?
5. *motivational climate.* How can I best demonstrate the importance of the subject I am discussing? Is there a need for me to motivate the audience to learn the material I will be presenting?

Having shifted the available "sayables" through these mental sieves, the speaker should be in the best possible position to select those few main ideas he would like his audience to remember. (In our subsequent discussions of the other dilemmas that confront the public communicator, we will focus on principles that allow a speaker to give shape to these central and sub-ideas.)

PRESENTING TOO MUCH INFORMATION

Now that you have generated your numerous thoughts, you might feel ready to go out and throw them at your audience by the bushel. However, in a communication situation, the complexity of ideas can be increased by the simple (and very human) expedient of saying too much. How then, do you determine how much is enough in public communication? Since the structural aspects of human memory continue to baffle researchers, there is no surefire solution to our dilemma. At present, all we have is a theoretical answer.

Most contemporary researchers assume that there are three different types of memory or storage systems:

1. A sensory storage or register (SR) which collects our impressions of the world around us.
2. A short-term store or memory (STM) which selects a small number of the impressions from the SR and stores them for a brief time.
3. A long-term store (LTM) which selects information from the STM for assimilation into the information already stored in the LTM.

Despite the newness of research on the three types of memory, one stable finding is that the STM has a relatively small capacity for processing information. Estimates of this capacity range from seven, plus or minus two items (Miller, 1956), to five, plus or minus two (Mandler, 1967). The point of all this is simple: such capacities do not allow an audience to retain unlimited information from a speech. What this means for the public communication is illustrated by Verner and Dickinson (1967):

In a lecture given by a brilliant scholar with an outstanding topic and a highly competent audience, 10 percent of the audience displayed signs of inattention within fifteen minutes. After eighteen minutes one-third of the audience and 10 percent of the platform guests were fidgeting. At thirty-five minutes everyone was inattentive, at forty-five minutes, trance was more noticeable than fidgeting; and at forty-seven minutes some were asleep and at least one was reading. A casual check twenty-four hours later revealed that the audience recalled only insignificant details, and these were generally wrong. (p. 90)

Based on current knowledge, then, many scholars suggest that no more than three main points should be covered seriously in a speech of average length. In the long run, however, your own experiences will be the best indicator as to "how much" you should present. The level of sophistication of the audience, the complexity of the material, and the capacity of the public communicator to arrange his speakable thoughts will do much to suggest optimum strategies.

Another approach to our "too much" problem is available. The limitations imposed on the public communicator by the limited capacity of the short-term memory demand that a speaker specify precise goals for his speech. In doing this, the speaker can learn from the teacher planning a lesson. One begins with objectives. What is it that you want your audience members to know or to be able to do when you finish? In what situations will they need to use that knowledge or those acquired skills? To be certain that you have conceived your goals in a meaningful way, ask yourself how you will know when your speech has been successful. What would you like to observe your audience doing and in what situations? Defining your goals in this way should provide some help to you when planning precisely how to say your "sayables."

Communication situations seem to operate on the premise that the speaker can reduce the complexity of ideas for listeners by insuring himself that he has *inclusively* covered the salient points when preparing his message and that, when presenting his material, he seriously reckons with listeners' limited capacities to process information. Remembering such a premise may not make you Communicator of the Year, but at least it might make your remarks *clear* to others.

clarifying information

Clarity does not simply "exist." It is produced by judicious interactions between how a speaker says what he says and the resources listeners have within them for dealing with such information. The producers of "Sesame Street" can teach youngsters the alphabet, not only because they are aware of efficient modes of making constructs observable, but also because they are aware of certain *needs* imbedded in their audience.

The list of such needs will not overwhelm (or surprise) you: *listeners usually prefer the specific to the general, and the concrete to the abstract.* But do not get carried away with this. When your boyfriend asks you why you love him, you should *not* reply, with all the specificity and concreteness in the world: "I love you because you make a good salami sandwich." Such a refrain might make things clear, but it sure would take the mystery out of life.

Another reason why you should not follow the letter of our "law" blindly is that it is often necessary for a listener to understand the *general* make-up of the forest before he is able to appreciate the characteristics of the stately maple. Similarly, unless a listener is able to build abstractions from concrete material (that is, produce constructs from observables), he is unlikely to truly grasp the import of his knowledge.

Gracefully passing through the horns of these dilemmas is not easy, as any beginning student teacher can heartily testify. Still, research, not to mention common sense, has offered the student of communication a number of clarification devices with which to enlighten the crania of his fellows. While the list of such "complexity reducers" presented in Table 5 (see pp. 192–193) is not complete, it is, hopefully, not complex.

One profitable application of this table might be as a checklist. When you are having difficulty finding a good way of explaining an idea, you could run through these standard clarification devices to see if anything "clicks." Since we are told that variety is the spice of life, it is probably wise to vary the methods of clarification used in a speech. It is also good to remember that some subjects lend themselves to the use of certain clarification devices more than others. (What physical education professor, for example, could resist *comparing and contrasting* the motor movements utilized in basketball with those used in football?) The most important thing to remember about these methods of clarification, however, is to keep their *functions* uppermost in mind: *these devices are used to support and clarify ideas—they should not "overtake" the general principle being explained lest the listener remember, say, the interesting story and forget the concept being discussed.*

intensifying information

One principle of intensity is that listeners are most able to comprehend information when their perceptions are somehow *sharpened.* However, listeners' perceptions must be sharp, but not too sharp.

OVER-INTENSITY AND UNDER-INTENSITY

Consider this problem metaphorically. To cut, a knife must be sharp. On the other hand, when a knife is honed too finely, its edges become thin and brittle—not worth much for slicing through ideas presented discursively by a speaker.

To a large extent, audiences are imitative creatures—if the speaker is intimately involved with his material, a kind of contagion effect oftentimes occurs in members of the audience—they, too, get excited. On the other hand, if the speaker appears to be "going through the motions" with little or no commitment to what he is saying, audience members are likely to adopt a *complementary*, but not *complimentary* posture. We have probably all encountered the salesperson who tells us all we need to know about the books, the vacuum cleaner, or whatever, while—at the same time—his deadpan manner assures us that he is doing his job, but he is not really excited about the product.

Strangely, a speaker can also be too intimately involved with his subject matter so that he fails to pay attention to his audience's needs. Slick Sam's case is merely one manifestation of over-intensity. Our interest and involvement in the material can often put blinders on us and we wind up disregarding the informational levels of our audiences. Thus, we are probably wise to take heed of Gilbert Highet's remarks (1950) concerning student oriented teaching:

> ... The main danger in lecturing on this plan is not that one's notes will be sketchy. It is that, if one establishes real rapport with the class, one will become so interested in talking to them that one fails to make them remember what one is talking about. For unless a lecture leaves in the minds of the class a lasting result—a new interpretation of facts, a technique of experiment, a chain of argument—it is only a display of learning or of acting. They must be interested. Yes; and also they must be taught. (p. 104)

It is the wise public communicator, therefore, who prepares for his assignment by asking himself questions such as: How can I best demonstrate the importance of the subject I'm discussing? Is there a need for me to motivate the audience to learn the material I'll be presenting? How can I best tap their needs and desires in order to focus their attention on my message? In short, how can I most appropriately sharpen listeners' perceptions so that they can attend to the information I'll be presenting without becoming overwhelmed?

FACTORS OF ATTENTION

In adapting your message to a particular audience, it is often good to remember the elementary fact that a person cannot learn a thing until he first attends to it. Because it is so basic, this proposition is an easy one to forget. Also, because listening is such a complex process, audience members have many "claims" on their attention in any given public communication setting—the seats are hard, the blonde in the front row is attractive, meal time is approaching, and—oh, yes—the speaker is up there talking!

A learner's attention is an undulating phenomenon. It rises and falls and changes both in force and direction over time. We are wise to remember that an audience member is always *attending to something*; hence, the speaker's job is one of *focusing* that person's attention on himself and the topic at hand.

The research on attention is limited, but we know that at least eleven elements seem to command attention rather regularly. The speaker might use the following list as a prespeech checklist to insure

table 5
methods of clarification (what is a "reference group"?)

TYPE	FUNCTIONS	EXAMPLE
Serial examples	Adds "totality" to a speaker's remarks by presenting, in scattered fashion, numerous manifestations of the same phenomenon.	Parents can act as our reference groups, as can friends, political groups, religious organizations, social fraternities, etc.
Extended example	Adds "vivacity" to a speaker's remarks by presenting a detailed rendering of a single event or concept.	Let's consider what happened to John Jones, an undergrad who has had trouble "sorting out" his reference groups. John started school like most people and soon . . .
Quantification	Adds a feeling of "substantiveness" to a speaker's remarks by means of concrete, enumerative assertions.	Some experts estimate that 70 percent of our decisions are affected by our reference groups and that one out of every three people experiences tensions in relation to reference group choice.
Isolated comparisons	Adds "realism" to a speaker's remarks by drawing analogically upon a listener's past experiences.	A reference group is like a spouse—you can't live without them, but sometimes it's darn hard to live with them!

Extended comparisons	Adds psychological "reference points" to a speaker's remarks by successively structuring his perceptions along familiar lines.	A reference group is similar to a mother—it nurtures our feelings when we are hurt, it disciplines us for violating its norms, it helps us mature by . . .
Testimony	Adds to the "inclusiveness" of a speaker's remarks by quoting appreciatively from known or respected sources or depreciatively from sources of ill-regard.	Sociologist Carolyn Sherif has said that none of us can really escape the influence of the groups we identify with—our references groups.
Pictorialization	Adds to the "concreteness" of a speaker's remarks by presenting graphic representations of the speaker's assertions.	
Definition	Adds to the "specificity" of a speaker's remarks by delimiting the speech topic in some fashion.	Let's consider what is *not* meant by a reference group. It is not just *any* group we belong to nor is it always identifiable. Rather it is . . .
Contrast	Adds a "dramatic" quality to a speaker's remarks by depicting opposed elements.	Those who identify with many groups have very different attitudinal structures from those who resist such identifications.

that he has built materials into his speech that will assist him in sharpening listeners' perceptions and cause them to focus on the information he offers:

1. *activity:* depicting elements in a state of real or imagined motion
2. *proximity:* depicting elements as being close in space or time to listener
3. *specificity:* depicting detailed aspects of an element
4. *intensity:* depicting one element (the speaker) as being psychologically immersed in another element (the topic)
5. *novelty:* depicting new or unusual aspects of an element
6. *humor:* depicting incongruous, unexpected, juxtaposed, or familiar elements
7. *realism:* depicting and emphasizing the sensory qualities of an element
8. *conflict:* depicting two or more elements in opposition
9. *familiarity:* depicting elements as being psychologically close to the listener's past perceptions
10. *suspense:* depicting an element with uncertain consequences
11. *variety:* depicting a large number of apparently unassociated elements[3]

To make this list somewhat more concrete, let us assume that you have chosen to alert your classmates to the dangers of pollution. Following, are statements which you might make to incorporate the (verbal) factors of attention:

1. *activity.* No matter where you drive these days—from the wheat fields of Kansas, through the winding Rockies, and then down to the Great Salt Lake—our ecology is going to pot.
2. *proximity.* Heck, right here at the University we've got problems. Just look out that window and see how the power plant is polluting the air.
3. *specificity.* I have just returned from a trip to Connersville where the Mylon Paper Company has been fined for dumping pollutants into the Fairfax River. Some progress is being made.
4. *intensity.* I have been working my tail off for over three years trying to get this school to offer a curriculum in environmental problems. I've been buffeted and battered by every bureaucrat on campus, and I'm tired of it!
5. *novelty.* If we keep polluting the atmosphere at the rate we are now, in ten years you won't be able to walk in a city, without getting lung cancer.

[3]Adapted from John F. Wilson and Carroll A. Arnold, *Public Speaking as a Liberal Art,* 2nd ed. (Boston: Allyn & Bacon, 1968), pp. 99–100. Reprinted with permission.

6. *humor.* One report I've heard states that our forests are in such bad shape that Smokey the Bear has resigned from the Forest Rangers!

7. *realism.* Try driving through Gary, Indiana. Your nostrils burn, your breath becomes short, and your head starts to throb because of the noxious gases in the air.

8. *conflict.* Nature could do her job if man would stop battering the plant life, raping the land, and crushing the top soil.

9. *familiarity.* Think about the nature hikes you went on when you were in grade school. The water was fresh, the air clean, the plants resilient. Now look what we've got.

10. *suspense.* We can continue to overpopulate; we can continue to increase thermal pollution; we can continue to dump our wastes indiscriminately; but if we do,...

11. *variety.* Think about drinking toxic residues. Think about living in glassed-in cities. Think about seeing thousands of dead fish on the beach. Think about pollution.

Several facts are important to note about this matter of attention. Because of the basic biological and psychological nature of man, attention is easy to "get" but difficult to maintain. For example, a psychedelic light show will immediately arrest our attention, but unless the stimulus is changed, the variegated intensities and hues of the lights will soon become "old hat" and our attention will wander—our senses will have become saturated. Thus, while the tried-and-true, surefire joke in the speech may help the audience attend to the speech initially, the humor alone will not insure the *continued* adherence of the audience to the speaker's message.

As mentioned before, the speaker's job is not so much one of "getting" attention, but rather one of focusing attention on himself and his message. A listener's attention has a tendency to "scatter" when presented with a *fixed* stimulus (e.g., a speaker standing in front of the room talking). So, the speaker must constantly be on guard to be sure that the attention factors he employs are *constricting the attentive powers of the audience.* Walking a donkey into the room will surely serve to command the attention of the audience, but it is unlikely that such a tactic will *focus* their attention on matters pertaining to the space program.

timing of information

So far we have suggested methods by which the speaker can generate a sufficient amount of information for use in public communication circumstances. We were careful to admonish you not to "over-generate," lest the audience become buried in a verbal avalanche. Then we discussed relatively standard means by which speakers can clarify and intensify their remarks. But no matter how many clear and intense ideas you generate, you cannot give voice to them all at the same moment in time. Thus, in this section, and in the one which follows, we would like to stress the importance of appropriately timing and sequencing the information you wish to present.

FORMS OF EMPHASIS

If the information which we present as speakers is to have impact, in most cases we would like listeners to remember what we have said. Without looking at the cover of this book, can you remember the names of all three authors? There are probably many reasons for your forgetting our names, not the least of which is that you probably perceived no need to do so. So how is it that we come to remember? And how may a speaker insure that his listeners will at least retain the information *most crucial* to his message?

Researchers concerned with the structural aspects of human memory suggest that an important mechanism by which information is transferred from the short-term memory to the long-term memory is what they call oral/auditory rehearsal. This rehearsal may take the form of our using mnemonic devices, or of repeating the items over and over to ourselves. Given the limited capacity of the short-term memory *and* the time required for the rehearsal process, the public communicator, who wishes his information to be remembered, can profit from a thorough study of the methods for providing emphasis for ideas in his speeches.

Pace and Boren (1973, p. 164) suggest that three types of emphasis contribute significantly to the effectiveness of the rehearsal process. They are:

1. *proactive emphasis:* accomplished by any method which forecasts, cues, highlights, summarizes in advance, or underscores ideas to be presented and developed later in a message
2. *coactive emphasis:* accomplished by any method which intensifies the impact of an idea as it is being presented or that stresses the relationship of that idea to some other idea in a message
3. *reactive emphasis:* accomplished by any method which reviews or summarizes what has passed, or which highlights ideas that have already been developed in a message[4]

[4]From *The Human Transaction* by R. Wayne Pace and Robert R. Boren, Copyright © 1973 by Scott, Foresman and Company. Reprinted by permission of the publisher.

Sometimes called "previewing," *proactive emphasis* consists of highlighting, in advance, message components which you wish an audience to remember. This highlighting may take the form of an introductory statement of the main points you will cover in your speech, or it may take the form of blatant signposts (such as, "I want you to remember this") immediately preceding your making an important point. In either form, the function of proactive emphasis is to assist audience members in their "rehearsal" of the information you present, and to guide them in following along with your message.

Ray Ehrensberger (1945) found that 86 percent of the listeners he studied retained information preceded by a statement such as, "Now get this," whereas only 53.2 percent "got it" when no such emphasis was used. On a smaller scale, your own authors have observed that the mere hint that a certain bit of information is likely to be requested on the next examination is enough to get students to reach for their notebooks.

It might also be mentioned that proactive emphasis need not be verbal. Roger Wilcox (1967, pp. 110–111), for example, suggests that delivery techniques such as pauses, variations in vocal force, inflections, gestures, and other bodily movements can effectively supplement verbal modes of emphasizing. Most new teachers, for example, discover early in the game that pauses are often effective ways of suggesting that their next set of remarks will be especially worthy of the group's consideration.

As Pace and Boren's definition implies, *coactive emphasis* serves two functions: it intensifies the impact of your idea as you develop it, and it states the relationship of this idea to the other ideas in your message. That is, by both verbal and nonverbal means, we can use coactive emphasis to highlight the importance of the point we are making and to show how that idea relates to the overall structure of what we have said. The influence of multimedia, coactive emphasis on the retention of information is vividly reported by Wil Linkugel and David Berg of the University of Kansas (1970):

... Studies conducted at Atlanta show that when knowledge was imparted to a person by telling alone, the recall three hours later was 70 percent, and three days later, only 10 percent. When imparted by showing alone, the knowledge recall three hours later was 72 percent, and three days later, about 35 percent. A marked improvement. But does this mean that we should stop speaking and just show pictures? Obviously no. "When both telling and showing were the teaching tools ... the recall three hours later was 85 percent, and three days later, 65 percent. This should emphasize that recall increases markedly by using both speech and pictures." (pp. 68–69)

As any confirmed TV addict knows, advertisers have recognized for many years that our third form of reinforcement, *reactive emphasis* or repetition, is effective in getting listeners to recall products and brand names. Ehrensberger has found that directing attention to what has passed or pointing to a specific idea that is fundamental to information gain, are effective devices. He found that the simple expedient of scattering three repetitions throughout a speech was most effective in promoting retention of the speech material. Even more effective, however, was the use of "concentrated" repetition—state your idea, restate it as you develop the idea, and conclude the development of your idea with a final restatement.

In applying this latter principle to the key ideas of his speech, the public communicator is wise to remember that just saying something again and again will not enhance clarity significantly. If, for example, you are not familiar with "the linguistic-kinesic analogy," the repetition—"that's the linguistic-kinesic analogy"—will not be of much help. *Adapted and varied repetition seems to be the key to reducing the structural complexity of a spoken message.*

In summary (note the use of reactive emphasis!), the public communicator who makes a conscious effort to incorporate proactive, coactive, and reactive emphasis into his messages will assist his audience in retaining the information he chooses to present.

OTHER MATTERS OF TIMING

We are all familiar with the renowned lecturer who talks at a paragraph-a-minute clip and who covers the blackboard ten or so times in a fifty-minute class period. Rather than censure such a character, we should take pity on him. All speakers feel that there "just isn't enough time to cover all of the material adequately," and hence we all too often use "compressed speech." Unfortunately, such a device does not make practical sense. The short-term memory has a very limited capacity for processing information; hence, speaking quickly only serves to compound the possibilities of information loss. Thus, it should not be surprising to you that most studies indicate that "normal conversational delivery" is best suited to covering most material with both clarity and efficiency.

The other horn of the "timing" dilemma is all too apparent. The plodding, overly cautious, detailed speaker often fares just as badly as does the speed demon. Since most studies indicate that we can listen much faster than a speaker can talk, the snail's-pace speaker only serves to increase the "lag time" that results under even normal delivery conditions. Being the hedonists they are, audience members usually fill up such "dry spots" with thoughts of weekend dates, football games, and drinking bouts. The important thing to remember here, then, is that both excessively rapid and inordinately slow delivery of a speech will decrease audience comprehension.

sequencing information

By now you have learned how to generate a body of ideas that seem important enough to talk about, process those ideas through a series of mental filters, and develop some really telling methods of clarifying, intensifying, and reinforcing the ideas that remain. Having done this, you are still faced with a most vexing problem—how do you put it all together?

Unfortunately, because they are far from consistent, the research findings on the organization of speeches are only partially helpful. In fact, after reading the literature, we are not at all sure *how* the organizational aspects of a message serve to increase the audience's comprehension of information. The difficulties of the research seem to lie in the fact that the "organization of a speech" has been treated as being inherently present in the relations among the ideas of a speech. Thus, instead of thinking in terms of the psychological structures demanded by listeners, the research has focused on identifying the logical structure of the ideas in the message. Whatever the reason, if, as many psychologists contend, *people habitually think in patterned ways*, it makes sense that the way we sequence information will influence listeners' reactions to the complexity of spoken ideas.

To our way of thinking, therefore, a public communicator must give serious thought to methods of linking ideas together. People *will* respond differently to the messages: "I really like your course. Can I be excused on Saturday?" and "Can I be excused on Saturday? By the way, I like your course."

To assist us in making these sequencing decisions, some basic facts about human listeners may help: (1) listeners must have their attention focused on a matter before they can comprehend it, (2) listeners want to know *why* they should listen before they will listen, (3) listeners find it easier to move from the familiar to the unfamiliar than in the reverse direction, (4) listeners need to understand the simple before they can comprehend the complex, and (5) listeners like to move from the concrete to the abstract. While none of these elementary principles will shock you, it is surprising how often speakers violate such basic tenets of human communication. In their desire to "delve into the material," speakers often forget about their listeners' needs for pattern, and hence speakers foster confusion and frustration.

While no single method of organizing ideas will be satisfactory in all speaking situations, the system that has come to be known as

Monroe's Motivated Sequence is not a bad one for understanding the psychological demands that listeners place upon those who would communicate with them. Streamlined a bit, Monroe's system looks something like this:

1. *orientation.* Studies conducted at Stanford University have suggested that appropriate "frames of reference" must be established before a person can grasp unfamiliar material. This search for common ground between the audiences' knowledge-experience and the material to be discussed in the speech must be made if the speech is to be effective. By "reminding" the audience of experiences they have had previously, of things they have already learned, or of needs they are desirous of fulfilling, the speaker can "pre-cue" the speaking experience and thus make the subsequently presented material easier to comprehend.

2. *need.* From what we have said previously about attention and motivation, it should come as no surprise to learn that audiences operate best when they perceive that a potentially important topic is being dealt with by the speaker and that, by giving the speaker their attention, they will be able to improve their scientific, social, or philosophical welfare. Dramatizing the "need" to pay attention is not always easy, especially when the material being dealt with seems trite at first glance. Thus, many speakers begin by showing why the audience should pay attention and how the material to be presented will affect their lives.

3. *satisfaction.* If a listener's curiosity has been piqued by the general problem being dealt with, he is likely to "stay around" mentally for the solution. Listeners need "closure"—that is, the completion of the story—and hence, one of the major jobs the speaker has is to "process" or wrap-up the speech. Audiences do not appreciate loose ends and become frustrated if a problem has been presented and they are left without a means of resolving it. Consequently, the speaker must guard against the mistake that almost every novice speaker makes sooner or later: cramming too much material into too short a time, and thus leaving no time to summarize and thereby to satisfy the audience's need for completeness.

Armed with just these few casual observations of the audience's condition, the speaker can avoid many of the problems that develop because of poorly sequenced message components. Yet these general remarks about speech organization do not reveal the *specific* resources available to the speaker wrestling with the structures of his anticipated speech.

While any number of tried-and-true methods may give shape to a body of ideas, it is *not* true that the subject itself will suggest the most propitious method of organizing the message. For example, consider the case of the child development major who is dealing with the general topic of childhood autonomy. At first glance, it might appear that only a chronological presentation of the facts would be advantageous. But after a bit more reflection, it should be apparent that the same material can be structured in many different ways. Consider some of the standard forms of organization shown in Table 6 and let us see the options available to our Kiddie Koddler.

When deciding upon a method of organization, it might be helpful to keep in mind a few criteria: (1) Does the method of organization help present a comprehensive view of the topic? (2) Is the structure of the speech suited to highlighting the most significant aspects of the topic? And, most importantly, (3) does the method of structuring

table 6
methods of organization

TYPE	DESCRIPTION*	EXAMPLE
Chronological	Places time relationships of message topics in the foreground. Maintains a narrative line.	Even the infant's scream can be seen as his attempt to dramatize his unique needs. By the age of two, the child is beginning to experience the rewards and costs associated with independence. At around five years of age, the child has made a significant number of choices relative to dependence-independence.
Spatial	Shows coherence or differentiation among message topics in terms of space relationships.	The child soon learns that autonomy is a relative matter—at the dinner table, he is submerged in the family group; at the playground he must fight his siblings for Mommy's attention; but in his own bedroom, he is king!

*Based, in part, on remarks made by C. C. Arnold in an unpublished paper entitled "Form and Structure." Adapted by permission of Carroll C. Arnold.

table 6 continued

TYPE	DESCRIPTION*	EXAMPLE
Causal	Attempts to show the clear, sufficient, and/or practical implications of cause-to-effect or effect-to-cause relationships.	By the age of four, the child can be a fairly independent entity. This can be attributed to three acculturating influences: parents, siblings, and forces from the outside world. Let's consider each of them in order.
Ascending–descending	Places message topics in sequence according to their relative importance, familiarity, or complexity.	Parents undoubtedly exert the most influence on the child's capacity to be independent. Next come his brothers and sisters who positively or negatively reinforce such parental pressures. Outside forces (such as television) can also affect the young child, but generally less so than his immediate family.
Problem–solution	A standard pattern of organizing speech topics by means of dramatizing an obstacle and then presenting alternative remedies.	In his early years, the child fights a Herculean battle between dependency and autonomy. He is constantly torn between striking out on his own and bending to the will of the family. Typically, children handle such problems in one of three ways: submission, rejection, or compromise.
Topical	Perhaps the most common method of organization whereby selected but parallel elements of the same subject are focused on successively.	There are three areas in which the child's struggle for autonomy becomes pronounced: social development, intellectual maturation, and physical development. Let's first consider social development. . . .

the speech get my audience to see what I want them to see? Some speakers favor some methods of organization more than others, but experimenting with all of them from time to time may be worthwhile. While such trial and error approaches may not be totally comforting to you, it is still the best procedure we have in communicating effectively.

feedback and information

Perhaps the most important of the "dilemmas" afflicting public communication involves speeches and speakers who suffer unnecessarily because the clarity, amount, and sophistication of the *feedback* they receive from their audience is either excessive or nonexistent. While accepting feedback can oftentimes be tedious for a speaker ("That's a dumb thing to say, Bonnie."), it seems to be almost a "law" of human interaction that a speaker's behavior will not change appreciably unless he monitors the results of his communication and *acts* on the basis of such knowledge.

While it may seem strange, a communication system can also be "feedback rich." That is, a speaker can be overly concerned with how he's doing and hence forget his basic job of helping his audience in comprehending his message. While it may be better to err in this direction than to disregard feedback altogether, slavishly soliciting and responding to the apparent reactions of audiences may only serve to build congeniality—not to increase the audience's comprehension of facts and opinions.

In *public* communication, there is usually a dramatic imbalance in the "obviousness" of message cues given off by the speaker and his assembled auditors (What *does* a listener's furrowed brow mean, after all?) Thus, *public* speakers must often be quite creative when searching for ways to assess the "learning potential" of their speaking. Testing, of course, could tell what information is lost; but, even if you could get your audience to sit still for fifty true/false questions, the results would not tell you *why* the information was lost. Better methods of getting at these "whys" might be one or more of the following:

1. *selective feedback*. Monitor the reaction of one or two "representative" members of your audience and use these responses to bring about ongoing changes in your speech.
2. *overt feedback*. Many speakers use the "if-you-don't-understand-something-sing-out" technique; this is probably the most desirable type of feedback, but a speaker who uses such a technique must convince his audience that the invitation is a sincere one.

3. *delayed feedback.* Setting up a "feedback committee" is sometimes a practical device; if the feedback group is representative of the audience and insightful to boot, they can be most helpful to the speaker, despite the delayed nature of their feedback.
4. *indirect feedback.* Coaxing a friend to attend your speech can often be helpful since he is in a position to know what to look for.
5. *self-feedback.* With the advent of audio- and videotaping equipment, the speaker has a new ally; by reviewing your own speech in such a fashion, many important insights can be derived if one makes a conscious effort to keep self-bias to a minimum.

While any of these devices can provide a speaker with helpful, corrective information, combining two or more of the techniques would create an even more ideal set of feedback circumstances.

These few suggestions will have to suffice until American audiences adopt the system of Scottish universities where, "when they admire a phrase or an idea, the students applaud by stamping, none too gently; and when they miss something they shuffle their feet until the sentence is repeated." As Gilbert Highet says, "It may sound odd, but it is extremely helpful to the lecturer, and also ensures that the Scots get full value for their fees" (1956, p. 90).

conclusion

For those of you whose thinking is assisted by graphics, we might summarize this chapter by viewing the process of reducing complexity for listeners as a sort of sifting-redistributing set of procedures. Figure 9 is our simple representation of such a process.

Note that we are not suggesting that this is how the mind works when generating communicable thoughts. What we are suggesting is that some attention should be given to the various levels of the process if a complex idea is to be made clear, palatable, and motivating for human listeners. We believe that if public messages were created with such a winnowing-and-re-sorting procedure in mind, that *at least the speaker would be clear to himself what it was he wanted to say.* As we have intimated in Chapter 6, it is possible for a muddled speaker to make things clear to some listeners, but such a possibility does not generate effective communication consistently.

Whatever prior preparation you do, however, must also be supplemented by ongoing analysis and by adapting to listeners' needs as they develop *during* the interaction. Since the fortunes of mice and men change so dramatically in the unpredictable world of human communication, it is best to be prepared for anything—even the set

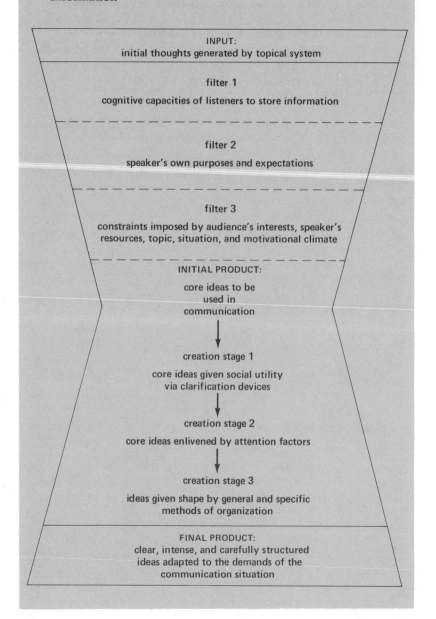

figure 9

generating material for reducing the complexity of information

INPUT:
initial thoughts generated by topical system

filter 1

cognitive capacities of listeners to store information

filter 2

speaker's own purposes and expectations

filter 3

constraints imposed by audience's interests, speaker's resources, topic, situation, and motivational climate

INITIAL PRODUCT:

core ideas to be
used in
communication

creation stage 1

core ideas given social utility
via clarification devices

creation stage 2

core ideas enlivened by attention factors

creation stage 3

ideas given shape by general and specific
methods of organization

FINAL PRODUCT:
clear, intense, and carefully structured
ideas adapted to the demands of the
communication situation

of circumstances that befell Barrett Wendell of Harvard many years ago (Simon, 1964):

When he gave his first lecture, he had it carefully outlined on cards and nicely calculated to last exactly an hour. As he lectured, he put the top card at the bottom of the pile and so worked slowly through the pack. Presently, he found himself faced again with the first card, and glancing at the clock, found that only twenty minutes had passed. Nervousness had made him talk more quickly in the lecture room than in the rehearsals. There was only one thing he could think of doing—start all over again. He did this and went through the cards three times without the class's knowing the difference. (p. 67)

sustaining attitudes, values, and behaviors

CHAPTER 8

Be seated.

I want you to remember that no bastard ever won a war by dying for his country.

He won it by making the other poor dumb bastard die for his country.

Men, all this stuff you've heard about America not wanting to fight, wanting to stay out of the war, is a lot of horse dung.

Americans traditionally love to fight.

All real Americans love the sting of battle.

When you were kids, you all admired the champion marble shooter, the fastest runner, the big league ball player, the toughest boxer.

Americans love the winner and will not tolerate a loser.

Americans play to win all the time.

(I wouldn't give a hoot in hell for a man who lost and laughed.)

That's why Americans have never lost and will never lose a war.

Because the very thought of losing is hateful to Americans.

Now, an army is a team.
It lives, eats, sleeps, fights as a team.
This individuality stuff is a bunch of crap.
The bilious bastards who wrote that stuff about individuality for the *Saturday Evening Post* don't know anything more about real battle than they do about fornicating!

Now, we have the finest food and equipment, the best spirit, and the best men in the world.
You know, my God, I actually pity those poor bastards we're going up against.
My God, I do.
We're not just going to shoot the bastards.
We're going to cut out their living guts and use them to grease the treads of our tanks!
We're going to murder those lousy Hun bastards by the bushel!

Now,
Some of you boys are wondering whether or not you'll chicken out under fire.
Don't worry about it.
I can assure you that you will all do your duty.
The Nazis are the enemy!
Wade into them!
Spill their blood!
Shoot them in the belly!
When you put your hand into a bunch of goo that a moment before was your best friend's face, you'll know what to do.

Now, there's another thing I want you to remember.
I don't want to get any messages saying that, "We are holding our position."
We're not holding anything.
Let the Hun do that.
We are advancing constantly and we're not interested in holding on anything except the enemy.
We're going to hold onto him by the nose and we're going to kick him in the ass!
We're going to kick the hell out of him all the time and we're going to go through him like crap through a goose!

Now, there's one thing that you men will be able to say when you get back home.

And you may thank God for it.

Thirty years from now when you're sitting around your fireside with your grandson on your knee, and he asks you, "What did you do in the great World War II?", you won't have to say, "Well, I shoveled shit in Louisiana."

All right, now, you sons of bitches; you know how I feel.

Go on.

I will be proud to lead you wonderful guys into battle anytime, anywhere.

That's all.[1]

T his is Hollywood's version of the words of General George S. ("Blood and Guts") Patton, as spoken to his men prior to the launching of an Allied attack in World War II. Patton's task was not that of reducing the complexity of ideas for his men, nor did he face collective hostility. Rather, his communicative job was that of heightening emotions and feelings, sustaining certain attitudes and values, and reinforcing the psychological stances and behaviors needed by his troops to reach their military objective—the destruction of other human beings. This chapter deals with the type of public communication needed to keep men marching, churchgoers praying, and footballers charging. Such public communication events, of course, span a wide range of emotional intensity—from very strong emotion (Patton's speech or Rockne's "Get One for the Gipper" oration) to rather mild, cathartic feelings (a speech of welcome to new freshmen students on campus). The sort of talk we will focus upon in this chapter helps to constitute some of our most "ordinary" experiences with public communication. We hear "pep talks" from teachers just before they give us exams, from parents prior to their sending us off to City U., and from preachers before they allow us to say "I do." All this chatter is designed not to inculcate new beliefs in us, but to remind us to keep the faith.

We can, of course, think of "sustaining talk" in a grander perspective. Every society has its set of values that constitute the basis for

[1]From the 20th Century-Fox release, *Patton*. Reprinted by permission.

that society's existence. But once values have been established so as to bring a cohesive society into existence, the perpetuation of that society, *as originally constituted*, requires that these values be continually refreshed, reinforced, and reheard. This process of reaffirmation is carried out, to a great extent, through public communication —oftentimes through highly institutionalized procedures and communicative rituals.

In Chapter 9 we will be concerned with how values, attitudes, and behaviors are modified through the process of persuasion; but in the present chapter, we shall focus upon how values already established and currently held by members of a group are "kept in place" and reaffirmed through public discourse. Thus, when considering how birds of a feather are continually urged to flock together, we will discuss (1) how shared motivations are reinforced through public communication, as well as how beliefs are maintained within us through the various agencies of (2) personality, (3) commitment and anchoring, (4) inoculation, and (5) public ritual.

As we go about our discussion, you might want to return from time to time to Patton's speech (if you can stomach it) to see how he attempted to overcome the fears and anxieties that threatened to undermine his troops' motivations, how he reinforced his audience's motivations to do battle for Old Glory, and how he performed his ritualistic task of pep-talker in a most difficult set of communicative circumstances. Should you choose to reread the speech you will find Patton relating past experiences which his men remembered fondly, the forces of evil which they denounced, the goals to which they aspired, and the obligations which they had imposed upon themselves when they chose to wear a uniform and carry a weapon. After considering such sobering realities, you might want to scout around in locker rooms on Sunday afternoons to see if Patton talk is still alive.

reinforcing shared motivations

Contemporary humankind is beset with numerous examples of public communication used to sustain and to intensify values and attitudes. Church services, pep rallies, fund-raising dinners, conventions of professional organizations, key-note addresses, and sales promotion meetings are but some of the occasions in which public communication is used to intensify and to reaffirm existing feelings. We are constantly surrounded by instances of such public communication— and for good reasons: we humans are a forgetful lot—failing to remember the eighth commandment, failing to recollect our commitments to the United Fund, and failing to recall our recruiting obligations to old IPT sorority. Thus, on any day, you will find persons convening in hotels, on university campuses, in municipal convention centers, and at business and industrial meetings throughout the nation. Thousands of sales meetings are in progress each week and religion is resold in tens of thousands of church services simultaneously. The fact that so many of these re-psyching conclaves are held each day is adequate evidence that someone out there always needs to be reminded of something and that someone else needs to do the reminding.

INTENSIFYING SOCIAL COHESION

One such type of reinforcing speech is that which seeks to intensify feelings of groupness. That is, since *groups* of people so often embody disparate, sometimes conflicting, motivations, public talk is often used to remind the group of the importance of their commonalities and of the basic irrelevance of their differences. Through such talk, people are made aware of their common, salient values and of their needs to strengthen their commitment to such *group* values.

One excellent example of this kind of "we're in it together" speech is Dr. Martin Luther King, Jr.'s "I Have A Dream," given in August of 1963. Almost a quarter of a million Americans had assembled at the Washington Monument for King's speech and had previously walked in two columns to the Lincoln Memorial to demonstrate for equality in civil rights. Later that afternoon, the high point of the entire day's activities was reached when Martin Luther King, Jr. gave his powerful, inspirational speech to the assembled crowd. Although somewhat dated now, it is still a superb example of public speaking aimed at drawing people together in a spirit of unity and cohesiveness. A segment of the speech, which demonstrates how the "elevated" feelings of the group can be used to overcome the more mundane notions of individuals, follows:

So I say to you, my friends, that even though we must face the difficulties of today and tomorrow, I still have a dream. It is a dream deeply rooted in the American dream that one day this nation will rise up and live out the true meaning of its creed—we hold these truths to be self evident, that all men are created equal.

I have a dream that one day on the red hills of Georgia, sons of former slaves and sons of former slave-owners will be able to sit down together at the table of brotherhood.

I have a dream that one day, even the state of Mississippi, a state sweltering with the heat of injustice, sweltering with the heat of oppression, will be transformed into an oasis of freedom and justice.

I have a dream my four little children will one day live in a nation where they will not be judged by the color of their skin but by the content of their character. I have a dream today!

I have a dream that one day, down in Alabama, with its vicious racists, with its governor having his lips dripping with the words of interposition and nullification, that one day, right there in Alabama, little black boys and black girls will be able to join hands with little white boys and white girls as sisters and brothers. I have a dream today!

I have a dream that one day every valley shall be exalted, every hill and mountain shall be made low, the rough places shall be made plain, and the crooked places shall be made straight and the glory of the Lord will be revealed and all flesh shall see it together.

This is our hope. This is the faith that I go back to the South with.

With this faith we will be able to hew out of the mountain of despair a stone of hope. With this faith we will be able to transform the jangling discords of our nation into a beautiful symphony of brotherhood.

With this faith we will be able to work together, to pray together, to struggle together, to go to jail together, to stand up for freedom together, knowing that we will be free one day. This will be the day when all of God's children will be able to sing with new meaning—"my country 'tis of thee, sweet land of liberty, of thee I sing; land where my fathers died, land of the pilgrim's pride, from every mountain side, let freedom ring"— and if America is to be a great nation, this must become true.

And so let freedom ring from the prodigious hilltops of New Hampshire.

Let freedom ring from the mighty mountains of New York.

Let freedom ring from the heightening Alleghenies of Pennsylvania.

Let freedom ring from the snow-capped Rockies of Colorado.

Let freedom ring from the curvaceous slopes of California.

But not only that.

Let freedom ring from Stone Mountain of Georgia.

Let freedom ring from Lookout Mountain of Tennessee.

Let freedom ring from every hill and molehill of Mississippi, from every mountainside, let freedom ring.

And when this happens, and when we allow freedom to ring, when we let it ring from every village and hamlet, from every state and city, we will be able to speed up that day when all of God's children—black men and white men, Jews and Gentiles, Catholics and Protestants—will be able to join hands and to sing in the words of the old Negro spiritual, "Free at last, free at last; thank God Almighty, we are free at last."[2]

Several things are important to note about King's approach. In trying to instill a sense of group destiny and renewed cohesiveness, King chooses to: (1) operate at a highly *abstract level* so that individual realities will not abrogate the more elusive aspirations of the collective will, (2) cite (albeit obscurely) a *great number* of specific and identifiable places and instances so that individual segments of

[2]From Roy L. Hill, ed. *The Rhetoric of Racial Revolt* (Denver: Golden Bell Press, 1964), pp. 373–375. Reprinted by permission of the publisher.

his public audience are brought into the fold, (3) emphasize *common enemies* in order to heighten the essential oneness of his audience, and (4) focus on *basic values* (e.g., a spirit of "Americanism") so that attitudes about specific aspects of civil rights (e.g., militancy) will not receive undue consideration by the group.

During the same year in which Martin Luther King gave his "I Have a Dream" speech, John F. Kennedy toured Europe speaking to the people, trying to revitalize and to strengthen the bond of union between the people of Europe and those in the United States. The highpoint of his highly successful tour came in West Berlin, where he was given a veritable hero's reception. Almost two-thirds of the population of West Berlin poured into the streets, throwing flowers, waving flags, clapping, and cheering. After visiting the Berlin Wall and city hall (where he signed the *Golden Book*), Kennedy mounted the platform erected on the steps of the city hall and gave his *Ich Bin Ein Berliner* speech. Schlesinger (1965, pp. 884–885) reports that "the crowd shook itself and rose and roared like an animal" and Kennedy remarked, following the speech, that if he had said, "March to the wall—tear it down," the crowd would have done so. There seems to be little question that Kennedy successfully cut across gaps of culture and geography and launched a vessel which, at the time, promised to bring together rather diverse peoples. It is said that when Kennedy proclaimed "I, too, am a Berliner!" there were few dry eyes in the audience—a rather remarkable set of circumstances, given the fragile American-German bonds that are said to have existed prior to Kennedy's speech.

Numerous examples could be given to demonstrate the importance of this sort of communicative coming-together, but the two cited above illustrate the cohesive impact sometimes unleashed by public communication. Whether it is the sermon given to reawaken religious unity, the talk designed to boost company morale, or the pep rally which attempts to make the commuters feel a part of Ivy U., public communication, *because it is public*, is a vehicle uniquely equipped to instill, at least, *aspirations* of collective endeavor.

INTENSIFYING COMMON GOALS AND VALUES

Naturally, there are some situations in which the cohesiveness of a group is beyond question, so that the speaker's main job is to direct such shared motivations toward the reawakening of a group's purpose for existence. Take, for example, the case of General Edwin Walker, a one-time major general in the armed forces, a sometimes candidate for governor of Texas, and a perennial John Bircher. On a rather blustery evening in February of 1962, General Walker addressed an overflowing crowd of fellow conservatives in Chicago's McCormick Auditorium. Because he was addressing a similarly committed group of individuals, Walker chose not to reinforce group identity in his speech, but rather to recommit the loyalties of his listeners to previously acknowledged goals and values. In part, he proceeded in the following way:

Yesterday I was a soldier—a Major General in your Armed Forces. Today I am a civilian. My aim and purpose has not changed. This is to keep the American eagle flying, and not to see it caged or become a "dead duck." My cause is national survival. . . .

Thirty years of military strategy and tactics have convinced me that we are not in "dire peril," but that the course of our national leadership has involved deception and misrepresentation of the American people. I would not degrade or limit the issue by unnecessarily criticizing individuals. Individuals as such, including card-carrying Communists, are not my basic concern. But I must criticize, and I give no quarter to, the total leadership responsible for our national peril from the date we recognized the Soviet Union 28 years ago. . . .

The American people are awakening. Who would have dreamed a year ago that we would be here tonight? When President Kennedy warned us of dire peril, he perhaps did not expect this response. He failed to realize the people of this Republic have been educated by the Tehran New Deal and the Camp David Coexistence Crusade. The United States has committed many national follies under the leadership of two decades of Potomac Pretenders, all in the name of One World. But the people of the United States are not going to commit national suicide by releasing their army from its responsibility when they are facing dire peril—even though they are being called *superpatriots*.

We have a duty to perform, and that is to restore and preserve the Constitution. We must release the Supreme Court and the State Department from the bonds of subversion and captivity. The Congress and the Military must be prevented from being captured by the enemy. Arouse your indignation and let it continue righteously until victory is achieved. Through faith in our Divine Savior, and loyalty to our beloved country, we shall meet the forces of darkness and destruction with light and truth that shatter their evil power to bits.

Put on the whole armor of God, so that *you* can speak boldly.

The order is: Attack on all fronts!

Your greatest weapon is the truth.

Man your weapon and speak boldly.[3]

Although it would be interesting to concentrate on the political and psychological dimensions of Walker's remarks, we shall refrain from doing so. Rather, let us consider these excerpts from Walker's

[3]Edwin A. Walker, *Walker Speaks Unmuzzled* (Dallas: American Eagle Publishing Co., 1962), pp. 47–48, 64–65.

speech as being representative of in-group rhetoric used to intensify common motivations. While Walker's words alone cannot reveal all of the techniques found in speeches used to reinforce values, his speech is suggestive of common strategies used in such circumstances, some of which are:

1. *contrasting emotions.* One characteristic immediately evident in virtually all speeches seeking to revitalize feelings and commitments to values is a balancing of emotional opposites. We might call such an approach the "carrot and the club" strategy. Any number of persons have identified the strategy, but Samuel Johnson stated it succinctly when he once said, "The two greatest movers of the human mind are the desire of good and the fear of evil." Stated another way (as it is applies to motivation) it involves urging an audience to accept our remarks because it will provide them with a tasty treat *and* prevent them from getting bashed over the head!

   Using both the carrot and the club in the same communication is rather like a "double whammy." This strategy is readily apparent in the Patton speech presented at the beginning of the chapter. Notice how the emotions of shame and pride, fear and security, and affection and hate are used contrapuntally by Patton to create a powerful emotional impact. Notice also how fellow militarist, Walker, contrasts God and Communism, individuality versus subjugation, and strength and defenselessness.

2. *visualizing through imagery.* If you are astute, you will notice eagles, dead ducks, and monsters trotting through Walker's speech. While Freud might have a field day with such metaphors, this sort of imagery is most necessary when relatively abstract goals and values must be reinforced through speech. Such aspects of language give "life" to otherwise dormant values, they enliven otherwise trite expressions of ends and means. Notice how Patton adapts his unquestionably earthy images to the dreary, grovelling life of the combat soldier. Notice, on the other hand, how King "elevates" his audience's perceptions with his talk of mountaintops, oases, and symphonies. Such "mind-pictures" are rich in their connotative trappings and serve to put new life into favored, but sometimes remote, goals and values.

3. *simplifying the group's values and goals.* More important than contrasting "enlivened" images is the uncomplicated expression of the group's aspirations. This simplification procedure is, perhaps, the essence of communication designed to heighten and sustain people's motivations. The speaker becomes the representative of the audience. They want or need certain values and goals stated

and restated, and the speaker is their agent designated to do the job. The successful inspirational speaker articulates feelings that individual members are unable to express themselves and does so in the manner deemed appropriate by that audience.

Moreover, the expression of such values and goals must be simple and straightforward. Whether they be Patton's troops or Walker's right-wingers, listeners usually demand that easily understood forces of good and evil be contrasted, that *an* answer to their problems be put forth, and that *one* overriding goal be proffered by the speaker. Should a speaker in such circumstances become too complicated in his discussion, or should he confuse the issue with a complex statement of goals, the very motivational core of the audience might be undermined.

4. *monitoring nonverbal elements.* At the risk of seeming obvious, it is especially important for the "inspiring" speaker to modulate carefully the nonverbal factors that affect his audience's perceptions. In the movie *Patton*, it was probably a bit more than the usual Hollywood schtick that determined that Patton should give his speech while standing before an American flag that measured some 20 feet by 30 feet. Similarly, the flower-strewing that surrounded Kennedy in Berlin and the civil rights banners and symbology that attended King's speech did much to increase the emotional impact of their respective addresses.

Equally, speakers who presume to articulate commonly accepted values and goals must do so with vigor and force, in the absence of tension and uncertainty. Nonverbal communication is important in any speaking situation, but it is *crucially important* in the inspirational speaking situation. It is imperative, in such instances, that the speaker say what the audience needs to have said *and say it well.* It is also important for his nonverbal behavior to validate the fact that his feelings and emotions are congruent with those of the audience. In such settings, the audience and the speaker are a team. They have the same goal for the occasion. They have the same feelings. His mood must be their mood, and those relationships will be revealed oftentimes through his gestures and vocal quality.

5. *encouraging audience participation.* Comedian Flip Wilson (among others) demonstrates that some fundamentalist congregations are often inhabited by an "Amen Charley," a character whose self-imposed job it is to assert, from time to time, "Amen, Reverend, Amen." When persons gather to share their common aspirations and allegiances, they usually do so with a good deal of powerful emotion welling up within them. Thus, it is not unreasonable for them to wish to be a part of the action, to give voice to their

approval of the speaker addressing them. Cheering, clapping, or more demonstrative signs of approval, are often part and parcel of speeches designed to intensify goals and values. As we saw in Chapters 1 and 5, such intra-audience responses can do much to further the cause of the speaker, and thus the speaker is often wise to permit and sometimes to encourage such reinforcings of his reinforcing.

So far in this chapter, we have painted a rather rosy picture of how public communication is used to reinforce and to sustain the motivations of human listeners. We have talked a bit about speakers who found themselves in very favorable circumstances, as they went about their business of intensifying the solidarity of the group to which they spoke or of revivifying that group's common goals and values. Our speakers were met with flowers, amens, and thunderous applause.

In the next section, we will darken the picture a bit. We will consider why our speakers spoke in the first place—*they had competition*. Walker, Patton, King, and Kennedy all apparently perceived that some exigence needed to be met with discourse, that some problem existed which threatened to pull their listeners away from the straight and narrow. General Walker knew that motivation for conservative ideals is not a constant thing; he also knew that for every self-respecting John Birch spokesman in the world, there is a liberal preaching some sort of gussied-up socialism. General Walker further knew that his remarks would form only a portion of the blanket of communication with which his listeners would be enveloped. Thus, he manned his weapons and spoke boldly!

sustaining beliefs through personality

Follow along for a moment, if you will, the case of Freddie Freshman, a lad who had always been the apple of his mother's eye. Freddie came from good, Midwestern stock, from a strong religious background. Freddie came from an environment of varsity sports, of clean-living, of Americanism. Freddie also came to college.

And what should return to good old Mom and Dad subsequent to Freddie's first semester at college? You guessed it. A dirty-living, pinko, beer-bellied slob! "How could this happen?", queried Mom. "Where have we gone wrong?" bellowed Dad. "Why have you forsaken all that we taught you?" exclaimed Mom and Dad in chorus.

What Mom and Dad had not reckoned with is that very special communicative techniques are required if listeners are to resist the influence of unseemly persuaders. They also failed to realize that while "good" attitudes and values can be strengthened in a listener, it is concomitantly necessary to help a listener "steel" himself against "bad" attitudes and values if the listener's original beliefs are to be truly sustained. Communication can act as an *inhibitor* of change, as a kind of serum designed to protect the mind from unsavory parasites. Because they had not reckoned with the inherent charms of campus life (e.g., roommates and liberal professors), Mom and Dad lost still another soul to the clutches of the campus liberals.

In this section, then, we will consider general research findings which shed light on how one's resistance to persuasion can be *increased*. In the sections which follow, we will see the options open to the public communicator for helping his listeners resist specific arguments and persuasive attempts. In Chapter 9, we will give the other side its due by discussing how resistance to persuasion can be *decreased*. Before doing so, however, let us now consider how Mom and Dad might have inculcated a "resistive stance" in Freddie before sending him off to the persuasive battles at The Big U.

There are two phenomena related to one's ability to resist persuasive efforts. One centers about personality factors and other internal psychological states, while the other has to do with the individual's belief structure itself. Although there are many psychological states and personality factors that relate to one's general ability to withstand persuasion, we will identify only three here. These three—self-esteem, hostility, and anxiety—are selected because they have been researched rather thoroughly. Such studies seem to indicate that when a listener possesses a good opinion of himself or when he is distraught in some fashion, he will be likely to resist the influence of others in rather wholesale fashion.

SELF-ESTEEM

Persons of high self-esteem are, other things being equal, better able to resist persuasion than are persons who think ill of themselves. Apparently, the strength of one's ego is related to one's ability to defend against "attack" and to withstand persuasive attempts by others. Moreover, Kelman (1950), Stukat (1958), and other scholars have discovered that providing a person with a "success experience" prior to a persuasive attempt makes that person quite resistant to change. Gelfand (1962), among others, has shown that the success experience need not be related to the issue subsequently discussed and that any success experienced immediately before hearing a persuasive message improves our "general resistance" to that message. Furthermore, it has been shown (Mausner and Bloch, 1957) that the success experience is especially effective for creating resistance if the prospective listener witnesses the simultaneous failure of the person who will later attempt to persuade him.

On the basis of such findings, it seems reasonable to suggest that a public communicator is wise to remind his audience initially of the wisdom of their holding their current beliefs, while simultaneously pointing out the many rewards their present beliefs have garnered for them in the past. Obviously, such *vicarious* "success experiences" will not be as potent resistance-inducers as would immediate, more tangible rewards.

Other research has discovered that these "success experience" approaches are especially bolstering to those low in self-esteem. Consider, for example, a speaker who is addressing a meeting of new members of the local chapter of Alcoholics Anonymous and whose job it is to encourage his listeners to continue to refrain from the grape. Having only recently been "cured," such listeners are probably still wallowing in the depths of depression and self-hatred. A speaker who adopts a Pollyanna approach in such a set of circumstances is obviously unwise. Rather, many trained professionals who deal with alcoholics extensively begin their remarks with the straightforward statement that "you people are alcoholics and always will be." Such speakers are quick to assert, however, that their listeners have already turned the corner by deciding to forsake further imbibing (Success Experience 1) and have demonstrated that commitment by joining with other alcoholics in a remarkably successful organization (Success Experience 2).

Drug rehabilitation centers operate in much the same way (although seemingly aware of another finding which shows that the "success experience" technique will not work if the attending persuasive arguments are highly involved and complex). In fact, research by Gollob and Dittes (1965) has shown that such an approach may actually backfire on the persuader since it gives the listener a false sense of security in his new, still-fragile attitudes. The rough-and-tumble, no-nonsense approaches used by drug rehabilitators indicate that self-esteem and "success" must be built into their clients, but not at the expense of providing the former addicts with still more rationalizations for renewing their self-destruction.

HOSTILITY

A second factor related to one's general ability to resist persuasion is aggressiveness or hostility. Research appears to indicate that raising a person's hostility by subjecting him to abusive treatment, for example, can have one of two opposite effects upon his resistance to subsequent persuasive attempts. It will make him either more susceptible or less susceptible to adopting new beliefs, depending on the characteristics of the persuasive arguments chosen to inculcate such beliefs. If the persuasive message that the aggressive listener receives is one which derogates others, then the receiver tends to be *more vulnerable* to the persuasive proposals than he would were the abuse directed his way. If the persuasive message, for example, asks that harsh or abusive actions be taken against others, the aggressive auditor is likely to acquiesce to the persuasion. If, however, the persuasive message is factual, emotionally colorless, or is based upon benign premises, the hostile person is quite likely to resist the persuasion (Weiss and Fine, 1956).

What such abstruse findings have to say about day-to-day public communication is not clear at present. Apparently, if we are to believe the reports, Patton chose wisely when detailing what his men should be prepared to do when meeting the German armies in battle. Assuming that Patton's troops were aggressive, that Patton's speech gave them ample opportunity to direct their frustrations toward others, and that the general's listeners were receptive to his colorful appeals to their basic, motivating drives, then such hearers would undoubtedly resist any *Saturday Evening Post* "nonsense" about individuality and would also turn a deaf ear on the preachments of those who urged human kindness in the battlefield situation. Interestingly, some commentators are now suggesting that it was the very lack of such aggressiveness on the parts of some GIs in Vietnam that rendered thm particularly susceptible to the persuasion of the Peace Movement in the late 1960s.

ANXIETY

Research in persuasion has discovered the interesting fact that anxious people are generally resistant to changing their attitudes but that *very anxious* people are sometimes quite suggestible. Nunnally and Bobren (1959) found that persons who received a threatening or anxiety-producing message on a topic were quite unwilling to receive further messages on that topic and that their resistance to the "other side" of the issue thereby increased. Janis and Feshback (1953) discovered, however, that if the anxiety level produced in listeners was quite high, the person might be unable to resist later persuasive attempts, so pronounced becomes his need for some sort of reassurance. The effect of anxiety on our subsequent ability to resist the influence of others is thus not easily predictable for a *group* of listeners.

Such findings may help to explain why the Freddie Freshmans of the world become subverted by the Forces of Evil on campus. Bereft of the sustaining influence of Mom, Dad, and his well-established reference groups back home, Freddie must now find new and local forms of social support. The life of the college freshman being what it is, the intense pressures of study and peer group begin to take their toll on Freddie. Friends are difficult to make. The grades come harder than they did in high school. Few people make the college varsity. All of this creates a relatively high amount of anxiety in Freddie, making him less responsive to the influence of the folks in Canyonville, and quite susceptible to the whims of all the other searching Freddies on campus.

In fact, there is every reason to suspect that Freddie's self-esteem has been lowered by the buffetings he must take during those first few lonely days on campus, and that this makes him aggressive to the folks back home who "allowed him to get into such a mess." Since he would thus combine all of the traits of the prototype nonresistor to persuasion, it is little wonder that Freddie becomes an attitudinal weather-vane until he is able to sort things out for himself.

sustaining beliefs through commitment and anchoring

While certain personality characteristics sometimes may combine to engender in us a particularly high degree of resistance to persuasion, it is also true that the ways in which our beliefs "hang together" will make some of us "easy marks" and others of us "tough customers" in a communicative sense.

If we start with the assumption that most of us like to maintain a certain amount of consistency among our beliefs, we are afforded a unique view of the forces which affect our suggestibility as auditors. That is, many of us seek to keep our attitudes "in line" with one another (e.g., If I like Richard Nixon, I should like the principle of executive privilege). Similarly, we seem to prefer that our attitudes and behaviors coincide (e.g., I like Richard Nixon and I voted for him). Called by various names (cognitive consistency, balance, the principle of congruity), this concept of attitudinal "sameness" does much to determine how, and to what extent, we will maintain our present beliefs, and consequently, what new beliefs we will consider adopting. In other words, we *structure* our beliefs, and it is not until these "structures" are upset in some fashion that we will be tempted to change our minds. Remembering this assumption of cognitive consistency, then, let us look at a few of the conditions (of belief) under which we will resist persuasion.

COMMITMENT AND INTENSITY

The intensity of a belief, or the extent to which we are committed to it, is an important factor in determining one's resistance to an attack on that belief. The more committed we are to a belief, the more we are willing to *do* on behalf of a belief, the more difficult it is for an "outsider" to change that belief. It seems to follow, therefore, that we will hold fast to a belief if we are required to demonstrate our commitment to it.

There are at least four things that can be done to facilitate greater commitment to beliefs we hold. First, we can be *continually reminded* that we hold the beliefs. After all, since we "believe" in so many things, our attention is often diverted from specific attitudes we supposedly hold. In one sense, at least, the weekly sermon is designed to remind us of (and hence to reinforce) our beliefs about the devil and the deep blue sea. In safety campaigns, in heart-fund appeals, and the like, we see the use of symbols and slogans designed to call to mind, easily and quickly, beliefs and values that demand continued reinforcement lest they become dormant.

A second strategy by which a speaker may strengthen commitment to a belief held by his listeners is to encourage them to make positive verbal statements about the belief, or even to *verbalize the belief* itself. A research summary by McGuire (1969) indicates that just writing the belief or writing positive statements about the belief to one's self (or in a relatively private setting) has the result of deepening one's commitment to the belief. Similarly, the effects of a third strategy, *public verbalization of the belief,* has been studied by a number of scholars and found (Fisher et al., 1956) to be superior to private opinion-stating with regard to increasing one's resistance to attack against the belief. After all, we know that people often try to avoid committing themselves to ideas they "really seem to hold" because, if they do so, they are "stuck with the belief" (or so run many native psychologies). We know also that it requires some loss of face, some inconsistency and admission of error, to later reverse ourselves on a belief we have admitted in public to holding.

This believe-say-believe-even-more technique is now widely used in public communication surroundings—rather notably, for example, by Weight Watchers. At a typical meeting of the organization, members of the group are encouraged, one by one, to sing their praises (if they have dutifully fasted) or to heap abuse upon themselves (if they have not lost weight). Besides reinforcing the value of a slim figure in the mind of the individual in question and making him later resistant to the pleadings of the Pillsbury Dough Boy, such verbal commitment also does much to inculcate similar feelings of remorse or exaltation in the other members of the audience.

Privately verbalizing a belief is good; publicly verbalizing the belief is better; but the best of all strategies is to have the person take some public, nonverbal action (e.g., picketing) which *irreversibly* links himself or herself with the belief. Such overt action is the nearest thing to a 100 percent guarantee that the belief will be subsequently unshakeable. Kiesler (1971) and others have demonstrated in their studies the powerful effectiveness of this strategy. They have concluded that involving people in public acts by which they are irreversibly identified with a belief renders them highly resistant to subsequent persuasive attempts in regard to that belief.

One further aspect of this fourth strategy has to do with the conditions under which the public behavior occurs. If the person performs the overt behavior of his own will, that is, with little or no social pressure and little or no public reward, his commitment to the belief will be even greater than if he is required to perform the act or is enticed to act through promise of high reward.

In summary, we have identified four strategies for increasing commitment to a belief: (1) keep the belief uppermost in one's attention or awareness, (2) verbalize the belief privately, (3) verbalize the belief publicly, and (4) link the belief to the person through his own overt, public behavior. Any of these strategies can increase our commitment to a belief and make us quite resistant to attacks on the belief from any source using any argument.

ANCHORING

A second factor related to one's belief structure can be called anchoring. If a specific attitude is anchored or tied to other salient beliefs the person holds, that belief will be more resistant to change than if it were not so anchored. If a cluster of beliefs are closely inter-related, anchored one to the other, then all "members of the cluster" may help to sustain any one of these which happens to "come under attack." However, anchoring may become a two-edged sword, working either *for* strengthening beliefs or *against* strengthening beliefs. Tying beliefs together may mean that, if a persuasive campaign can be generated that is strong enough to cause the one belief under attack to fall, then all the other beliefs tied to it may also fall—the straw which breaks the back of the attitudinal camel.

As this book was being written, a most interesting example of this anchoring-clustering phenomenon came to light. Consider the case of the average pre-Watergate Republican. His beliefs were "clustered" tightly: Richard Nixon = law and order = rejection of immorality = ethical conduct in government = good conservative principles, etc. As the facts concerning Watergate slowly were made known, the attitudes and values which anchored "Richard Nixon" in the belief system of such an individual came under significant bombardment. High ranking administration people had deceived the public. Cabinet officers came under indictment. Nixon himself became more reclusive and defensive than usual. As the various pieces and parts of the "Richard Nixon" cluster of beliefs were torn asunder, for many people, the target belief (Nixon) also began to crumble. Some persons were able to resist such cave-ins. But others gave up the ghost entirely —rejecting all of the beliefs in the cluster in question (e.g., why believe in political morality and ethical conduct? Nixon's like all the rest of the politicians—just a crook).

Thus, the anchoring process is a two-humped camel. It makes each individual belief quite resistant to change; but if an attack is strong enough to cause one belief to fall, then all beliefs in that cluster are apt to fall under certain conditions.

McGuire (1969) has identified three of the most effective strategies for insuring that beliefs will remain anchored: (1) link the belief to other related beliefs, (2) link the belief to one or more highly salient values, and (3) link the belief to an individual or group having high credibility for the individual holding the belief.

1. The first strategy is one we have discussed previously. Abelson and Rosenberg (1958) had subjects study several beliefs and then asked them to estimate the extent to which each belief was consistent with all others. The relationships among the beliefs were identified, and the subjects were then shown specifically how very great the inconsistency would be if they would change a single belief in the cluster. Being the consistency-seeking animals they were, such an anchoring strategy made the beliefs quite resistant to change for the subjects involved.

   The rationale behind such an anchoring strategy may help to explain why Nixon, during the Watergate investigation, attempted to protect *all* of his flanks—guarding tapes, defending former associates, refusing subpoenas—lest *one* chink in the armor cause the whole suit to disintegrate.

2. A second way to anchor a belief is to link it to a value or goal that is held strongly by the individual. Not only can such a linkage be clearly identified, verbalized, and continually strengthened through repetition by the individual holding it, but the particular value or goal can be called to the person's attention immediately *preceding* the persuasive attack against the belief. Keeping the value or goal in one's awareness makes it perceptually salient. Reminding the person of the goal, of its importance and value to him, and of the necessity of the particular belief to the realization of the goal, increases his resistance to attack against that belief.

Thus, during Watergate, we found Nixon continually urging that the people in the country forget the incident and turn their attention to more important *goals* such as world peace. Similarly, he argued from time to time that the *values* of executive privilege and separation of powers were being undermined by the Senate's excessive scrutiny of the whole affair.

3. The third strategy for anchoring a belief is to connect the target belief to a person or group held in high esteem by the individual. It has been discovered by Bennett (1955) that linking the belief to even an anonymous individual or group (reliable sources, other college students, experts, or even "they") has the effect of anchoring the belief and making it quite resistant to persuasion; but linking it to a known person and to a respected person or group is even better for holding the belief in place. Usually, almost any newspaper will have countless examples (e.g., "reliable sources verified" or "most experts") of anchoring and legitimizing opinions and conclusions through the strategy of linking their message with anonymous persons or groups.

It is not unreasonable to suspect that this is precisely what Nixon had in mind when he brought in Elliott Richardson and Archibald Cox to "clean house" and to lend their prestige to the Nixon administration in those first few post-Watergate days.

Another method of "anchoring" is also related to the issue of credibility. Numerous researchers have discovered that the attractiveness of a persuasive proposal can be diminished if the *person* backing such a proposal can be shown to be untrustworthy or otherwise corrupted. Thus, when trying to hold onto his following, Nixon (through intermediaries) cast aspersions on the integrity and motivations of the Senate investigators. Because they wished to believe only the issues backed by reputable sources, many Republicans bought into Nixon's reasoning—thus avoiding attitudinal inconsistency.

We have covered rather a lot of ground lately, so it might be appropriate to recap a bit at this point. We have seen that people are generally resistant to changing their beliefs if their self-esteem is intact, if they have rather aggressive feelings at the time of communication, and if they are not particularly anxious. More recently, we have looked at two general strategies useful for a speaker who wants to keep the faithful in line. In a number of ways, our beliefs can be buttressed against change if we are constantly required to make commitments to those beliefs, and especially if we make such commitments to those beliefs in the presence of others. Further, we noted a number of ways in which the public communicator can cause certain of our beliefs to "hold fast," a process often accomplished by continually anchoring such beliefs to highly valued ideas or persons.

sustaining beliefs through inoculation

Return with us, if you will, for one final look at the plight of Freddie Freshman. Although we have been somewhat facetious in our treatment of Freddie, you should not let our jocularity mislead you. Many college undergrads undergo great psychological upheaval during that first painful year. Academic and psychiatric counselors are deluged with the countless Freddies who are suddenly barraged with new and strange persuasive messages that push them all over the psychological countryside. And the Moms and Dads of the world often receive the brunt of such sortings-out by their Freddies (or Francines). In this section, we would like to discuss one of the reasons which may account for the Jekyll and Hyde turnabout Freddie effected during his freshman year.

Social psychologist William J. McGuire has been interested in what he has called the "immunization" or "inoculation" approach to sustaining attitudes, values, and behaviors. In a number of studies, McGuire validated a metaphorical explanation of the Freddie Freshman phenomenon which runs something like this: beliefs are susceptible to disease (i.e., persuasion) if they are not immunized (usually through communicative contacts) in some fashion prior to the infestation of (persuasive) germs which intend to feed upon those beliefs.

While argument by analogy is not the strongest mode of proof, McGuire's conceptualization makes sense. For example, when back home in Canyonville, Freddie knew nothing of drugs, alcohol, atheism, and loose coeds. Obviously, his parents were not inclined to mention such indelicate subjects to him. Thus, neither forearmed nor forewarned, Freddie came to campus—ripe for the social ills he would face at a liberal school and with no attitudinal "antibodies" with which to ward them off.

If we follow through with McGuire's analogy, Mom and Dad could have attempted to immunize Freddie against such "sickness." By discussing frankly and openly alternative life-styles with Freddie *prior to* his arrival on campus, the parents could have hedged their bets a bit more insightfully than they did with their see-no-evil-hear-no-evil approach. That is, by having been given a weak dose of the disease he was about to encounter, Freddie could have generated his own psychological defense system against untoward persuasive messages. Naturally, as in medical treatments, this inoculation should be weak enough so as not to overcome the person but strong enough to encourage Freddie to discover why he believed what he believed *before* he entered a hostile environment.

Freddie, then, could have been "guided through" a particular way of experiencing the expected persuasive message before it was actually presented to him. The message of liberalism, when it did come, would not have caught Freddie off guard, and the pattern of thinking suggested by his collegiate chums would not have been the *only* pattern available to him. Rather, he would have had available an alternative route, over which his mind had traveled already. In short, the pretreatment message would have reduced his vulnerability to the later persuasive attempt.

MODES OF INOCULATION

There are at least three ways of inoculating a person against subsequent persuasive attempts: first, warning of future attack; second, providing counterarguments against the assertions he will receive in the real attack; and third, identifying weaknesses in the arguments he will receive in the real attack. When attempting such inoculation, it is wise *both* to strengthen the "good" beliefs (via the methods we have already discussed) *and* to prepare the patient for the onset of the "bad" attitudes. McGuire (1961) found, in fact, that a combination of strengthening and reinforcing existing beliefs (taking a vitamin pill) and giving the person a weakened form of the persuasion (the immunization shot) results in optimal resistance. However, let us now consider the three inoculation strategies briefly:

1. *forewarning strategy.* One of the most efficient strategies is that of previewing the coming attack. The mere warning of future attack has been found to decrease later suggestibility. Apparently, a child who is reared into adulthood in a shielded and protected environment may not be able to maintain his beliefs, values, and behaviors as well as could a person who has been exposed to other ideologies, philosophies, values, and life styles when growing up. A person could be shielded so well from other points of view that, although his beliefs are constantly reinforced as to their "goodness" and "rightness," he would be highly susceptible to persuasive influences once *outside* that sheltered environment.

   McGuire and Papageorgis (1962) have hypothesized that forewarning calls all of a person's defenses into action against the expected argument, and that the mere knowledge of an impending threat motivates him to put his defenses to use. Forewarning can be especially effective when the person has strong, supportive arguments for the relevant belief that is to be attacked, but needs time to recall them and motivation to rethink them.

2. *creation of counterarguments.* A second inoculation strategy is to give the person a weakened form of the expected persuasion so that counterarguments can be created to refute the impending assertions. Two types of procedures (passive or active) may be used to acquire such counterarguments. One procedure is simply to furnish the "patient" with possible counterarguments, or, at least, to provide him with a maximum amount of information. This technique treats the listener somewhat passively, but helps to build *immediate* resistance to persuasion. It has been found, however, that this type of inoculation decays over time and that "booster shots" are required *before each persuasive attack.*

The second technique requires the person to construct his own counterarguments. With this procedure, the person becomes active; no information or ready-made counterarguments are given to him. Rather, he receives the weakened dose of the expected attack and is left to create his own counterarguments. Such a procedure is recommended for long-range resistance to persuasion. It requires some time for such a type of inoculation to "take," but it does *not* subsequently decay as does the former type of resistance. In fact, this type of active protection tends to become more virulent over time.

3. *identification of weaknesses.* A third inoculation strategy is that of identifying weaknesses in the anticipated arguments so that one can refute them rather than simply offering counterclaims. As with the creation of counterarguments, if the person actively discovers the weaknesses and creates the refutational stance himself, the inoculation will be more effective than if the refutations are handed to him ready-made.

To summarize, in this section of the chapter we have identified a number of approaches which can help us resist persuasive attempts and, thereby, to guard and to sustain beliefs that we currently hold. While few of us are as naive of the pitfalls of collegiate liberalism as was our friend, Freddie, none of us can hope to maintain our cherished attitudes and values if we are unaware of the alternatives to those attitudes or if we are without sufficient means of convincing ourselves of their veracity.

sustaining beliefs through public ritual

Thus far, much that has been said in this chapter applies to private as well as to public talk. Let us now turn our attention to public discourse exclusively and to a *public* vehicle by which we sustain attitudes, values, and behaviors. There are certain public speech situations which require neither the rendering of complex ideas nor the overcoming of significant persuasive resistance. There are speech settings which simply are meant to reinforce our beliefs and to express our emotions in very public ways. Often ritualized in form and stylized in content, such speeches seek only to give collective voice to our joys and sorrows as a society.

Some of our "best remembered" speeches are of this type. If someone were to ask you to name a famous oration, what speech would you name? Probably, it would be Lincoln's "Gettysburg Address." It is not surprising that such speeches would be remembered so clearly, since they deal with our feelings, emotions, and our strongest values. They hit us where we live, so to speak. Moreover, in such situations, the speaker becomes the personification of his audience. He is their representative, their mouthpiece. He is "expressing" for them. He is not "teacher," or "advocate," but simply "conducts" or presides over the ritual chosen to reaffirm deep-seated beliefs. We might classify such forms of discourse into two categories—echoic speeches and ceremonial speeches.

ECHOIC SPEECH

Echoic speeches are those in which the feelings and emotions of the audience are simply reverberated by the speaker. He expresses the emotion the audience is feeling. Such speech situations are institutionalized and ritualized in form and in content. The where, the who, the how, and the why are often defined and standardized, thus creating self-conscious predictability. Conventional, collective behavior results in such situations from the working out of established expectations in regard to mode of communication, roles of speaker and audience, situational expectations, and other rules that govern participants in their collective expressions of emotion. Let us consider some of the emotions that groups seem accustomed to express through public communication rituals.

Sometimes a community or group wishes to express its pride collectively. Parents are proud of their children's accomplishments (commencements), or the townsfolk want to boast of the new city hall (dedications). In times of national disaster, or in other situations in which a society feels sadness, people gather together to express that sorrow. In these latter situations, they need not only a means for ritualizing their sadness, but also require someone to articulate their hopes and to recharge their motivational batteries.

A powerful illustration of the latter is Winston Churchill's speech given on June 4, 1940. At the time, the British army had suffered a painful defeat at Dunkirk. The loss in lives and equipment was heavy and the nation was overrun with fear and despair; also, there was hope, loyalty, and perserverance that needed to be identified, expressed, and hence renewed. Churchill responded to the task admirably:

> We shall go on to the end, we shall fight in France, we shall fight on the seas and oceans, we shall fight with growing confidence and growing strength in the air, we shall defend our Island, whatever the cost may be, we shall fight on the beaches, we shall fight on the landing grounds, we shall fight in the fields, and in the streets, we shall fight in the hills; we shall never surrender. . . .[4]

At other times and in quieter moments, people assemble to give voice to their happiness (victory banquets), to their nostalgic yearnings (class reunions and homecomings), or to their patriotism. In addition, we flock to Las Vegas, to the Catskills, and to Lake Tahoe to hear nightclub "speakers" entertain us. In all such cases, we seek not to solve the great problems of the day, nor do we desire to expand our informational or attitudinal horizons. Rather, we just seek some respite from the worlds of rape, war, and financial problems.

CEREMONIAL SPEECH

A second type of public communicative ritual is ceremonial in nature. Speeches of this sort serve to "punctuate" a collective act and to verbalize a social amenity. Thus, when a person dies, our culture demands that *talk of a public sort* accompany the departed on his or her way to the final resting place, that some suitable words be spoken in a funeral address, at a memorial service, or at the interment in the cemetery. The need for this particular sort of ceremonial speech is dramatized in almost every Western worth its salt. Only the cowboy's pal, the sheriff's wife, and little Johnny are there at Boot Hill, but they manage to carry out the talking ceremony in their awkward, inept way. The audience, of course, feels great pity and sorrow because the deceased has been denied proper, *ritualized* treatment (i.e., preacher plus *crowd*). But, we feel affection and admiration for our trio for having done the best they could under adverse circumstances, and for having had their hearts in the right communicative places.

Death is only one of many situations demanding ritualized public talk in our society. When someone deserves to be recognized, for example, there is an expected procedure for handling it. We award people gold pins, gold watches, and then treat them to gold-plated eloquence. Sometimes, we need public talk to say "hello," "good-bye,"

---

[4]Winston S. Churchill, *Blood, Sweat, and Tears* (New York: Putnam, 1941), p. 297.

"thanks," "you've done a fine job," etc., and so a ceremony comes about. Every society has such needs and develops rituals to fulfill those desires. Ralph Linton (1945) has identified and described in most interesting detail the ceremonies and rituals of the Comanche Indians. Many of their ceremonies had to do with four areas of their life—medicine, puberty rites, religious beliefs, and death, and most ceremonies require public communication of a sort.

Like echoic talk, ceremonial speeches serve many of the functions we have discussed in this chapter. They help us rededicate ourselves to our beliefs. They give us a shot in the attitudinal arm so as to ward off unsavory, intruding beliefs. They rebuild our spirits, refocus our motivations, and help us to recoup our emotional losses.

A clear example of such functions being served through public talk is provided by the late Adlai E. Stevenson, a man who was particularly sensitive to the demands of public ritual but who also could create telling variations on the prescribed themes. In a speech given at the National Cathedral in Washington D.C., on the occasion of Winston Churchill's death, Stevenson began by acknowledging his ritualistic duties:

Today we meet in sadness to mourn one of the world's greatest citizens. Sir Winston Churchill is dead. The voice that led nations, raised armies, inspired victories and blew fresh courage into the hearts of men is silenced. We shall hear no longer the remembered eloquence and wit, the old courage and defiance, the robust serenity of indomitable faith. Our world is thus poorer, our political dialogue is diminished and the sources of public inspiration run more thinly for all of us. There is a lonesome place against the sky.

So, we are right to mourn. . . .

He concludes the eulogy by reaffirming some of the more salient values of his audience:

In the last analysis, all the zest and life and confidence of this incomparable man sprang, I believe, not only from the rich endowment of his nature, but also from a profound and simple faith in God. In the prime of his powers, confronted with the apocalyptic risks of annihilation, he said serenely: "I do not believe that God has despaired his children." And in old age, as the honors and excitements faded, his resignation had a touching simplicity: "Only faith," he said, "in a life after death, in a brighter world where dear ones will meet again—only that and the measured tramp of time can give consolation."

The great aristocrat, the beloved leader, the profound historian, the gifted painter, the superb politician, the lord of language, the orator, the wit—yes, and the dedicated bricklayer—behind all of them was the man of simple faith, steadfast in defeat, generous in victory, resigned in age, trusting in a loving providence and committing his achievements and his triumphs to a higher power.

Like the patriarchs of old, he waited on God's judgment and it could be said of him—as of the immortals that went before him—that God magnified him in the fear of his enemies and with his words he made prodigies to cease. He glorified him in the sight of kings and gave him commandments in the sight of his people. He showed him his Glory and sanctified him in his faith. . . .[5]

conclusion

In this chapter, we have attempted to demonstrate that remarks such as Stevenson's constitute a significant bulk of the public communication visited upon us daily. Our discussions have focused on that sort of discourse which is created because certain beliefs and motivations would be in jeopardy without such a communicative response. We have seen too that, because we are human, social, and complex, we need to make contact with others if our beliefs and attitudes are to "stay put." We have seen also that beliefs are prone to change under some circumstances, and that our attitudinal insurance policies are underwritten by ritual, by personality, by commitment and anchoring, and by a host of other communicative options.

In the next chapter, we will discuss those people who would rather we did not maintain our present attitudes, but instead encourage us to give them up and take on others. These mutual tuggings between maintaining and adopting, between staying put and trying out, will probably not cease as long as there is someone who likes us as we are, and another who wants us to be more like him.

Before we move on to consider how resistance to persuasion can be diminished in individuals, it might be profitable to stop for a moment and to consider how intertwined the exigences of sustaining beliefs and overcoming resistance to persuasion sometimes become in *public* discourse—where there always seems to be some listener behind you and another one against you. Perhaps it is this sort of complexity that comedian Pat Paulsen was responding to when he remarked that,

. . . A lot of (political) candidates burden themselves with different speeches to fit the mood and political complexion of each audience. I have found that one basic speech will usually suffice:

My fellow (Americans) (housewives) (patriots) (soul brothers):
Our nation faces an insidious threat from an evil coalition which I call the (eastern liberal establishment) (military-industrial complex) of the radical (right) (left).

[5]*Washington Post*, January 29, 1965, p. A5.

This is a combination of two elements: the military (war lords) (dissenters) and the creeping influence of (profit) (drug)-crazed (industrialists) (hippies). Their philosophies are based upon the selfish belief that no one should be required to take (orders) (baths).

How do we recognize this festering menace? It is the (crime) (pollution) in our streets. Our lakes and rivers are crowded with (sewage) (naked hippies). But it does not always assume the form of a (factory) (revolutionary) spewing forth ugly (smoke) (profanity). It is sometimes the innocent-looking programs of the media, our press and television, secretly controlled by the (pseudo-intellectual leftists) (materialist pigs). We see it in the vague and untelling arguments of those who would make us give up our (guns) (grass), those with bleeding (hearts) (heads) who call themselves the (establishment) (anti-establishment). Other nations look at our once-proud republic and cry "shame," taunting us for dropping our (ideals) (profits) (pants).

How can we regain our lost (moral) (market) values? We must restore the traditional meaning to that great cornerstone of our national heritage, the Bill of (Rights) (Sale).

I can promise, if (nominated) (drafted) (elected) to (eliminate) (assist) those who see to (split) (restore) our great nation under the banner of (truth) (ambiguity)![6]

[6]From *How to Wage a Successful Campaign for the Presidency* by Pat Paulsen. (Los Angeles: Nash Publishing Co., 1972), pp. 83–84. Copyright © 1972 by Pat Paulsen Company, Inc. Published by permission of Nash Publishing Corporation, Los Angeles.

overcoming resistance to persuasion

CHAPTER 9

Meeting a new girl is like meeting a new anyone. You don't plunge right in and begin discussing the most sensational or gory details of your or their sex life. You sort of edge in. When you first meet a new girl, the object is to casually warm her up. Start off with something general, something that won't frighten her or put her on guard. *Then,* as the conversations heat up, try edging her further and further into a corner so that she begins revealing important things about herself. Once you get her to do this, she's made sort of an emotional commitment to you. She'll feel you understand her. She'll feel close to you. And she'll want to feel even closer.

. . .

A large part of picking up girls is hanging on to them once you've made initial contact. Just because you've been successful at flagging some broad's attention doesn't mean she's going to come with you right then and there, or accept a date, or even give you her phone number.

. . .

If you commute to work or school by bus or train, keep your eyes open for girls you like. Chances are you're going to see them at least two or three mornings a week. Pick out one and try to get a seat near her. After a few mornings you'll sort of automatically become old friends—without even speaking. Before long you should feel quite free to say something to her like, "If this train is late one more time I'm going to personally murder the engineer." Or, "Where do you work?"

. . .

When you approach a woman with an intense, serious expression on your puss, you frighten her. She doesn't know whether you're going to ask directions to the nearest deli or snatch her purse.

Conversely, a good smile automatically melts a woman. Girls want to feel loved and appreciated. And when you smile at them, it makes them feel you love and appreciate them. It makes them feel *secure.*

. . .

Here's a great little technique to use once you've made contact. As soon as you can, find out the girl's name. Then, as soon as you do, use it. Plenty. Carol and Jane and Claire and Bernice her to death. She'll love it . . .

Women feel the same way you do. Their name is literally music to their ears. When you say a woman's name with warmth and feeling, it makes her feel warm. It flatters her. It makes her like you.

. . .

The moral of this little story is that one of the best ways to compliment a woman is to tell her you dig something about her she had no idea was particularly digable. Pick out some insignificant little feature she's probably overlooked. Tell her she's got fantastic eyebrows or beautiful slender fingers. Tell her anything as long as its nice. And don't be afraid to really lay it on thick. Because when it comes to discussing their looks, women are insatiable. They can't get enough![1]

[1]From *How to Pick Up Girls!* by Eric Weber. Copyright © 1970 by Eric Weber. Published by Bantam Books, Inc. and The Symphony Press. Reprinted by permission.

These remarks, made by Eric Weber in a book entitled *How to Pick Up Girls!*, can be dismissed on numerous fronts. Many would react negatively to his objectification of women—the crass way in which he suggests that females are but things to be dangled on the end of a great persuasive yo-yo. Equally passionate objections could be made to his arrogant male chauvinism. Your authors are distressed with his comments, for these and for one other reason—these comments are dumb.

Essentially, Weber is trying to suggest that his years of experience in singles bars have qualified him to wax knowingly on the art of influencing others to lower their resistance to persuasive change. In the book, he seems to argue that there are certain surefire, never-fail "rules" according to which any red-blooded American male can ply his seductive wares. But your own experience with meeting people discounts such a claim. *You* are aware that the minute you would attempt to apply Weber's type of persuasion to the women in your life, you probably would fall flat on your face. *You* know that to posit incontrovertible "rules" about human communication is at best short-sighted and, at worst, just plain ignorant. Most importantly, *you* undoubtedly have found that when it comes down to the nitty-gritty *people* interactions that compose our everyday existence, all the canned lines, the detailed seduction strategies, and the standard one-liners seem to escape you just when you are ready to address the woman in your life.

Although we will talk a good deal about persuasion in this chapter, we will not attempt to compound error by offering you unfailing techniques for dealing with recalcitrant audiences. Rather, we will try to present you with some of the findings, theories, and (when all else fails) hunches that researchers in persuasion have generated over many years of studying public influence. In addition, we will attempt to describe what some apparently successful speakers have done when confronting difficult audiences. In all cases, our attempt will be to *present you with options* for handling communicative situations. We will not presume to lay out a series of laws about human persuasion. When it comes to law-generating in communication, the individual speaker is his own legislature.

In this chapter we will consider such topics as: (1) What are the root causes of dissension in human affairs? (2) What makes us see some communicators as "reasonable" and others as "unreasonable"? (3) What insights for building reasonability and for overcoming discord are offered to us by previous research in persuasion? (4) What general approaches to persuasion seem to be viable for use in the rapidly changing world of human interaction? (5) What specific strategies for overcoming resistance should we be aware of when attempting to exert influence on our social environments? While the answers we will present to such questions will not allow you to rush out and immediately win the world for whatever cause you espouse, we do hope to improve a bit on the advice Barbara Walters (1970) offers:

Even normally gracious and poised people tend to become rattled by someone very famous, or very rich, or very intellectual, or in a position of power. Many older adults have trouble talking to anyone under thirty without becoming overly hearty (or angry) and there's something about approaching a stranger sitting behind a big desk that gives the most poised of us stomach flutters.

Nevertheless, we can't avoid meeting people who alarm us, and we would miss a lot if we could. I maintain it is possible to make sure meetings are enjoyable on both sides every time, with a few simple tips on how to launch the conversation, and a little practice to build up confidence—and a deep breath. (p. 6)

It is not the deep breath that is so tough—it is what to do after we exhale that presents the difficulties!

the nature of resistance to persuasion

Even Pollyanna would admit that people disagree with one another. Exactly *why* they do, *when* they do, and about *what* issues they disagree are queries not easily answered. Recent theorists on conflict have argued that disagreements, even violent ones, are part and parcel of the human condition. Others have argued that conflict and confrontation are not to be eschewed in our day-to-day interactions with others and that such mutual resistances are among the healthiest signs of being human. Herbert Simons (1972) of Temple University has suggested that the traditional "drawing room" techniques of persuasion are relatively incapable of dealing with the blood-and-guts sorts of spoken confrontations that have become the heritage of twentieth-century humankind. Simons argues that the "power" forces in human relationships are potent factors in determining who will be persuaded to do what under which conditions. Whether they concur with Simons or not, most contemporary students of conflict agree that the nature of resistance must be understood before techniques for overcoming it can be intelligently devised.

In this chapter we are concerned with public communication situations in which speaker and audience initially harbor significant disagreements with one another. Thus, it is especially important that we discuss some of the basic sources of human discord, even though we will not be addressing ourselves to the potentially violent sorts of confrontations to which Simons and others have addressed themselves.

GENERAL SOURCES OF RESISTANCE

In his book *Future Shock*, Alvin Toffler seems to suggest that the possibility of *change* is one of the most frightening prospects that confronts modern man. According to Toffler, it is not so much the specific changes that worry us, but it is a pervasive, exponentially increasing aura of change that worries us (sometimes literally) to death. If this is true, then it would seem to follow that *any* persuasive proposal to alter one's attitudes, beliefs, or values in any important fashion would meet with resistance—so disconcerting is the prospect of still more change.

Naturally, we cannot get carried away with such doomsday thoughts. All of us change our attitudes, jobs, tastes in liquor, sometimes even our life styles. But before we do so, many of us take the "show me" approach of the Missouri farmer. In a very real sense, persuasion is a *way of showing*. Showing that current beliefs will reap fewer dividends than will alternative beliefs; that listeners' present behaviors run contrary to values they hold, or should hold; and that, if change must come, the listeners might as well engage in it on the persuader's terms.

Research has suggested, however, that some of us are more resistant to attitudinal and behavioral change than are others, as we have already seen in Chapter 8. In the language of Chapter 3, some listeners have "potentials" within them that render them peculiarly distrustful of persuasive communications. Simons (1971) has suggested that the following types of persons are likely to be particularly resistant to persuasion:

1. *those who are highly ego-involved in the issue under consideration.* Researchers have discovered that when a person's psychological and behavioral investments in a particular issue have been prodigious, that person will be especially resistant to changing his positions on the issue (e.g., the fraternity president who, in defending Greek life, is also affirming his own life style).

2. *those who have already taken an extreme position on the matter under consideration.* By taking a polar position on an issue, we necessarily cut down severely on the range of attitudinal options open to us. Sherif, Sherif, and Nebergall (1965) report that the more extreme the position we take on an issue, the greater is the psychological mandate to reject alternatives to that position. The father who states that his son will *absolutely not* have the car for that weekend date would probably find it most difficult to save face *and* to relent from his position after listening to his son's woeful pleas.

3. *those who have a well-ordered, highly consistent system of atti-*

tudes. The key here is the word *system.* Some of us, for one reason or another, tend to lock all propositions into a well-integrated matrix of attitudes. The Ku Klux Klanner, for example, is typically quite resistant to persuasion on issues that run counter to his *system* of beliefs. Thus, he embraces *rigid* law and order, *rigid* religion, *rigid* Americanism, and *rigid* ethnocentrism, not because of the issues themselves but because of his passion for *rigidity.*

4. *those who have certain highly specialized personality traits.* Research has demonstrated that dogmatic persons, those low in self-esteem, and those who have authoritarian tendencies seem to resist persuasion in wholesale fashion. Especially when the issue is highly ego-involving for such individuals, their very personality structures do not·permit them to dally with the possibilities of attitudinal change.

5. *those who have certain demographic characteristics.* While the research is not totally in agreement on such matters, it often appears that males, older persons, intelligent individuals, and those who avoid anxiety are generally hard to persuade. These findings must be interpreted with caution. All of us know, for example, that intelligent males are persuaded day-in and day-out. As a *group,* however, they may present special problems for the public persuader.

SPECIFIC SOURCES OF RESISTANCE

Let us now consider more detailed explanations for the "persuasive resistances" that exist in some public audiences. Such an excursion is not fatuous. If the public communicator is to achieve any semblance of success via spoken influence, it is best that he be aware of the *reasons* underlying his audience's recalcitrance.

In a book entitled *Conflict Among Humans* by Robert Nye (1973), several explanations for the existence of conflict are offered. Extrapolating from Nye's postulates, we might suggest that persuasion becomes difficult when

1. Both the speaker and listeners are authoritarian.
2. There is a clash between speaker and listeners over basic needs and values.
3. Listeners have been previously rewarded for their present opinions.
4. Listeners have received too little information (or too much "wrong" information) about the speaker's position.
5. There has been minimal previous contact (of any sort) between speaker and listeners.
6. Speaker and listeners hold differing orientations toward authority.

7. Speaker and listeners embrace competing identifications (i.e., they admire different groups).

These seven sources of conflict seem to imply their own palliatives. Speakers who face such a set of conditions are, of course, wise to (1) avoid making "authority" an issue in the persuasive situation, (2) minimize the effects of contrasting values and identification, (3) maximize the availability of information favorable to the speaker's position, and (4) devise some sort of persuasive "punishment" for the listeners' current beliefs and behaviors. While there is much value in having these persuasive goals in mind, actually carrying out such techniques in pragmatic ways is much more difficult. As we shall see later in this chapter, there are specific methods available for increasing the adherence of an obstinate audience to a speaker's viewpoint, but it would be impossible to attempt to give you a set of recipes for Instant Persuasion. Nevertheless, these four approaches to persuasion might provide you with some of the ingredients.

In addition, it can be suggested that speakers should approach resisting auditors in what we might call a spirit of "conditional positive regard." *Positive* in the sense that they demonstrate a good deal of commitment to their audiences, and *conditional* in that they retain a sufficient amount of commitment to their messages. That is, no persuasive battles are likely to be won if the speaker becomes a human chameleon *or* if he adopts an "untouchable" strategy. By saying this, we are simply echoing what we have said throughout this book—it is how we *think about* communication that will determine our success in sustaining meaningful interactions with both friendly and non-friendly audiences. Simply "being aware" of the general and specific sources of resistance to persuasion will not win us persuasive garlands, but being unaware of such important sources of insight (and assistance) is bound to lead to trouble in communicating our messages.

BELIEFS AND RESISTANCE

Still another view of why it sometimes becomes so difficult for us to alter each other's behaviors is afforded by considering the *structures* of listeners' belief systems. As you will remember from our discussions in Chapter 4, Rokeach (1968) has discovered that there are a number of different types of beliefs within us and that these beliefs are differentially vulnerable to persuasion. Following Rokeach's lead (but not his terminology), we might profitably think of an individual's belief system as constituting a set of "building blocks." Figure 10 is a clear, albeit simple-minded, version of such a construct.

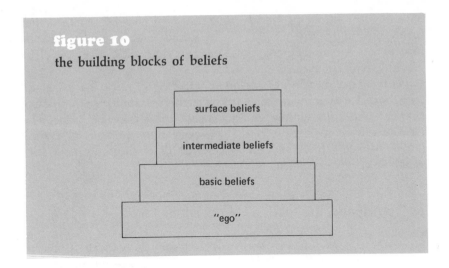

figure 10

the building blocks of beliefs

The most obvious conclusion that we can draw from our model is that the beliefs are hierachially related. That is, surface beliefs are less ego-involving than are intermediate or basic beliefs, and hence are more easily altered through persuasion than are the latter two. Consistent with our building block metaphor, changes in basic beliefs (e.g., I believe in God) will in many cases mandate changes in our intermediate beliefs (e.g., I should follow God's law) and surface beliefs (e.g., I should go to church on Sundays)—a sort of "earthquake" effect.

The reverse relationship does not necessarily hold. A person may not attend church regularly, but this does not necessarily imply that he or she will compromise more basic beliefs or give the ghost up entirely. There can, of course, be "avalanche effects" in a person's belief system. Usually, however, such changes would be the result of a long series of persuasive communications and belief restructurings.

As we "move down" our model, it is probably safe to say that the need for social reinforcement of our beliefs successively decreases, since our personal involvement with the belief would be increasingly higher. It also seems to follow that we are generally more protective of our basic beliefs than we are of the beliefs at the upper levels. Thus, it is not difficult to imagine that, if *basic beliefs* are changed, severe alterations in attitudes, opinions, behaviors, and sometimes even in personality itself may follow.

The practical implications should be clear. It is undeniably important for a persuader to know "where" he is attempting to operate in a listener's hierarchy of beliefs. For a speaker to operate in casual fashion when, for instance, attempting to effect changes in a listener's basic beliefs, would be to commit persuasive suicide. On the other hand, for a source to "bring in the big guns" to effect changes in surface beliefs would not only be foolhardy but, most likely, will be insulting to listeners.

Thus, resistance to persuasion is not created solely by a general reluctance to be influenced, or by certain personality or attitudinal characteristics alone, or even exclusively by speaker-audience relationships. In many situations, it is the position of the "target" feeling in the listener's hierarchy of beliefs that determines the ease with which he can be persuaded.

resistance and the logic of persuasion

Still another view of resistance to persuasion is available. Consider the hypothetical case of Perry Mason *before* he became the darling of the TV-rerun set. Fresh from a brilliant tour of duty at Ipsilanti Law School, Perry knew all of the precedents, all of the legal and logical intricacies, all of the arguments and counterarguments surrounding his specialties: first-degree murder and slip-and-fall cases. It was now time for his very first courtroom appearance. Armed with weighty legal tomes and a three-month supply of yellow legal pads, he sashayed into court ready to do battle. He built his case carefully, intricately. He produced documents, tapes, affidavits, previous legal decisions, photostats, statistics, note cards, testimony from the great figures of jurisprudence, more facts, more figures, until he finally collapsed with the satisfaction that only a young attorney can have at knowing that he has built a *perfectly logical* case.

The jurors sat in amazement—impressed with Mason's verbal adroitness, his clever twists of logic, his dazzling array of data. They could hardly turn their attention to the bumbling, stumbling country lawyer who called but one witness. Mason smugly watched the proceedings, sat back, mentally rending the logical fabric of his adversary, amazed at the verbal ineptitude of his opponent. Then Mason walked out of court . . . a loser.

Later, after his sixth martini, Mason looked woefully at his resourceful Della Street. "What happened?" he queried. It was all Della could do to recount the tearful, home-spun plea of Mason's opponent —a plea replete with folksy stories and gingham prose. "How dare he," retorted Mason as he ordered his seventh martini, "doesn't he know that a courtroom is run on the basis of *cold, hard logic?*" Apparently not.

It really was not Mason's fault. For many years now, the logic of persuasion has not been very well understood. In the past, it was common to assume that communication could best be understood by knowing the logical fallacies, the rules of scientific reasoning, and the dictates of formal logic (syllogisms, Venn diagrams, etc.). What Mason did not know was that *human* listeners reason differently than do logic books; people can be influenced by considerations such as: "Oh, how could she have killed him? She looks just like my sister."

CONSTITUENTS OF PERSUASIVE LOGIC

Illogical? Well, obviously not for many of us. In order to get some understanding of how human persuasion works, we probably should revise our conceptions of what is "reasonable" in communication. For some years now, Carroll Arnold of Penn State has mused about the logic of human interactions. Arnold and other researchers argue that in persuasion we must be less concerned with how scientific or formal logic works and concentrate more on how ordinary human beings reason. Says Arnold:

> In general communication, 'reasonable' and 'logical' occur as terms *people* use when they want to report that something 'hangs together' for *them,* seems adequately developed for *their* purposes, seems free of inconsistencies insofar as *they* noticed. It seems to me we *must* admit that in rhetoric and drama at least, 'reasonable' is in the final analysis what the consumer is willing to call 'reasonable'.
>
> But I would hasten on to make a second point: that it is a general characteristic of men and women that they *hunt* for interconnections among things and ideas, especially when they are uncertain or beginning to doubt. That is part of their nature—a fact well documented. It isn't *all* of their nature, of course. We must admit that, too. Maybe we need not be uniformly regretful. I, for one, think it is rather nice to illogically allow people to fall in love instead of logically mating them by bloodlines as we do with apparently more important creatures like dogs and horses! I do not really see that admitting that people do not always hunt for reasons denies that relation-hunting is *there* in people; and communicators *must* be ready to deal with these "rational" demands or they will most surely fail whenever they encounter the indifferent or the doubters. Accept that much, and now, there is *reason* to reason![2]

What Arnold seems to be saying is that in persuasion (especially in persuasion designed to overcome significant resistance), we should adopt a "psycho-logic" approach: that as analysts of persuasion, we should think less of what constitutes *inherent* reasonableness, and think more about what listeners *do* to a message when processing it. Although we know very little at present about the psycho-logic of

---

[2]Carroll Arnold, "What's Reasonable?" *Today's Speech,* vol. 19, no. 3, Summer, 1971, p. 4. Reprinted by permission of the publisher.

persuasion, Hart (1973) and others see the following propositions to be central to the way listeners reason:

1. *in persuasion, logic is created jointly by the speaker and his listeners.* This proposition stems from our considerations of the process of communication in Chapter 3. Listeners do not sit listening with empty heads. They have experiences, feelings, and prejudices which they "add to" a speaker's message as they filter and complete his remarks. In a very real way, listeners *make* sense, through an active process of "matching up" their feelings with those espoused by the speaker. Because communication is transactive—involving joint "contributions" from both speakers and listeners—no speaker can be *inherently* "logical" unless, of course, he is talking to himself.

2. *in persuasion, the psycho-logical "connections" that a listener makes determine the reasonableness of a communication.* To understand the logic of persuasion, we must develop a new lexicon. Instead of talking about "proof," we must speak of the "sufficiency" of a speaker's remarks—has he *tapped* enough of his listener's potentials? Rather than speaking of the "validity" of an argument, we must look to the associations listeners are likely to make as they match-up what a speaker has said with what they already know or feel. When your recalcitrant classmates fall asleep as you drone on in your 3-to-5 minute persuasive speech, they probably do so, not because of any inherent fallacy in your remarks, but because you did not deal with *enough* of their potentials.

3. *in persuasion, "logic" is measured not by what is, but by what seems to be.* This is a bitter pill to swallow for the scientists in the crowd. After all, many of us cling desperately to facts—cold, hard explanations of how the world *is*. Unfortunately, there are few "real" facts in the world of human interactions. As Arnold points out, there *are* people who believe that the world is flat. Call them foolish, or illogical, as you will; they do exist; and only some force of persuasion will encourage them to see the geometry of the world as you do. We live in a world of probabilities, and it is the most persuasively probable set of assertions that wins the day in the realm of human interaction.

Again, it must be said that it is the way you think about communication that will determine how you approach others with your message. If you believe that your message can be inherently logical, that it need not measure up to the petty biases and strange experiences of your listeners, then you will proceed differently than you would if you believed that you as the speaker contribute at best one-half of the logic-making in persuasion. While, in the eyes of the Campus Crusader, the Bible may contain all of the "truth" and "pure logic" worth knowing, it is not until a human contact is made that the questioning heathen is intrigued enough to open the book.

PERSUASIVE LOGIC AS DECISION-MAKING

When approaching obstinate listeners, it might be useful to remember that listening is a process of decision-making. A speaker is seen as psycho-logically credible by a listener only if that listener can render favorable judgments at a set of crucial decision points. Consider, for example, the "logic" of the following message created by an undergraduate philosophy student for an audience of history majors:

I would like you to give generously to the Campus Hunger Crusade for the following reasons: (1) your great grandchildren will appreciate it; (2) apples, pears, and bananas; (3) when I miss my daily caviar I know what it means to be hungry; (4) 99 out of every 100 people starve to death; (5) hunger, when it progresses to the stage of malnutrition, inhibits numerous enzymatic reactions, and, over the long period of time, can lead to terminal illness; and (6) the Catholic Church urges us to help starving people. Thank you for your kind attention.

Quite illogical, is it? No. It is nonpsycho-logical! We could, of course, look at the speech and find some undistributed middles, some unscientific premise-connecting, and the like; but such a procedure would miss the basic foolishness of the message.

Perhaps the best way to view this attempt at persuasion would be to consider the *types of decisions* listeners would be likely to make while and after listening to it. In response to statement 1, a listener might ask: "who cares?" To statement 2, he might say, "huh?" Statement 3 would hardly bring a tear to his eye, and he would label 4 as blatant foolishness. Unless he understands biochemistry, our listener would not know what to think about statement 5, and if he were a Protestant, he would be walking out of the room by the time the speaker got half way through the last statement. The problem with our message is that it would be incapable of meeting the criteria that listeners seem wont to apply when deciding who shall influence them. Rather than helping the situation, our philosopher's speech has *inhibited favorable decisions* from being rendered by the audience.

Listeners probably meet countless and complex such "decision points" when matching up a speaker's remarks with their own preferences. Figure 11 presents six of the most common.

credibility decision

Our model is based upon what seem to be common psycho-logical needs that listeners bring to a persuasive situation. As we mentioned

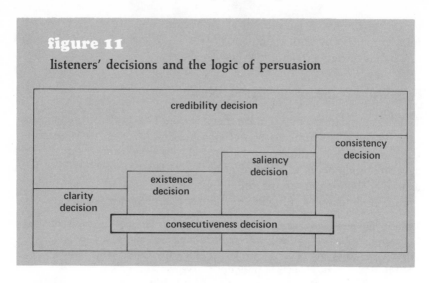

figure 11

listeners' decisions and the logic of persuasion

in Chapter 2, it is almost impossible for a listener to divorce his perception of a speaker from that of the speaker's message. Because of this, and *because credibility is always at issue in oral communication,* our model implies that a listener never strays very far from considering the *person* standing behind the persuasive message. At other moments in time, a speaker's own remarks (e.g., statement 3 in the previous example) *force* decisions to be made about the speaker's credibility. In addition, the credibility decision colors all other decisions and in turn is affected by the judgments listeners render at all points during the communicative experience. If this were not true, how could we explain the common reaction: "I don't know what he said, but didn't he say it well?"

clarity decision

When deciding whether or not a speaker is reasonable, a listener must also know what he is being asked to do or to believe. "Apples, pears, and bananas" does not come across as a clear statement. The clarity decision was placed first in our model since, if listeners are unable to determine what is being asked of them, they are unlikely to stay around mentally for further remarks from the speaker.

existence decision

Assuming that a listener understands what he is being asked to "give" in persuasion, he must then determine whether he has what it takes. Unless a listener is a scientific whiz-kid, he is unlikely to respond favorably to statement 5 in our previous example. The psycho-logical potential for "enzymatic reactions" probably does not reside in the intellectual repertoire of the average history major. While the statement might be factually true and scientifically logical, it has, in our example, run up against a stone wall.

saliency decision

One of the most crucial bases for decision-making residing within all of us is the matter of saliency. In everyday terms, saliency is a measure of the *immediacy and importance* of an issue. Statement 1 in our example loses on both accounts. The matter of saliency also helps explain the cry for "revelance" heard resounding through the halls of academe in the late 1960s—an apparent reaction to the nonsalient material that students felt was being ingested into the educational tube. The speaker who can demonstrate that his proposal can cause *immediate and important* benefits to accrue to his listeners has overcome one of the most serious hurdles to their appreciating the reasonableness of his persuasive message.

consistency decision

If we view listeners as "comparers"—people who *compare a speaker's remarks with what they have experienced or otherwise know to be fact, with what they themselves believe to be right, or with what the speaker has said on a previous occasion*—we can see why the consistency decision is central to the logic of persuasion. As hearers make "intellectual connections" while listening to a speaker, they do so in the presence of a storehouse of beliefs and recollections, all of which potentially can be brought to bear on a given persuasive stimulus. Should a speaker's remarks contradict what a listener values dearly or with what the listener believes to be true, then the speaker might very well lose the psycho-logical battle. Arnold (1971) makes the point well:

> Thirdly, I would want to drive home the most practical point I believe I know about making communications reasonable, as I have defined the term. That point is that when listeners *want* reasons spelled out, they mercilessly put down as stupid or too sloppy to be trusted communicators who do not reason or who do it badly. It is easy to show that general absence of clarity, consistency, completeness, and consecutiveness in discourse is, in the world's eye, the mark of the fool. I remind you that Bottom in *A Midsummer-Night's Dream* is a jackass, not because of his headgear. He has been a jackass for 375 years because Shakespeare would not let him talk clearly, consistently, with full awareness of what was gong on, or with "reasonable" coherence. It makes no difference who plays the part, when he speaks Bottom's lines, he plays the fool. (p. 4)

consecutiveness decision

A final type of decision which listeners seem inclined to make when assessing the remarks they hear, might be called a consecutiveness decision. The mandate for our making such kinds of decisions arises out of our human need to perceive some sort of discernible *pattern* in the world about us. As we saw in Chapter 7, there are many sorts of patterns (e.g., chronology, cause-effect, etc.) with which listeners find it especially easy to work. When looking at the above remarks in our example, we notice an almost random set of claims being made, a total lack of any "signposting" or bridging between thoughts, and no attempts on the part of the speaker to pre-cue or post-cue the listener. Such a potpourri of assertions (i.e., enzymes, Catholics, great grandchildren, etc.) made in such a short period of time would hardly facilitate the listener's task of working his or her way through this cacophony of data. People in such a situation would probably want to know how the individual assertions "connect"; they would want to discover if they were being presented with a "package" of statements or with a series of unconnected pieces and parts; finally, they would want to know if all of the assertions "add up" to anything in particular. Because the speaker in our example has failed to take his listener's need for pattern into consideration when generating discourse, he is likely to be viewed as being misguided, foolish, or both.

This rather lengthy discussion of the logic of persuasion might seem a bit unreasonable to you. Obviously your authors feel differently. The details of our discussion are not as important as is the state of mind that underlies our remarks. *If we view persuasion as a psychological process whereby listeners continually render decisions by comparing the speaker's assertions with their own values, beliefs, and sources of information,* then we as interactants will remember that communication is not a push–pull process whereby information travels on some mythical railroad car from speaker to listener. The speaker who fully *acknowledges* that he is aware that his listeners "do things" when listening, that they have the capacity to tune out at any moment, and that their adherence is a prized, yet fragile, entity does much to increase his chances of interacting in meaningful and profitable ways with them.

dealing with resistance to persuasion

Necessary as it may be for a speaker to be aware of listeners' tests for persuasive logic, and important though it is for him to understand the subtle, complex forces which feed potential resistance to his message, eventually, he must talk. In this section we will focus on some modes of thinking that may help you overcome the attitudinal and psycho-logical impediments to successful human influence. While we will be focusing primarily on public communication, you should not fail to reap the benefits of your own persuasive experiences. Any five-year-old who has used the wiles of Mom to overcome the reluctance of Dad has a head start on generating effective methods of coping with interpersonal resistance.

In the sections which follow, we will consider three topics: (1) behavioral research on "hostile" persuasion, (2) general modes of coping with resistance to persuasion, and (3) specific techniques for undoing those whose attitudes would stand against us.

RESEARCH ON HOSTILITY AND PERSUASION

Although behavioral research in persuasion is still in its theoretical infancy, the student of public communication can generate some important insights for dealing with communicative resistance by considering the findings in the area. Of course, not all research in persuasion has dealt with our special topic for this chapter and not all research in persuasion is now capable of offering specific, practical advice to the would-be persuader. Still, research summaries by Karlins and Abelson (1970), Simons (1971), and McCroskey (1969) are useful for our purpose. Consider the following propositions we might derive from past research in persuasion:

1. Material acceptable to the audience should be presented first in a persuasive speech in order to short-circuit mental "counter-arguing" on the parts of listeners.
2. Speakers addressing hostile audiences must exhibit some semblance of speaker-audience commonality even though that commonality may be irrelevant to the topic at hand.
3. An explicit proposal for change should not be stated initially by a speaker if a hostile audience is being addressed.
4. A speaker should at least mention the opposition's point of view when listeners are initially opposed to his proposal.
5. Factual evidence is especially effective when the speaker's credibility is low.
6. When listeners are minimally involved in the issue to which the speaker is addressing himself, especially strong arguments should be placed in the beginning of the speech.
7. Speakers are often advised to invite audience participation in order to overcome their listeners' resistance to persuasion.
8. Speakers who explain *why* a given audience might be opposed to them and to their proposal are often advised to do so.
9. Fear appeals are best used when the audience views the issue under consideration as being important.
10. For a number of reasons, speakers should be aware that fear appeals reach a point of diminishing returns when used excessively.

11. Speakers facing hostile audiences are advised not to attempt total conversion but rather to *change specific beliefs gradually.*
12. Strange as it may seem, the more attitude change asked for in a persuasive message, the more actual change one is likely to get.

As stated, these twelve principles are relatively general, abstract, and certainly not lawlike. As usual, the hard part of persuasion lies in actually putting such advice into practice. Some people are capable of doing so:

> ... **Let me start this speech off by saying that I am very, very grateful and deeply moved to be addressing my own university after five years of speaking at colleges all over the country. I am very grateful for the opportunity afforded me by the academic community. It is the last (as far as I'm concerned), it is the last vestige of free speech left in the country. Sorry to say it is usually accorded me by liberals. Conservatives are usually too chicken to let me speak. And I want to again say how grateful I am [to be invited here] regardless of the politics of [the sponsoring organization]. I am most grateful to them for the fight they have put up to see there's also free speech for anticommunists. . . .**
>
> **I am not here to agitate. You see no uniforms. There are no party buttons. There will be no attempt in any way to agitate. I am here to present, to the best of my ability, facts and ideas which changed me from an ordinary student at Brown University—as many of you are—to the point where I am proud to stand before you as a National Socialist. . . .**
>
> **And I am going to try to give you some insight tonight into the facts which came to my attention which I believe you have been denied [and] which caused me to make that change. All I can do, ladies and gentlemen, is to present to you a few, a very few, samples of what I consider to be shocking facts. And ask you to do what I had to do after I found out these things and go check 'em out for yourselves. . . .**[3]

Well, how would you start a speech if you were George Lincoln Rockwell, late head of the American Nazi Party, telling a liberal university audience (and a goodly number of riot-control policemen) that they should be sympathetic to the neo-Nazi movement in America?! Rockwell's approach seems to point up a canny, shirt-sleeved awareness of some of the twelve persuasive principles we have just discussed. Rockwell starts his speech in a complimentary fashion, reminds his audience of certain bonds they already share with him, withholds any specific proposal for change from his introduction, promises to present factual evidence, acknowledges that there is an opposing point of view, and, although he goes on in the speech to ask for at least tacit sympathy for the National Socialist movement, is probably

---

[3]George Lincoln Rockwell, Speech at Brown University, 1966. Reprinted by permission of the National Socialist White People's Party, Arlington, Va.; previously the American Nazi Party, headed by George Lincoln Rockwell.

aware that the best he can expect is "open-mindedness" from his audience.

While it is highly doubtful that Rockwell was aware of our list of research findings when making his speech, his remarks should indicate that practical methods of carrying out persuasive insights are capable of being developed. As we move on in this chapter and consider various approaches to persuasion, you might want to consider, from time to time, what other options for response were open to Rockwell when attempting to peddle his racism.

general modes of overcoming resistance

In this section, we will consider two of the most common methods speakers use when attempting to have impact on resisting auditors. We hope that much of what we have to say will appear commonsensical to you—for, being reminded of sensible insights based upon common experiences (that's what common sense is) is one of the most distinctively human methods we have of increasing knowledge about human communication.

THE COMMON PREMISE APPROACH

Let us start with a kind of a self-quiz. Read the following remarks and see if you can guess who the speaker is, when the speech was given, and under what circumstances.

Three hundred years ago a man who gave his name to this state, William Penn, a Quaker, was prevented by an Act of Parliament from speaking in his church, from giving a sermon. So he went out and he gave his sermon in the streets of London, on Gray Street. He was arrested and charged . . . with inciting to riot . . . and he was brought before a magistrate at the Old Bailey in London.

And the magistrate said, "Mr. Penn, you've been charged with crime. How do you plead?" And Penn said, "What is the charge against me?" And the magistrate said, "That's no consequence to you. How do you plead?" And William Penn (and I brought his remarks in here tonight), William Penn said, "Shall I plead to an indictment that hath no foundation in law? Tell me, please, what is the nature of the indictment, so that I may determine whether I am innocent or guilty." The judge said, "You are a saucy fellow. Speak to the indictment." And Penn said, ". . . I say, unless you show me and the people the law you ground your indictment upon, I shall take it for granted your proceedings are merely arbitrary."

The judge said, "The question is whether you are guilty of the indictment." And Penn said, "Where there is no law, there is no transgression, and that law which is not in being is so far from being common that it is no law at all." And the judge said, "You are an impertinent fellow. Will you teach this court what law is?" . . . And Penn said, "You tell me what the law is, I mean no affront, and I shall answer with my plea." And the judge said, "Sir, you are a troublesome fellow, and it is not for the honor of the court to suffer you to go on." And Penn answered, "I have asked but one question and you have not answered me, though the rights and privileges of every Englishman be concerned in it." And the judge said, "If I should suffer you to ask questions till tomorrow morning you would be never the wiser." And Penn said, "That depends on the answers."

And the judge said, "We must not stand to hear you talk all night." And then Penn said, . . . "I design no affront to the court but to be heard in my just plea, and I must plainly tell you that, if you will deny me knowledge of that law which you suggest I have broken, you do at once deny me an acknowledged right and evidence to the whole world your resolution to sacrifice and arbitrary designs." And the judge said, "Bind and gag him." And that's what happened to William Penn.[4]

Now let us play "Would You Believe?" Would you believe that the speech was given in the early 1970s at Pennsylvania State University? Would you believe that what you have just read was part of an introduction to a speech dealing with the Chicago Eight conspiracy trial? Would you believe that the speaker was William Kunstler, lawyer for the Chicago Eight and an unofficial patriarch of the New Left movement? Finally, would you believe that the audience he was addressing was largely composed of middle-of-the-roaders?

You may find this a rather strange way to begin a speech. However, Kunstler probably knew that he was not facing a group of hard-core radicals, but a group of middle-class Penn State students who were confused and upset about the turmoil that was sweeping college campuses in the late 1960s and early 1970s. Yet, what seems most incredible about the speech is the amount of *time* that Kunstler spent on his William Penn story. Why?

For want of a better term, we might label Kunstler's approach the common-premise strategy—one of the oldest and most viable methods available to persuaders who expect significant resistance from their audiences. Essentially, the common-premise approach operates in an analogical fashion, by comparing two apparently disparate elements and then using the one to reinforce the other. By beginning with the Penn story, Kunstler apparently reasoned that he was on safe ground —that most students of Pennsylvania would be able to identify and to admire a personage of Penn's stature. By building this common premise as carefully as he did, Kunstler was then in a position to ap-

[4]From a tape recording of Kunstler's May, 1970 speech at Pennsylvania State University. Reprinted by permission of William Kunstler.

ply the clincher—if we respect and admire Penn's stand against improper conduct by a judge, how then can we condemn the Chicago Eight for giving Judge Julius Hoffman such a rough time in court? In essence, *the common premise strategy is a technique for inhibiting listeners from spending their listening time thinking up counterarguments.*

The common premise strategy takes advantage of two of the findings of persuasion research we discussed previously—the proposal should be withheld initially and speaker-audience agreement *on some issue* must be established early in the speech. As with all human behavior, there is nothing surefire about this approach. Still, it seems to work reasonably well on many occasions and generally proceeds in somewhat the following fashion:

1. *Identify* a belief or opinion that is already held by a listener or by a group of listeners.
2. *Build* the saliency of that belief or opinion so that it becomes "operational" in the communicative situation.
3. *Demonstrate* that you, the speaker, also share that belief or opinion. (This makes it a *common* premise.)
4. *Connect* the common premise to the proposal which you are advocating as a speaker.

Naturally, the procedure is not as easy as it seems. You might, for example, select a belief or attitude that is not held strongly by your audience. You might fail to make it really salient for your listeners. Your hearers might distrust your own commitment to the proposal or they might fail to see any important connection between the common premise and the proposal. If he were not especially careful, Kunstler could have failed to persuade because of any or all of these four factors. Indeed, Kunstler, on that evening in 1970, probably succeeded in winning no wild-eyed converts. But he did, perhaps, encourage some open-mindedness on the issue, and that's not a bad night's work.

THE DETACHMENT APPROACH

Again operating at a rather global level, we can envision a second overall persuasive approach, whereby a speaker attempts to "detach" certain of the listeners' beliefs that serve to anchor another belief that the persuader is particularly interested in altering. For instance, in an antipollution campaign, ecologists oftentimes reason that John Q. Citizen will not take his refuse to the recycling center because of certain ingrained, habitual feelings he has toward disposing trash. Instead of coming on strong with the "it's your moral obligation to recycle" argument, ecologists sometimes attempt to "cut loose" the more basic attitudes holding the no-recycling belief in place. By assuming that the underlying reasons for resistance to modern ecological practices might be due to a penchant for tidiness, the advent of mechanical "aids" (such as compactors), or simple human laziness, recyclers attempt through persuasion to detach such values from the individual's belief system so that the *target belief* (recycling) will be loosened from the underlying or *anchoring beliefs* (tidiness, compactors, and laziness) after the latter are changed. Consider the following examples, which, hopefully will illustrate that the approach is not as confusing as it may sound.

When attempting to rise to power in post-World War I Germany, Adolph Hitler knew that several forces militated against his establishing a fascist regime. Chief among these "retarding forces" were the press, organized religion, and the government then in power. In rather systematic fashion, Hitler attempted to neutralize the persuasive effects of such powerful determiners of German attitudes (i.e., the religious and political anchoring beliefs) and then *later* set out to destroy (coercively, for the most part) the German people's allegiance to the target belief (i.e., a non-Nazi government). Had he not opted for such an indirect approach and instead attempted to change the target belief by means of more frontal techniques, he very well might have failed, so powerful were the countervailing forces of persuasion.

To use such an approach effectively, the persuader obviously must know which underlying attitudes are holding the target belief in place. Sometimes, such knowledge is difficult to obtain. In fact, at times, listeners themselves are unaware of the feelings which anchor a given target belief. In such a situation, by simply pointing out these anchoring beliefs and then arguing against them, a persuader has relatively little trouble in subsequently "cutting loose" the target belief.

For example, an advertisement recently appeared in many campus newspapers which asked for contributions to the East Pakistani Relief Fund. Instead of *beginning* with the "help an orphan" approach, the ad asserted and developed the following points: "We can well understand why you might refuse our plea. After all, giving has become impersonal and involuntary; we've lost the ability to be shocked by man's inhumanity to man; and we've all got our own problems." By thus reckoning directly with the "opposition's" point of view, the creators of the appeal were in a position to alter anchoring beliefs. Later on in the ad, of course, they presented more "positive" reasons for supporting the East Pakistani fund (i.e., the new belief they wished to instill).

The detachment approach and the common premise strategy have much in common. Both acknowledge that when resistance to the speaker's proposal is expected to be high, a frontal attack on listeners' basic beliefs is oftentimes unwise. With the common premise approach, the speaker refrains from dealing with potentially dangerous material until sufficient speaker-audience agreement (on some issue) has been developed. The detachment technique operates a bit more directly by dealing immediately with the attitudinal forces which threaten to withhold acceptance of his proposal. Still there is much overlap between the two strategies. The important thing to note about both strategies, however, is that each is peculiarly useful for speakers operating in distant or unfriendly surroundings. Few of us, when talking to our friends, have to go through such persuasive gymnastics.

AN ETHICAL DIGRESSION

Before we go any further, it is probably as good a time as any to comment on the ethics of persuasion. We are talking in this chapter about *strategies*. We are talking about *methods of influencing*. We are talking about *persuasion*. Without getting into a detailed discussion of morality, your authors would like to make one simple point: no matter how "evil" these terms may sound, we as people in a complex society have little choice but to understand persuasion, and to use it effectively. For every persuader of the ilk of George Lincoln Rockwell or Adolph Hitler, there are mass mobilizers like Mahatma Ghandi and Jesus Christ. For every left-winger like Kunstler, there is a John Bircher such as Robert Welch. It is our very simple-minded belief that if you do not choose to influence, if the word *strategy* gets stuck in your throat as you attempt to utter it, or if you believe that human beings are capable of *not* influencing one another (either intentionally or unintentionally), you should retreat from human society. To forsake persuasion and the techniques for making it effective might be to forsake some of your deep-seated beliefs and to insure that the world will progress (or regress) without the benefits of *your* views, *your* concerns, and *your* ideals.

specific approaches to persuasion

We intend the final section of this chapter to be the practical culmination of many of the things we have been saying in the preceding pages. So far, we have discussed the attitudinal and psychological reasons listeners might have for rejecting a speaker's proposal. More recently, we have considered two general approaches to persuasion that are peculiarly appropriate for use in attempting to overcome listeners' resistances.

Research in persuasion has more to say on the subject. On the pages that follow, we have listed and explained a number of specific

table 7

strategies for overcoming resistance to persuasion

TYPE	DEFINITION	EXAMPLE	COMMENTARY
1. Inclusion	The process of connecting the immediate audience's attitudes, values, and goals to those of a prized reference group.	All the folks on the block are buying these battery-operated can openers.	Particularly useful with listeners who possess a high need for social affiliation.
2. Maximization	The attempt to demonstrate graphically the superiority of the speaker's proposal over that of competing propositions.	The Dale Carnegie course will bring you untold amounts of health, wealth, and happiness.	Particularly useful after alternatives to the speaker's proposal have been dealt with and dismissed.
3. Minimization	The process of deprecating the views of those opposing the speaker and/or of slighting apparently detrimental aspects of the speaker's proposal.	If you want high gas bills, buy a Chrysler. Despite it's initial cost, a Cadillac is your best buy in the long run.	A very necessary approach when there are obvious disadvantages to the speaker's proposal or when the listeners have been recently made aware of proposals opposed to that of the speaker.
4. Association	The method whereby the speaker shows relationships between himself or his proposal and beliefs that are positively valued by the listener.	If you like plump, fresh-roasted peanuts like I do, you'll love Skippy peanut butter.	One of the most fundamental aspects of persuasion. Particularly valuable when an audience has a well-defined, highly contiguous value system.
5. Disassociation	The process by which the speaker depicts the lack of relationship between himself (or his proposal) and beliefs that are negatively valued by the listener.	Like you good folk, I don't want any Big-Brother-creeping-federal-bureaucracy here in the good old U. S. of A.	An obvious reversal of the association approach. Particularly helpful after a speaker has "reminded" an audience of the things they dislike.

6. Simplification	The method whereby a speaker reduces the positive aspects of his proposal (or the negative aspects of his opponent's proposal) to its lowest common denominator.	When all is said and done, you can't beat Joe's Bar for having fun.	Simplicity should, of course, characterize any attempt to communicate efficiently. Simplification is particularly useful when a speaker desires to treat complex or detailed arguments in a skeletal fashion or when a detailed examination of an issue would raise too many issues to be resolved easily during the interaction.
7. Unification	An attempt to demonstrate graphically the underlying similarity among a series of otherwise disparate elements.	If you start to think about who's raising taxes, starting wars, and spreading immorality, you'll know for whom to vote.	Especially helpful in campaign or movement persuasion when the issues, arguments, and evidence are numerous and complex.
8. Involvement	The actual or simulated attempt to engage the audience directly in communicative interaction.	Could I have a volunteer from the audience come up here and sample Dr. Ewbank's Magic Elixir?	While a difficult strategy to employ in many *public* communication situations, involvement of an audience (or members of an audience) can do much to generate a "sense of interaction" between a speaker and his listeners.
9. Gradualism	A technique whereby the speaker argues that the acceptance of his proposal does not necessitate radical restructuring of an audience's belief system.	Look Barbara, you've been going to school for sixteen years now. What's another two years for a Master's degree?	Research conducted by Osgood (1962) has suggested that interpersonal conflict can be lowered by a gradual process of concession-making. When dealing with a hostile audience, a speaker who asks for a series of moderate changes will probably avoid frightening an audience to death!

table 7 continued

TYPE	DEFINITION	EXAMPLE	COMMENTARY
10. Over-kill	The oftentimes subtle procedure by which a speaker asks for far more attitude change than he can hope to get in order to at least obtain some concession from his audience.	Mommy, can I have a lollipop, some ice cream, a jawbreaker, some bubble gum . . . well . . . at least give me a lollipop.	The reverse of gradualism, the over-kill strategy takes advantage of the research findings which show that in some cases, the more change you ask for, the more you are likely to get. Particularly useful in the *beginning* of a persuasive movement since such a blatant approach tends to call attention to that movement (e.g., "nonnegotiable demands").
11. Projection	A common device whereby a speaker hypothesizes the outcomes of the audience's wrongly following the course of action he opposes and/or rightly embracing the proposal the speaker endorses.	Just picture it—your own little retirement bungalow, away from the noise, the pollution, and the hustle and bustle of the city.	A particularly safe device to use when speaking before a hostile audience, where a detailed discussion could raise more issues than it could resolve. Takes advantage of many of the attention factors discussed in Chapter 7.
12. Elimination	The process by which a speaker successively sets aside alternative approaches to the solution he supports (often accompanied by minimizing strategies).	Jones is too far left, Smith is too far right. How about a nice middle-of-the-roader like your candidate and mine, Mark Lane?	Takes advantage of persuasion research which indicates that a "two-sided" approach is quite necessary when a hostile or intelligent audience is being addressed.
13. Idealization	A kind of abstracting technique by which the speaker suggests that certain superordinate goals are more important than any disagreements the speaker and his listeners might harbor.	Of course you and I are of different religions. But that doesn't mean that we can't engage in ecumenical dialogue in order to better do our Christian duty.	Research by Sherif (1958) has indicated that agreement on general ends can often obviate serious disagreements between persons of opposing viewpoints. Especially useful when a discussion of ends, not means, is relevant to the persuasive situation.

14. Legitimization	The tangible counterpart to the idealization strategy whereby a speaker argues that some person, document, or institution demands the acceptance of the speaker's proposal.	Ok, so we disagree about busing. But if I read the constitution right, it guarantees all students, regardless of color, the right to a good education.	Nye (1973) indicates that allegiance to a common institution or ideology can sometimes help to settle differences between conflicting factions. By appealing to a "sponsoring" force external to the interaction, a speaker can sometimes make the dispute at hand seem quite petty by comparison.
15. Self-deprecation	A frequently used persuasive strategy in which the speaker admits to certain inadequacies in order to build reciprocity between himself and his listeners.	Let's talk frankly. Of course I haven't always voted in the ways you would have liked me to. But I have followed my conscience, and that's my job as your congressman.	An especially effective device for use in hostile situations, since the speaker can take the initiative by temporarily directing the audience's attention to aspects of himself that are irrelevant to the acceptance of his proposal but which will depict him as "fair-minded."
16. Apprehension	Better known as the fear-appeal approach, apprehension is a device whereby a speaker graphically illustrates a threatening set of events or depicts the deleterious consequences of an audience's not following the speaker's advice.	Our environment has become so polluted that medical researchers are now finding that some industrial pollutants are capable of producing skin cancers.	As mentioned previously, research has shown that fear appeals are effective only up to a point, after which listeners regard the appeal as incredible or insulting. A modicum of apprehension is helpful in dramatizing a speaker's proposal, but listeners are unable to assimilate information under conditions of high anxiety.

persuasive strategies that may be of considerable help to you in preparing persuasive messages. These are offered as communicative options. They are *not* sixteen infallible steps to health and happiness through persuasion. By being aware of these options for responses, however, we hope that you will be able to add to your communicative repertoire, which is, of course, the purpose of this entire book.

conclusion

It probably need not be said that several problems abound in our categorization of appeals: (1) The strategy types we have listed here are not mutually exclusive nor, perhaps, are they at the same level of abstraction in all cases. (2) Furthermore, most persuasive messages will be composed of a veritable network of such persuasive approaches. (3) Research has also not yet delineated the exact conditions under which these individual strategies will be effective in helping a speaker overcome resistance to his proposal. (4) Undoubtedly, certain of the strategies listed here are appropriate for use only by certain persuaders with certain audiences under certain conditions.

But we will apologize no further for our listing. As with most aspects of communication, it is the *thinking about* the persuasive situation that separates the dynamos from the ne'er-do-wells. Strategies, attention factors, methods of reinforcement, forms of clarification, and so forth, cannot alone do the job of effective communication. Such devices are, of course, helpful. But devices are forgotten and *attitudes toward communication* remain. In this chapter, and for that matter throughout this book, we hope to have left you with one major impression: *effective communication (or persuasion) is not something that is done to people, but is an outgrowth of a complex process of exchange in which both speakers and listeners pool their intellectual and emotional resources and, on occasion, achieve some measure of human accord.* If we are not able to come to grips with such an intellectual realization, then we will follow the Dale Carnegie road of life —desperately searching for, but never finding, the ten magic rules for effective existence.

Communicative contacts are often taxing, sometimes frustrating, and rarely predictable. Still, from the few scraps of insight we have attempted to offer you in this book, we hope you will at least be able to improve upon the communicative style of that notorious (but probably apocraphyal) senator who is said to have opined:

You asked me how I feel about whiskey. All right, here is just how I stand on this question:

If, when you say whiskey, you mean the devil's brew, the poison

scourge, the bloody monster that defiles innocence, yea, literally takes the bread from the mouths of little children; if you mean the evil drink that topples the Christian man and woman from the pinnacles of righteous and gracious living into the bottomless pit of degradation and despair, shame and helplessness and hopelessness, then certainly I am against it with all of my power.

But, if when you say whiskey, you mean the oil of conversation, the philosophic wine, the stuff that is consumed when good fellows get together, that puts a song in their hearts and laughter on their lips and the warm glow of contentment in their eyes; if you mean Christmas cheer; if you mean the stimulating drink that puts the spring in the old gentlemen's step on a frosty morning; if you mean the drink that enables a man to magnify his joy, and his happiness, and to forget, if only for a little while, life's great tragedies and heartbreaks and sorrow, if you mean that drink, the sale of which pours into our treasuries untold millions of dollars, which are used to provide tender care for our little cripple children, our blind, our deaf, our dumb, our pitiful aged and infirm, to build highways, hospitals, and schools, then certainly I am in favor of it.

This is my stand. I will not retreat from it; I will not compromise.[5]

[5]From the Associated Press.

EPILOGUE

the systems of public communication

EPILOGUE

At last week's 45th Academy Awards no one anticipated that the revered tribal ceremony would be graced by the presence of a real Indian, who proceeded to steal the nationally televised show. The fringed and beaded mystery guest was Apache Sacheen Littlefeather, who had been sent by Marlon Brando to refuse the Oscar awarded him as Best Actor for his performance in *The Godfather*. To a mixture of boos and cheers, Miss Littlefeather explained that Brando wanted to protest Hollywood's degrading portrayal of Indians.

"Perhaps at this moment," ran the text of Brando's statement, "you are saying to yourself what the hell has all this got to do with the Academy Awards? Why is this woman standing up here, ruining our evening . . . ?" Brando was ambushing the Oscars, he said, because the movie industry has been "making a mockery of [the Indians] character, describing him as savage, hostile and evil."

Angry: Hollywood is still abuzz over Brando's stunt. "I was backstage getting into

my tux," the show's producer, Howard Koch,
told *Newsweek*'s Martin Kasindorf, "when
a page told me that an Indian was expected to
show up for Brando. I got a little nervous.
What if it was a whole tribe?" When Miss
Littlefeather arrived, Koch rushed to the lobby
for a quick powwow. Blanching at the sight
of her three-page script, he first nixed her bid
to speak on stage. They compromised on a
45-second appearance and Koch ushered Miss
Littlefeather to her seat, harboring strong
suspicions that Oscar was about to get scalped.

Reaction has been mixed: Academy president Daniel Taradash contrasted the incident
with radical activist Jane Fonda's subdued
acceptance of her Oscar last year. "It's the
difference between a real person and a gifted
fool," he snapped. But several of Brando's
fellow winners were sympathetic to him.
"Brando is sincere and honest in what he
believes," said *Godfather* director Francis Ford
Coppola. "He saw a chance to use something
good that happened to him for what he considered good for an oppressed minority."

Both Liza Minnelli and *Godfather* producer
Al Ruddy admired Brando's realism but took
a dim view of his in absentia heroics. "He
could have been more effective if he had
shown up himself to make an eloquent statement before 75-million people," commented
Ruddy. And Miss Minnelli thought that
"Sending someone else is a bit of a copout."*

---

*"Ambushing Oscar," *Newsweek*, April 9, 1973, p. 104.
Copyright *Newsweek*, Inc. 1973, reprinted by permission.

Some things just never go right. This seems to be especially true of the Academy Awards. Since they were first shown over national television, the Academy Awards have had just about every sort of plague visited upon them—dropped cue cards, streakers, broken TV cables, award recipients who talked too long (or who did not show up at all), and, last but not least, American Indians!

Your authors find the preceding commentary on the 1973 Academy Awards most interesting, especially when viewed from the vantage point of public communication. Before commenting upon this situation in detail, however, we would first like to present a rather general perspective from which to view public communicative acts. After all, we expect that after having considered the many communication principles discussed in this book, you are hankering for some method of tying it all together. Thus, we would like to present a method of conceptualizing public communication, an approach that we hope will allow you to "put the pieces together" as you think back about the topics we have treated. And never fear—we *shall* return to the saga of Oscar and the Indian Princess.

thinking systemically

If you can imagine yourself as a Britisher viewing his first American football game, you might be able to understand why it is necessary to have "the big picture" when looking at the individual pieces and parts of communication. Think what our foreign visitor is likely to perceive during those first few moments in the Astrodome. He sees a whirl of colors—brilliant scoreboards, flamboyant uniforms, and the green-and-white zebra pattern of the playing turf. He is barraged by a cacophony of sounds—shrieking whistles, bellowing fans, barking hot-dog vendors, and thumping shoulder pads which muffle endless grunts and groans. Our visitor is beset with what must appear to be incredible amounts of movement—movement among players, fans, and marching bands. He is beset with strange, grotesque objects—goal posts, martianlike helmets, and, of course, that oddly shaped spheroid which receives the total attention of players, fans, and officials alike.

In short, our foreign visitor has been confronted with a *system* of objects and relationships which he cannot comprehend. It is not so much the pieces that present difficulties, but rather the "fitting together" that befuddles him as he attempts to understand our Sunday afternoon spectaculars. Should he attempt to figure out the parts, he loses the pattern. By looking for pattern, he fails to discern the details.

The process of public communication can be equally confusing. It too is comprised of a *system of relationships*, relationships which scholars are only now beginning to understand. It is our contention in this book that if you as a student of communication are able to appreciate these systems and subsystems of relationships, you will improve your chances of *effectively* communicating in public. After all, it is only after he has understood the multiple "systems" which comprise a football game that our foreign visitor can begin to predict the options available to the quarterback on a third-and-one.

components of public communication systems

Without attempting to overload you with extraneous information, we would like to suggest that there are certain basic elements to the system of public communication. We have attempted to diagram such a systems view of public communication in Figure 12. Incomplete though our picture is, we hope that it will help you realize how many mosaics and submosaics contribute to any act of public communication.

While the following list hardly constitutes an exhaustive view of a public communication system, it is, we hope, complete enough to suggest the complexity and intra-actions present when the one speaks to the many:

1. *speaker and audience.* Public communication involves an interaction between two human elements. These elements are complex, changing, and continually responding to the variety of moods that afflict all communicating humans.
2. *speaker/audience relationships.* When two humans come into communicative contact, they establish a relationship. All public communication situations are colored by these speaker/audience relationships—bonds that have developed in part because of past interactions between this speaker and these auditors. Coupled with these past interactions, the present exchange between speaker and listener will add to or subtract from the relationships they will share in the future.
3. *communication problem.* As we have seen in Unit III of this book, a number of exigencies or problems present themselves to the public communicator. Some of these problems stem from the nature of the interactants themselves, from the kind of relationships they share, or from their individual experiences and belief systems. Usually, of course, a host of communication problems will infiltrate any given public system of interaction. As they do,

figure 12

the systems of public communication

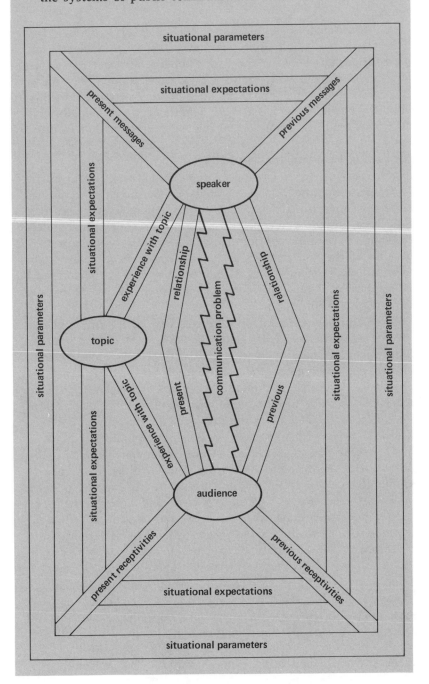

such problems will "act upon" the interactants as, in turn, the speaker and his audience attempt to address themselves to such exigencies.

4. *topic.* It is not difficult to imagine the kinds of *systems effects* that certain discussable topics can have on speaker, audience, and the relationships between the two. Should a preacher remark on the Ten Commandments to his weekly congregation, all will be in order. Should he, however, attempt to discuss Presidential politics, he will be ostracised from many a congregation. Not only do topics condition what can be said by a speaker, but in many cases the topic itself can affect many of the other subsystems comprising public communication events.

5. *experience with topic.* Obviously, the outcomes of certain public communication contacts are affected by how much the audience knows (or how strongly they feel) about the topic being discussed. Equally, a speaker who is perceived as having had minimal understanding or commitment to the topic he treats, will have to—because of the requirements of the system—behave in ways not expected of "experts." Thus, Gloria Steinem and Pat Nixon must be responsive to very different "systems forces" when discussing, say, role liberation.

6. *speaker's messages.* An important conditioner of the effects of any given communicative experience is the type and quality of remarks the speaker has made on previous occasions. For example, in 1973, during the Watergate affair, Richard Nixon's 1972 campaign promises concerning law and order greatly affected the public responses he made when attempting to explain (or explain away) the illegal acts surrounding the break-in.

7. *listeners' receptivity.* As we have seen throughout this book, a main determinant of the effect of any communicative act is the "subsystem" of attitudes and experiences that listeners conceal within them. If a given set of listeners, for instance, has been previously receptive to a passionate plea extolling the benefits of capital punishment, a speaker can sometimes reason that this will increase their motivation to hear him speak on the very same topic. However, this would only be true *if all other elements in the system were the same* on both occasions.

8. *situational expectations.* One collection of overriding factors affecting any system of public communication is the anticipations both speakers and listeners have for that situation. Should these expectations be violated and the violations not effectively counteracted by the speaker (or if listeners are unable or unwilling to make the necessary accommodations themselves), the system could very

well run wild, hurting the speaker's chances for achieving his or her desired communicative impact. For example, when students file into a lecture hall, they expect certain systems relationships. They expect to be addressed by a trained professor, they expect him to speak on matters germane to his discipline, they expect that their fellow classmates will sit quietly and take notes. Should any of these expectations be violated, "entropy" will be introduced into the system, and the public communication situation will take on a new tone.

9. *situational parameters*. A parameter can be thought of as a kind of boundary. In communication, these situational boundaries help to define what is communicatively permissible. Such boundaries are "constructed" by all of the above mentioned subsystems comprising the communicative event. In addition, forces external to the communication situation help to draw the boundaries. Matters of time, place, media, outside interference, and so forth, all contribute to the distinctiveness of the situation. Such forces also determine how much and what type of communicative business can be transacted. For example, the speaker-audience relationships, topic, and situational expectations being what they are, it is uncommon for us to protest our love for our sweetheart over the P. A. system at the intermission of a Boston Bruins hockey match. The spatial, legal, social, and psychological parameters surrounding hockey matches simply do not allow for such declarations of love. Unless the *system* is unusually responsive to immediate change and unpredictability, your communicative outburst will probably fall on the deaf ears of your embarrassed lover and of her outraged fellow auditors.

Although we have listed these nine elements separately, it must be remembered that in order to understand public communication as a *system* of relationships, it is necessary to view these elements in a holistic fashion. Thus, we can hypothesize that *public communication is comprised of a network of relationships in which any element (or combination of elements) is capable of affecting any other element (or combination of elements)*. From the standpoint of the speaker, the extent to which he is capable of understanding, monitoring, and adapting to such elements and systems-of-elements is a measure of his effectiveness as a public communicator.

The last two sentences may seem complicated, but actually, the principle is simple: as a speaker, you know that anything you say must be adapted to the peculiar set of conditions that surrounds you; such insights increase your chances of directing that communicative system in ways you deem desirable.

public communication systems: an example

As a practical example, let us consider how the network of relationship comprising the annual Academy Awards ceremony got upset on that cold night in March of 1973. First, we shall describe the *usual* systems of elements contributing to such ceremonial and echoic acceptance speeches:

1a. *speakers.* The usual "speakers" are the gushing, blushing recipients of awards. They are either actors or actresses or are otherwise associated with the film industry.

1b. *audience.* Stars, producers, directors, would-be recipients, Hollywood's "beautiful people," numerous hangers-on to the film industry, and, of course, the TV viewers across the United States.

2. *relationships.* Sometimes a bond of warmth, sometimes one of jealousy. Usually, however, the audience feels that the recipient is "one of us." Sometimes, when an "old timer" receives an award, he or she can build upon a firm, established relationship with the audience. At other times, the recipient is a "newcomer" and has only recently found his or her way into the hearts of movie buffs.

3. *communication problem.* Usually relatively simple. Probably not one of overcoming hostility, but rather one of sustaining motivation for hard work and dedication to the film industry. Part of the exigence is formed by the ritualistic necessity of thanking those who made the star what he or she is today.

4. *topic.* Direct and straightforward. Mention of the recipient's humility, surprise at having received the award, gratitude for all the back-up people without whom ..., and dedication to the ideals of the Academy.

5. *experience with topic.* Again highly ritualistic. The audience has been through all of this on previous occasions, probably knows the stock refrains, but takes delight in any *acceptable* variation on the themes of unworthiness and appreciation. The speakers' previous experiences with the topic varies. Some have been through all of this before, thus having had long since developed an appropriate repertoire of responses. The newcomers quickly learn the cues, and, for the most part, mimic the responses of their elder statesmen.

6. *speakers' messages.* Present message usually dovetails with the speaker's "image". Thus, Angry Young Man receives his award firm-lipped and unsmiling, while Young Starlet tries to say something light and effusive.

7. *listeners' receptivity.* Usually quite constrained. Listeners "pro-

gram" themselves to accept only the traditional acceptance speech. Awardees who thank too many people are looked down upon, as are those who introduce politics or other causes into the proceedings. Audience usually has a wide latitude of acceptance for tear-stained issuances.

8. *situational expectations.* Many of these have been hinted at previously. Acceptable speaker roles, topics, and communicative responses are all well defined. Humorous deviations from the norm are permitted—but only humorous ones.

9. *situational parameters.* Extraordinarily tight. Television literally forces the speakers to give conscious attention to how long they talk, where they stand, and even how loudly or softly they speak. This is a ritualistic communicative encounter in which all participants play their accustomed roles. Speakers must eschew their personal preferences and the audience must not be obstreperous.

Into this set pattern strode a lovely young American Indian to "accept" Marlon Brando's award for the *Godfather.* Because this "foreign element" was introduced into the communication system, things went predictably haywire. The speaker addressed herself to a topic which was unacceptable to the system. She badly violated situational expectations and exhibited little regard for the boundary conditions of such a speech occasion. Having had no prior experience with Miss Littlefeather, the audience's receptivity (for the most part) became increasingly truculent as she spoke. Rather than try to sustain motivation, she tried to deal creatively with the hostility. Some in the audience might have anticipated such shenanigans from a representative of Brando, one of Hollywood's Bad Boys. Others in the audience applauded—probably the same persons who supported Jane Fonda's appearance and George C. Scott's nonappearance on previous award shows. In short, the communicative applecart was overturned through the simple expedient of introducing *one* speaker and *one* new topic into an otherwise predictable and self-sustaining setting.

The "system" responded quickly, with boos for the most part. Subsequent presenters and awardees made snide comments about the introduction of "causes" into the ceremony proceedings. Such comments constituted futile attempts to return the system to its former state of affairs. Because of this system violation, it is not inconceivable that, in the future, listeners' receptivity and their situational expectations will be altered, so that a subsequent appearance by the Littlefeathers of the world would have minimal impact. It is equally likely that the producers of the Academy Awards show will tighten the parameters even more, prescreening all potential recipients for undesirable tendencies. It should be pointed out, however, that Miss

Littlefeather seemed to be well aware of the constraints of the communication system she presumed to enter. Indeed, by means of carefully chosen, precise, and sensitive remarks, she probably got more communicative mileage out of the event than could have most "intruders" under similar circumstances.

We have presented this rather detailed example in order to suggest the *practical* necessities of understanding the system within which you, as a speaker, are attempting to operate. Systems are incredibly complex and changeful and, while some are not nearly as "ordered" as the one we have just described, all public communication systems share common elements. In some fashion, the public communicator must be aware of the *system demands*, the *system potentialities*, and the points at which *system breaks* are most likely to occur.

But awareness alone is not enough. We have tried throughout this book to depict public communication as a creative experience, one which demands from speakers sensitive and sensible adaptations to listeners. We also hope to have impressed upon you how integral public communication systems are to a complex (multisystem) society, as they give voice to our highest aspirations and to our most perverse insanities. Finally, we hope that you now have some appreciation for the resources available to you as a speaker for educating, influencing, and charming those fellow humans who contribute to the bump and grind of our daily existences.

bibliography

Abelson, R. P., and Rosenberg, M. J. 1958. "Symbolic Psychologic: A Model of Attitudinal Cognition." *Behavioral Science* 3:1–13.

Adler, M. J. 1967. *The Difference of Man and the Difference It makes.* New York: Holt, Rinehart & Winston.

Andersen, K. 1971. *Persuasion: Theory and Practice.* Boston: Allyn & Bacon.

Andersen, K., and Clevenger, T. 1963. "A Summary of Experimental Research in Ethos." *Speech Monographs* 30:49–78.

Applbaum, R., and Anatol, K. 1972. "The Factor Structure of Source Credibility as a Function of the Speaking Situation." *Speech Monographs* 39:216–222.

Arnold, C. C. 1970a. "Form and Structure." Unpublished paper, Department of Speech, Pennsylvania State University.

———. 1970b. "Speech as Action." *The English Record* (October) pp. 36–43.

———. 1971. "What's Reasonable?" *Today's Speech* 19:19–23.

Bennett, E. 1955. "Discussion, Decision, Commitment and Consensus in Group Decisions." *Human Relations* 8:251–274.

Berelson, B., and Steiner, G. 1964. *Human Behavior.* New York: Harcourt Brace Jovanovich.

Bitzer, L. 1968. "The Rhetorical Situation." *Philosophy and Rhetoric* 1:1–14.

Borden, G.; Gregg, R.; and Grove, T. 1969. *Speech Behavior and Human Interaction.* Englewood Cliffs, N.J.: Prentice-Hall.

Brooks, R., and Scheidel, T. 1968. "Speech as Process: A Case Study." *Speech Monographs* 35:1–7.

Brown, C., and VanRiper, C. 1966. *Speech and Man.* Englewood Cliffs, N.J.: Prentice-Hall.

Carlsmith, T. M.; Collins, B. E.; and Helmreich, R. L. 1966. "The Effect of Pressure for Compliance on Attitude Change Provided by Face-to-Face Role Playing and Anonymous Writing." *Journal of Personality and Social Psychology* 4:1–13.

Cherry, C. 1966. *On Human Communication.* 2nd ed. Cambridge, Mass.: M.I.T. Press.

Clevenger, T. and Matthews, J. 1971. *The Speech Communication Process.* Glenview, Ill.: Scott, Foresman.

Cronkhite, G. 1969a. *Persuasion: Speech and Behavioral Change.* New York: Bobbs-Merrill.

———. 1969b. "Out of the Ivory Palaces: A Proposal for Useful Research in Communication and Decision." In R. J. Kibler and L. L. Barker, eds., *Conceptual Frontiers in Speech-Communication.* New York: Speech Association of America.

Ehrensberger, R. 1945. "An Experimental Study of the Relative Effects of Certain Form of Emphasis in Public Speaking." *Speech Monographs* 12:94–111.

Fisher, S.; Rubinstein, I.; and Freeman, R. W. 1956. "Intertrial Effects of Immediate Self-Committal in a Continuous Social Influence Situation." *Journal of Abnormal and Social Psychology* 52:200–207.

Fulbright, W. 1970. *The Pentagon Propaganda Machine.* New York: Liveright.

Gelfand, D. M. 1962. "The Influence of Self-Esteem on the Rate of Verbal Conditioning and Social Matching Behavior." *Journal of Abnormal and Social Psychology* 65:259–265.

Gibson, J. W.; Gruner, C. R.; Kibler, R. J.; and Kelly, F. J. 1966. "A Quantitative Examination of Differences and Similarities in Written and Spoken Messages." *Speech Monographs* 33:444–451.

Goffman, E. 1963. *Behavior in Public Places: Notes on the Social Organization of Groups.* New York: Free Press.

———. 1967. *Interaction Ritual, 1965.* New York: Doubleday.

Gollob, H. F., and Dittes, J. E. "Effects of Manipulated Self-Esteem on Persuasibility Depending on Threat and Complexity of Communication." *Journal of Personality and Social Psychology* 2:195–201.

Hart, R. P. 1973. "On Applying Toulmin: The Analysis of Practical Discourse." In G. Mohrmann, C. Stewart, and D. Ochs, eds., *Explorations in Rhetorical Criticism* pp. 75–95. University Park, Pa.: Pennsylvania State University Press.

Hart, R. P., and Burks, D. M. 1972. "Rhetorical Sensitivity and Social Interaction." *Speech Monographs* 39:75–91.

Highet, G. 1956. *The Art of Teaching.* New York: Vintage.

Hollingsworth, H. L. 1935. *The Psychology of the Audience.* New York: American Book.

Janis, I. L., and Feshbach, S. 1953. "Effects of Fear-Arousing Communications." *Journal of Abnormal and Social Psychology* 48:78–92.

Johnson, B. 1972. "Implicit Communication Theory." Unpublished paper, Department of Speech, Pennsylvania State University.

Karlins, M., and Abelson, H. 1970. *Persuasion: How Opinions and Attitudes are Changed*. New York: Springer.

Kelman, H. C. 1950. "Effects of Success and Failure on 'Suggestibility' in the Autokinetic Situation." *Journal of Abnormal and Social Psychology* 45:267–285.

Kelman, H. C., and Hovland, C. 1953. " 'Reinstatement' of the Communicator in Delayed Measurement of Opinion Change." *Journal of Abnormal and Social Psychology* 48:327–335.

Kiesler, C. A. 1971. *The Psychology of Commitment: Experiments Linking Behavior to Belief*. New York: Academic.

Laing, R. E. 1969. *The Divided Self*. New York: Random House.

Lazarsfeld, P. F.; Berelson, B.; and Gaudet, H. 1944. *The People's Choice*. New York: Columbia University Press.

Linkugel, W., and Berg, D. 1970. *A Time to Speak*. Belmont, Calif.: Wadsworth.

Linton, R. 1945. "The Comanche.'" in A. Kardiner, ed., *The Psychological Frontiers of Society*. New York: Columbia University Press.

Littlejohn, S. W. 1971. "A Bibliography of Studies Related to Variables of Source Credibility." N. Shearer, ed., *Bibliographic Annual in Speech Communication, 1971 Annual*. New York: Speech Communication Association.

Mandler, G. 1967. "Organization and Memory." In K. W. Spence and J. T. Spence, eds., *The Psychology of Learning and Motivation*, vol. 1. New York: Academic.

Martin, L. 1970. "Science is Polluted by Printed Words . . . Billions." *Chicago Tribune*, June 7.

Maslow, A. 1962. *Toward a Psychology of Being*. New York: Van Nostrand Reinhold.

Mausner, B., and Bloch, B. 1957. "A Study of the Additivity of Variables Affecting Social Interaction." *Journal of Abnormal and Social Psychology* 54:250–256.

McCroskey, J. 1969. "A Summary of Experimental Research on the Effects of Evidence in Persuasive Communication." *Speech Monographs* 36:169–176.

McGuire, W. J. 1961. "The Effectiveness of Supportive and Refutational Defenses in Immunizing and Restoring Belief Against Persuasion." *Sociometry* 26:189–197.

———. 1969. "The Nature of Attitudes and Attitude Change." In G. Lindzey and E. Aronson, eds., *The Handbook of Social Psychology*, vol. 3, pp. 136–314. Reading, Mass.: Addison-Wesley.

McGuire, W. J., and Papageorgis, D. 1962. "Effectiveness of Forewarning in Developing Resistance to Persuasion." *Public Opinion Quarterly* 26:24–34.

Milgram, S. 1963. "Behavioral Study of Obedience." *Journal of Abnormal and Social Psychology* 67:371–378.

Miller, G. A. 1956. "The Magical Number Seven, Plus-or-Minus Two: Some Limits on Our Capacity for Processing Information." *Psychological Review* 63:81–97.

Minnick, W. 1968. *The Art of Persuasion.* 2nd ed. Boston: Houghton Mifflin.

Morris, D. 1971. *The Naked Ape.* New York: Dell.

Mortensen, D. 1972. *Communication: The Study of Human Interaction.* New York: McGraw-Hill.

Nelson, W. 1970. "Topoi: Functional in Human Recall." *Speech Monographs* 38:121–126.

Nichols, R., and Stevens, L. 1957. *Are You Listening?* New York: McGraw-Hill.

Nunnally, J., and Bobren, H. 1959. "Variables Influencing the Willingness to Receive Communications on Mental Health." *Journal of Personality* 27:38–46.

Nye, R. 1973. *Conflict Among Humans.* New York: Springer.

Osgood, C. 1962. *An Alternative to War or Surrender.* Urbana, Ill.: University of Illinois Press.

Pace, W., and Boren, R. 1973. *The Human Transaction.* Glenview, Ill.: Scott, Foresman.

Phillips, G. M. 1968. "Reticence: Pathology of the Normal Speaker." *Speech Monographs* 35:39–49.

Postman, N., and Weingartner, C. 1969. *Teaching as a Subversive Activity.* New York: Delacorte Press.

Ringwald, B. E.; Mann, R. D.; Rosenwein, R.; and McKeachie, W. J. 1971. "Conflict and Style in the College Classroom—An Intimate Study." *Psychology Today* 9:45–49.

Rokeach, M. 1968. *Beliefs, Attitudes, and Values.* San Francisco: Jossey Bass.

Ross, R. 1970. *Speech Communication: Fundamentals and Practice.* 2nd ed. Englewood Cliffs, N.J.: Prentice-Hall.

Scheidel, T. 1972. *Speech Communication and Human Interaction.* Glenview, Ill.: Scott, Foresman.

Schlesinger, A. M. 1965. *A Thousand Days.* Cambridge, Mass.: Riverside Press.

Sherif, M. 1958. "Superordinate Goals in the Reduction of Intergroup Conflict." *American Journal of Sociology* 63:349–356.

Sherif, M.; Sherif, C.; and Nebergall, R. 1965. *Attitude and Attitude Change.* Philadelphia: Saunders.

Simon, H. W. 1964. *What is a Teacher?* New York: Collier.

Simons, H. 1972. "Persuasion in Social Conflicts: A Critique of Prevailing Conceptions and a Framework for Future Research." *Speech Monographs* 39:227–247.

————. 1971. "Persuasion and Attitude Change." In L. Barker and R. Kibler, eds., *Speech Communication Behavior,* pp. 227–248. Englewood Cliffs, N.J.: Prentice-Hall, 1971.

Stachowiak, J. G. 1968. "Decision-Making and Conflict Resolution in the Family Group." In C. Larson and F. Dance, *Perspectives on Com-*

munication, pp. 113–125. Milwaukee: University of Wisconsin, Department of Communication.

Steele, E., and Redding, W. C. 1962. "The American Value System: Premises for Persuasion." *Western Speech* 26:83–91.

Stukat, K. G. 1958. *Suggestibility: A Factorial and Experimental Study.* Stockholm: Almquist and Wiksell.

Verner, C., and Dickinson, G. 1967. "The Lecture: An Analysis and Review of Research." *Adult Education* 17:85–100.

Vick, C., and Wood, R. 1969. "Similarity of Past Experience and the Communication of Meaning." *Speech Monographs* 36:159–162.

Walters, Barbara. 1970. *How to Talk to Practically Anybody About Practically Anything.* New York: Dell.

Weiss, W., and Fine, B. J. 1956. "The Effect of Induced Aggressiveness on Opinion Change." *Journal of Abnormal and Social Psychology* 52:109–114.

White, R. K. 1970. "A Postscript for Peace Workers: Some Concrete Advice." In M. Rosenberg, S. Verba, and P. C. Converse, eds., *Vietnam and the Silent Majority: The Dove's Guide.* New York: Harper & Row.

Wilcox, R. 1967. *Oral Reporting in Business and Industry.* Englewood Cliffs, N.J.: Prentice-Hall.

Wilson, J., and Arnold, C. C. 1968. *Public Speaking as a Liberal Art.* 2nd ed. Boston: Allyn & Bacon.

Winans, J. 1938. *Speech Making.* New York: Appleton.

Wood, R.; Yamauchi, J.; and Bradac, J. 1971. "The Communication of Meaning Across Cultures." *Journal of Communication* 21:160–169.

INDEXES

author index

subject index

80 81 82 10 9 8 7 6 5 4 3